ΌΛΥΜΠΟΣ.

ZEUS

MANUAL

OF

MYTHOLOGY:

GREEK AND ROMAN,

NORSE, AND OLD GERMAN, HINDOO AND

EGYPTIAN MYTHOLOGY.

BY

ALEXANDER S. MURRAY,

DEPARTMENT OF GREEK AND ROMAN ANTIQUITIES, BRITISH MUSEUM.

REPRINTED FROM THE SECOND REVISED LONDON EDITION.

WITH 45 PLATES ON TINTED PAPER,

REPRESENTING MORE THAN 90 MYTHOLOGICAL SUBJECTS.

DETROIT

Gale Research Company • Book Tower

1970

This is a facsimile reprint of the
1885 edition published in New York
by Charles Scribner's Sons.

Library of Congress Catalog Card Number 75-130452

PUBLISHERS' NOTE.

MURRAY'S MANUAL OF MYTHOLOGY has been known to the American public thus far only through the English edition. As originally published, the work was deficient in its account of the Eastern and Northern Mythology; but with these imperfections it secured a sale in this country which proved that it more nearly supplied the want which had long been felt of a compact hand-book in this study than did any other similar work. The preface to the second English edition indicates the important additions to, and changes which have been made in, the original work. Chapters upon the Northern and Eastern Mythology have been supplied; the descriptions of many of the Greek deities have been re-written; accounts of the most memorable works of art, in which each deity is or was represented, have been added; and a number of new illustrations have been inserted. This American edition has been reprinted from the perfected work. Every illustration given in the original has been carefully reproduced; and the new chapters upon Eastern and Northern Mythology have been thoroughly revised by Prof. W. D. Whitney, of Yale College, who has corrected some minor inaccuracies which had escaped observation in the English edition. The volume in its revised form is without a rival among manuals upon this interesting subject. For the purpose of a text-book in high schools and colleges, and a guide to the art student or general reader, it will be found invaluable.

CONTENTS.

PREFACE.

THE rapid sale of the first edition of "THE MANUAL OF MYTHOLOGY" was so signal an assurance of public favour, that in preparing the second edition, which is now called for, every effort has been made to render it efficient as a standard text-book. The descriptions of the Greek deities have been largely re-written, and at the end of each has been added, in smaller type, an account of the most memorable works of art in which each deity is or was represented. Among the legends of the Greek heroes, those of the labours of Herakles have been re-written and greatly enlarged. The chapters on the Eastern and Northern Mythology are entirely new, and have been further made more readily comprehensible by the addition of new illustrations.

With these alterations, it is hoped that the MANUAL will now justify its claim to be a trustworthy and complete class-book for Mythology. This much it may also claim: to be no longer described as founded on the works of Petiscus, Preller, and Welcker. Not that in its new form it owes less to the splendid researches of Preller and Welcker. On the contrary, it owes more than ever to them, but this time as masters whose works have rather been an assistance which it is a pride to acknowledge, than models to copy with exactness.

LIST OF PLATES.

INTRODUCTION.

THERE is a charm in the name of ancient Greece; there is glory in every page of her history; there is a fascination in the remains of her literature, and a sense of unapproachable beauty in her works of art; there is a spell in her climate still, and a strange attraction in her ruins. We are familiar with the praises of her beautiful islands; our poets sing of her lovely genial sky. There is not in all the land a mountain, plain, or river, nor a fountain, grove, or wood, that is not hallowed by some legend or poetic tale. The names of her artists, Pheidias, Praxiteles, Apelles, and Zeuxis; of her poets, Homer, Pindar, Æschylus, Sophocles, Euripides; of her philosophers, Socrates, Plato, Epicurus; the names of her statesmen and orators, Pericles and Demosthenes; of her historians, Herodotus, Thucydides, and Xenophon; of her mathematicians, Archimedes and Euclid, are familiar to us as household words. We look back over a period of more than two thousand years with feelings of wonder at her achievements on the battle-field and in the arts of peace. We emulate her in many ways, but always confess to failure; and when we have no desire of emulation, we are still ready in most cases to admire.

How far we may find just cause for admiration or the contrary with regard to her religion remains to be seen. But whichever way it be, we shall at any rate find abundant evidence of the intense hold it had upon the great mass of the people, and of the important influence it was calculated to exercise on their civilization. For it was in the firm belief of his interests being the special care of a deity that the husbandman sowed his seed, and watched the vicissitudes of its growth; that the sailor and trader entrusted life and property to the capricious sea. The mechanic traced the skill and handicraft which grew unconsciously upon him by practice to the direct influence of a god. Artists ascribed the mysterious evolution of their ideas, and poets the inspiration of their song, to the same superior cause. Daily bread and daily life, the joy and gladness that circulated at festal gatherings, were duly acknowledged as coming from the same high source. Everywhere in nature was felt the presence of august invisible beings: in the sky, with its luminaries and clouds; on the sea, with its fickle, changeful movements; on the earth, with its lofty peaks, its plains and rivers. It seemed that man himself, and everything around him, was upheld by Divine power; that his career was marked out for him by a rigid fate which even the gods could not alter, should they wish it on occasion. He was indeed free to act, but the consequences of all his actions were settled beforehand.

These deities to whom the affairs of the world were entrusted were, it was believed, immortal, though not eternal in their existence, as we shall see when we come to read the legends concerning their birth. In Crete there was even a story of the death of Zeus, his tomb being pointed out; and, further, the fact that the gods were believed to sustain their existence by means of nectar and ambrosia, is sufficient proof of their being usually deemed subject to the infirmities of age. Being immortal, they were next, as a consequence, supposed to be omnipotent and omniscient. Their physical strength was extraordinary, the earth shaking sometimes under their tread. Whatever they did was done speedily. They moved through space almost without the loss of a moment of time. They knew all things, saw and heard all things with rare exceptions. They were wise, and communicated their wisdom to men. They had a most strict sense of justice, punished crime rigorously, and rewarded noble actions, though it is true that they were less conspicuous for the latter. Their punishments came quickly, as a rule; but even if late, even if not till the second generation, still they came without fail. The sinner who escaped retribution in this life was sure to obtain it in the lower world; while the good who died unrewarded enjoyed the fruit of their good actions in the next life. To many this did not appear a satisfactory way of managing human affairs, and hence there frequently arose doubts as to the absolute justice of the gods, and even the sanctity of their lives. These doubts were reflected in stories, which, to the indignation of men like the poet Pindar, represented this or that one of the gods as guilty of some offence or other, such as they were believed to punish. Philosophers endeavored to explain these stories, some as mere fictions of the brain, others as allegories under which lay a profound meaning. But the mass of the people accepted them as they came, and nevertheless believed in the perfect sanctity of the gods, being satisfied that human wickedness was detested and punished by them.

Whether the gods were supposed to love the whole of mankind, or only such as led good lives, is not certain. It would seem, however, from the universal practice of offering sacrifice and expiation on the occasion of any wrong, that they were believed to be endowed with some deep feeling of general love, which even sinners could touch by means of atonement. At all events they were merciful. They hated excessive prosperity among individual men, and would on such occasions exercise a Satanic power of leading them into sin. They implanted unwritten laws of right and wrong in the human breast. Social duties and engagements were under their special care, as were also the legislative measures of states.

There were tales of personal visits and adventures of the gods among men, taking part in battles, and appearing in dreams. They were conceived to possess the form of human beings, and to be, like men, subject to love and pain, but always characterized by the highest qualities and grandest form that could be imagined. To produce statues of them that would equal this high ideal was the chief ambition of artists; and in presence of statues in which success had been attained, the popular mind felt an awe as if in some way the deity were near. But while this was the case with regard to the renowned examples of art, such as the statue of Zeus at Olympia, by Pheidias, it was equally true with regard to those very ancient rude figures of deities which were believed to have fallen from heaven, and were on that account most carefully preserved in temples, the removal or loss of such a figure being considered an equivalent to the loss of the favour of the deity whose image it was. This was idolatry. At the same time, owing to the vast number of beautiful and grand statues of gods, there gradually arose a feeling of the deification of man and a struggle to become more and more like these beings of nobler human form and divine presence. For it is one of the advantages of having gods possessed of human form that mankind can look up to them with the feeling of having something in common, and the assurance of pity and favor. This was a powerful element in the Greek religion, and led more than any other to the extraordinary piety of the Greek race, in spite of all the awkward stories which we are accustomed to ridicule.

It would seem that the gods were not looked on, at any rate popularly, as having created the world. Perhaps the mass of the people cared nothing for speculation as to the origin of what actually existed, their chief thoughts being concentrated in the changes that took place in what existed and directly affected their interests. In this spirit they looked on the gods as only maintaining and preserving the existing order and system of things according to their divine wisdom. Hence it was that the Greeks never arrived at the idea of one absolute eternal God, though they very nearly approached that idea in the case of Zeus, who occasionally exercised control or sovereignty over the other gods who presided in particular departments in the management of the world. Their natural tendency to polytheism may have been further aggravated by the peculiar circumstances of their early history as a race. It has been suggested with much plausibility that a number of their deities, as Dione, Hera, Gaea, and Demeter, resemble each other so much as to warrant the reasonableness of the conclusion that their separate existence in the mythology was due to a coalescence at some remote early time of distinct tribes of the Greek race, each possessing beforehand a god or gods of their own, with separate names and slightly different attributes, though in the main capable of identification and a common worship. It is probable that, in consequence of such amalgamation, some of the earliest gods have disappeared altogether; while others. who in after times, as in the case of Dione, held subordinate positions, may have originally been deities of the first order.

At the time with which we are here concerned, the Greek nation inhabited the country still known by the name of Greece, though its present population has small claim to be descendants of the ancient race. It was spread also in colonies over the islands of the Archipelago and Mediterranean, along the coasts of Asia Minor and the Black Sea, in the Crimea, on the north coast of Africa, and on the south coast of France. In many of its features the mainland of Greece may be compared with England, both having the same comparatively vast extent of sea coast, very few parts of the country being out of sight of the sea. Both are well supplied with mountains that invigorate the climate, and stir the spirit of adventure. In both cases it may be that this proximity of the greater part of the population to the sea, with its horizon tempting young minds to penetrate beyond its ever-receding line, was the main cause of the general desire of commerce and distant colonization. At any rate, the natural features of Greece, her beautiful bays, the vivid lines of her mountain peaks, her delightful groves and valleys, made a deep impression on the people; and colonists, wherever they spread, retained the warmest recollection of them; of snow-clad Olympos, where the gods lived; of the lovely vale of Tempe; of the smiling banks of the Peneios; of the sacred grove at Delphi; of peaceful Arcadia, with its pastoral life; of the broad plain of Olympia, with its innumerable temples, statues, and treasure-houses of costly presents to the gods; of Corinth, with its flag that ruled the sea; of Athens; of Thebes, with its ancient citadel founded by Cadmus; of Eleusis, and many other places.

We propose now to examine more particularly the religious belief of the Greeks and Romans, with the view of preparing the way for the descriptions that follow of the gods individually. But first of all let us explain the meaning of the word "mythology." According to its derivation from the Greek *mythos*, a tale, and *logos*, an account, it would mean "an account of tales," the tales in this case being confined to the origin, character, and functions of the ancient gods, to the origin of mankind, and the primitive condition of the visible world. To understand these stories we must try to understand the circumstances under which they were invented, and must endeavour to comprehend the condition and circumstances of a nation in the early stage of its existence. For this purpose we can compare the early tales relating to the gods of other nations, of the Indian on the one hand and the German on the other; or we may also compare the condition of races at present in an uncivilized state. From these sources it would seem that the youth of a nation, like that of an individual, is the period at which the activity of imagination and fancy is greatest in proportion as knowledge is least. The mystery of surrounding nature strikes forcibly on the mind, its phenomena on the senses. There is a feeling of alarm when thunder crashes on the ear, of gladness in the warm light of day, of terror in the darkness of night, and of a strange dread at the darkness of death. The accidents of daily life bind men together, and repel the rest of the animal creation, over which the human superiority soon becomes known. Men learn to know each other when as yet they know nothing else. They know their own passions and instincts. They measure everything by themselves, by feet, paces, palms, and ells; and when they seek to fathom or measure the cause of the phenomena of nature they have no standard to employ at hand, except themselves. They might, it is true, imagine the cause of the thunder under the form of a great invisible lion; but in that case

they could not commune with and implore the thunderer for
pity, as they are moved to do. He must therefore be conceived as fashioned like a man, endowed with the highest imaginable qualities of a man. As knowledge and civilization
advance, those qualities become higher and higher. It seems
probable that the first phenomena that appealed to the mind
were those of the change of weather, of seasons, the revolving
day and the revolving year. At any rate, the earliest deities,
as well as we can trace them, appear to be those who presided
over the movements of the celestial sphere.

We seem to recognise the influence of such phenomena in
the chief characteristics of mankind in a primitive stage of
existence—the sense of order and regularity, the feeling of
fatality, the conviction that whatever temporary disturbances
might arise, the course of human life obeyed some fixed law,
coming with bright light, and departing in darkness, but only
to commence another day of happy life elsewhere. We know
that the name of the highest god of the ancients signified the
"light of the world," in a literal sense. In time, as the per-
ceptive faculties expanded, and the wants of men multiplied,
the other phenomena of the world became the subject of inquiry, and were, as usual, ascribed to the direct influence of
deities. The singular part, however, of this process of invent-
ing deities is, that having, at the commencement, obtained
one great powerful god, they did not simply extend his functions to all the departments of nature, instead of finding a
new god to preside over each. It may be that the apparent
conflict frequently observed between the elements of nature
was hostile to such an idea, while on the contrary nothing
was more readily imaginable than a quarrel among different
gods as the cause of such phenomena. By a similar process

the combination of different elements, as, for example, warmth and moisture, was appropriately described from the human point of view as a prolific union or marriage of two deities. The sun and moon were called brother and sister.

Another opinion, somewhat at variance with this, is, that the primitive stage of all religions is a universal belief in one great god—such a belief, it is said, being as natural to man as the use of his arms and legs. But this earliest and pure form of belief became, they say, in course of time debased into a belief in the existence of many gods, originating in such a method of explaining the phenomena of nature as we have described.

On the other hand, the oldest religious records we know of —the Vedas—speak of hosts of divine beings; while in the primitive religion of the American Indians the Great Spirit is surrounded by a crowd of lesser spirits, who represent the various phenomena of nature. It would seem that when the notion of one god did arise, it was of the one true God as opposed to the other and false gods, and this did not take place till a high stage of civilization was reached. In the best times of Greece, no doubt, thinking men acknowledged but one supreme being, and looked on the crowd of other gods as merely his servants, and in no sense really different from our idea of angels.

In due time the religion of the ancients became a polytheism on a very extensive scale; every phase of nature, sky, sea, and earth, every phase of human life, its habits, accidents, and impulses, being provided with a special guardian and controlling deity. In all the varying circumstances of life men turned to one or other of these divine persons in gratitude or for help. Temples, sanctuaries, altars, were erected to them everywhere, one being worshipped with special favour here, and another there; one with special favour at one season of the year, another at another season. Many of them were only known and worshipped in particular localities; as, for instance, marine deities among people connected with the sea. Others belonged to particular periods of the national history. This limitation, however, with regard to local differences, applies only to the vast number of minor deities whose names and attributes have come down to our times; for a belief in the superior order of gods was the common property of the whole nation, whether learned or unlearned, and of whatever occupation. The mysteries of Eleusis united the people in honour of Demeter; the national festivals united them in honour of other gods, as of Zeus at Olympia. Every one believed in the oracular power of Apollo, in the might of Poseidon, in the grim character of Hades, that Hera was the wife of Zeus, that Athene was his daughter, that Aphrodite was the goddess of love, Artemis of the moon, and Ares the god of war.

It was believed that these higher deities inhabited Olympos, living together in a social state which was but a magnified reflection of the social system on earth. Quarrels, love passages, mutual assistance, and such incidents as characterize human life, were ascribed to them. It must however be borne in mind that these human attributes, and the stories connected with them, whether they represent admirable qualities or the reverse, were not in the first instance ascribed to the gods out of a desire to make their resemblance to man more complete, but were the natural result of identifying the gods with the elements of nature over which they were supposed to preside, of conceiving and representing the combination or conflict of elements visible in nature as the result of the combination of invisible beings of human form. In later times of higher civilization and greater refinement, when the origin of the gods as personifications of natural phenomena was lost sight of, many of these stories came to be viewed as disgraceful, and by being made the subject of public ridicule in plays tended largely to uproot the general faith in the gods. Philosophers attempted to explain them as allegories. Others, who did not themselves see their way to believing them, yet advised that the popular faith in them should not be disturbed. But we who live in other times, having no need of a religion that has long since passed away, and desiring only to trace its origin and the source of its long and deep influence on a great nation, may look at them in a calmer mood. It is our part to admire as far as possible, and not to condemn without first taking into account every extenuating circumstance.

Turning now to the rites and ceremonies by which the Greeks and Romans expressed their belief in and entire dependence on the gods, we would call attention first to the offering of sacrifices. These were of two kinds, one consisting of fruits, cakes, and wine; the other of animals, which were led to the altar decked with garlands and ribbons, after various ceremonies slain, and part of the flesh consumed upon the altar fire, the smell of it being supposed to rise agreeably to the gods. It was necessary that the animals selected for this purpose should be spotless and healthy, that the persons participating in the ceremony should be cleanly in person and in mind; for no costliness could make the offering of a sinner acceptable to the gods. The colour, age, and sex of the animal were determined by the feeling of appropriateness to the deity for whom it was slain. The time chosen for the ceremony was the morning in the case of the gods of heaven, the evening in the case of the gods of the lower world. To these

latter deities the victim was always offered entire, as it was
not deemed possible that they could share in a feast in company with men.   The fire on the altar was considered holy,
and special care was taken that it should be fed with wood
that gave a pure flame.   In early times it would seem that
even human beings were offered as sacrifices to certain gods,
the victims in such cases being occasionally, to judge from the
instance of Iphigenia, closely connected by ties of blood and
affection with the person required to make the sacrifice.   But
these were, perhaps, mostly cases in which the will of the
gods was specially communicated through a seer or prophet;
whereas sacrifice generally was a spontaneous gift to the gods,
either for the purpose of expressing gratitude for the blessings
bestowed by them, or of atoning for some sin of which the
person sacrificing was conscious.   Sacrifices were not presented intermittently and at mere pleasure, but regularly when
occasion offered, as at harvest time, when the fruits of the
fields and gardens were gathered in.   The herdsmen sacrificed
the firstlings of his flock, the merchant gave part of his gain,
and the soldier a share of his booty in war. The gods to whom
all prosperity and worldly blessings were due expected such offerings, it was thought, and punished every instance of neglect.

There was, however, another class of sacrifices, springing
from a different motive, and with a different object in view;
for example, to obtain by means of an examination of the
entrails of an animal an augury as to the issue of some enterprise,—a form of sacrifice which was held of great importance
at the commencement of a battle; or to sanctify the ratification
of a treaty, or some important bargain between man and
man; or to obtain purification for some crime.   In this last
case it was supposed that the victim took the sin upon its own

head, and that both perished together. Hence no part of such victims was eaten.

How the gods were supposed to partake of the share of sacrifices allotted to them is not always clear, though in the case of burnt offerings they may be imagined to have been satisfied with the smell that rose in the air, and in the case of libations with the aroma of the wine. With regard to the sacrifices in honour of the deities of the lower world, it seems to have been the belief that the blood of the victim, if poured into a hole in the ground, would sink down to them, and be acceptably received. In the same hole, or near by, were buried the ashes that remained on the altar on which the victim was consumed. The portions assigned to marine or river deities were sunk in deep water.

It was the duty of the priests to perform the ceremony of offering up the sacrifices brought to the gods in whose service they were. The first part of the ceremony was to take a basket containing the sacrificial knife, some corn, and perhaps also flowers, and to pass it, along with a vessel containing water, round the altar from left to right. The water was next purified by dipping a brand from the altar in it. Thereupon the people who had brought the sacrifice sprinkled themselves and the altar, and taking a handful of corn from the basket, scattered it on the head of the victim as it approached. The priest then, after shearing a lock of hair from the head of the animal, and distributing it among the bystanders to be thrown on the altar fire, commanded silence, prayed that the offering might be acceptable to the god, and slew the victim. The blood, except in the case of the deities of the lower world, as has been observed, and the entrails, were mixed with wheat, wine, and incense, and placed upon the fire.

The strong feelings of piety, gratitude, dependence, or consciousness of guilt, which gave rise to such offerings, gave rise
also to a universal habit of prayer, and a desire to frequent on
all possible occasions the temples and altars of the gods.
Morning and evening, at the beginning of meals, at the opening of business in the courts of justice and public assemblies,
a prayer was offered up, now to one god, now to another, or,
if no particular deity appeared to be an appropriate guardian
for the time and occasion, to the gods generally. There was
this peculiarity in the Greek prayers, which we must not omit
to mention, that after calling on a deity by his usual name a
clause was added to save the suppliant from any possible displeasure of the deity at the name employed; for how could
man know the true name of a god? We have an example of
such a prayer in Æschylus: "Zeus, whoever thou art, and by
whatever name it please thee to be named, I call on thee and
pray." In praying to the gods above it was the custom of
the Greeks to lift the hands and turn the face towards the
east; of the Romans, to turn towards the north. A suppliant
of the sea gods stretched out his hands towards the sea, and a
suppliant of the gods of the lower world beat the earth with
his hands. When a prayer was offered up in a temple the rule
was to turn towards the sacred image. In cases of great distress the suppliant would carry an olive branch, or a rod with
wool twined round it, throw himself on the ground before the
sacred image, and embrace its feet. Pythagoras, the philoso-
pher, taught his followers to pray with a loud voice; but loud
prayers do not appear to have been customary. On the contrary, it happened not unfrequently that the prayers were written on tablets, sealed and deposited beside the image of the
god, that no human being might be aware of the request con-

tained in them. Here is a specimen of what seems to have been the usual form: "Zeus, our lord, give unto us whatever is good, whether we ask it of thee or not; whatever is evil keep far from us, even if we ask it of thee."

Besides sacrifice and prayer there is still another class of ceremonies, in which we recognize the deep piety of the Greeks: first, the custom of consulting oracles, especially that of Apollo at Delphi, in times of great perplexity; and secondly, the universal practice, in cases of less or more sudden emergency, of trying to interpret the will of the gods by means of augury or divination in a vast variety of ways. Sometimes the augury was taken from the direction in which birds were observed to fly overhead. If to the right of the augur, who stood with his face to the north, good luck would attend the enterprise in question; if to the left, the reverse. At other times an animal was slain, and its entrails carefully examined, the propitiousness of the gods being supposed to depend on the healthy and normal condition of these parts. But the gods were also believed to communicate their will to men in dreams, by sending thunder and lightning, comets, meteors, eclipses, earthquakes, prodigies in nature, and the thousands of unexpected incidents that occur to men. As few persons were able to interpret the bearing of these signs and wonders, there was employment for a large class of people who made this their particular business.

Finally, we must not forget to mention as a proof of the widespread religious feeling of the Greeks the national festivals, or games, as they are called, established and maintained in honour of certain gods. While these festivals were being celebrated it was necessary to suspend whatever war might be going on between separate states, and to permit visitors to pass unmolest-

ed even through hostile territory.   These festivals were four
in number: the *Olympian*, *Pythian*, *Nemean*, and *Isthmian*.

The first-mentioned was held in honour of Zeus, on the plain
of Olympia, in Elis.   It occurred every fifth year, and the usual
method of reckoning time was according to its re-occurrence,
by Olympiads, as we say.   The games with which it was celebrated consisted of running, wrestling, boxing, a combination
of the two latter, horse-racing, either with chariots or only
with riders.   The prize of victory was simply a wreath of olive,
and yet athletes trained themselves laboriously and travelled
great distances to compete for it.   Kings sent their horses to
run in the races, and counted a victory among the highest honours of their lives. The fellow-townsmen of a victorious athlete
would raise a statue in his honour.   Occasionally writers, as
we are told of Herodotus, took this occasion of a vast assem-
blage of their countrymen to read to them part of their
writings.   The Pythian games were held in honour of Apollo,
in the neighbourhood of Delphi, and occurred every fifth year,
there being competition in music as well as in athletics.   The
prize was a wreath of laurel.   At the Nemean games, which
were held in honour of Zeus, the prize was a wreath of ivy.
The Isthmian games were held in honour of Poseidon, on the
Isthmus of Corinth, and occurred every third year; the prize
was a wreath of pine.

It is remarkable and surprising that, with all the piety
and religious ceremonies of the ancients, there existed among
them no established means of instruction for the mass of the
people, as to the character and functions of the gods whom
they worshipped.   There was, indeed, a regular priesthood,
whose duty it was to conduct the public ceremonies, to offer
up sacrifices, and to perform other offices peculiar to the god in

whose service they were. But there their duties ceased. These
ceremonies had been handed down from time immemorial, and
that was perhaps sufficient guarantee of their importance to
make the ordinary Greek assiduous in his observance of them.
At any rate, this assiduity is not traceable to a clear and
explicit knowledge of the character of the gods derived from
public instruction. In regard to that, whatever unanimity
existed was unquestionably due in the first instance to the
influence of poets like Homer and Hesiod, and in the second,
to the exertion of the persons connected with the oracle at
Delphi. The effect of this state of things was a great amount
of confusion in the popular mind, and not only in the popular
mind, but also in the minds of men like Socrates, who confessed he did not know whether there was one Aphrodite or
two, and wondered why Zeus, who was believed to be one
god, had so many names.

The preceding remarks, it should be here observed, apply
for the most part only to the mythology of the Greeks, and
do not extend to that of the Romans, except so far as they
refer to the most primitive class of myths, such as those concerning the origin of the world. For the practice of identifying the mythologies of those two nations has no foundation
in fact. Both races, it is true, belonged to one and the same
great branch of the human family, and from that source derived a common kernel of religious belief. But before this
kernel had developed far the two nations parted, and formed
for themselves distinct and isolated settlements in Europe.
In the long period of isolation, that followed, the common seed
of religious belief with which both started grew up, was propagated under quite different circumstances, and assumed a
very different aspect. The Romans—in the early period of their

2

history a pastoral, agricultural, simple, and more or less united people—had no need of a various multitude of deities, such
as the Greeks found necessary, scattered and separated as they
were into a variety of tribes with a variety of occupations.

From this, among other causes, it happens that many, even
of the very early Greek myths, were quite foreign to the Romans.   To this class belong, for instance, the myths that describe the conflict between Uranos and his sons: Kronos de-
vouring his children to escape, as he thought, being dethroned
by them, and Zeus placing his father, Kronos, in durance in
Tartaros.   No less strictly peculiar to the Greeks were those
accounts of quarrels among the gods, wounds, and occasionally the banishment of certain gods to a period of service on
earth.   To these we may add the carrying off of Persephone
by Pluto, and several other stories.   With regard to the ceremonies which accompanied the worship of certain gods, we
observe the same great difference between the two nations,
and would cite as an example the wild unrestrained conduct
of those who took part in the festivals of Dionysos, remark-
ing that when in later times of luxury a festival of this kind
was introduced into Italy in honour of Bacchus, the Roman
equivalent for the Greek Dionysos or Bakchos, the new festival was forbidden, and those who took part in it were viewed
as persons of unbridled desires.   Nor did Mercury ever obtain the wide-spread worship and honour paid to Hermes in
Greece; and even **Saturnus**, in spite of the Roman poets,
was a very different god from the Greek **Kronos**.

At the time when the Roman poets began to write, "Greece
captured was leading her captor captive."   Greek literature
was the usual means of education; Greek philosophy, Greek
art,—everything pertaining to the Greeks,—constituted the

principal pursuit of educated men.　Many would rather employ the Greek than their own language in writing.　Poets, constructing their poems often in close imitation of Greek models, replaced the names of gods that occurred in the Greek originals by names of native deities possessing some similarity of character, and told a Greek story of a native Italian god; or, failing such, employed the Greek name in a Latin form.　At the same time no real adaptation or coalescence of the two religious systems ever took place.　The Roman ceremonies and forms of worship remained for the most part distinct from the Greek, and peculiar to the race.　In modern times, however, the literature (especially the poetry) of the ancient Romans was more familiarly known than the facts relating to their ceremonies and forms of worship.　It was more early and familiarly known than the literature of Greece, and instead of upon the latter, the modern notions of Greek mythology were founded on the statements of the Roman poets. Hence, arose a confusion which our own poets, especially those of the last century, only made worse confounded.　To meet this confusion we shall give the accredited Roman equivalent by the side of the Greek gods, throughout our descriptions, and point out as far as possible the differences between them.

Thus far our observations have been confined to the mythology and religious ceremonies of the Greeks and Romans, especially of the former.　We have had very little to say of the Romans, because, though equal perhaps to the Greeks in their piety and trust in the gods, they appear to have been very deficient in that quality of imagination which could readily invent some divine personification for every phenomenon of nature that struck the mind.　As, however, it is our intention to include a description, even if very brief, of the mythology of the Indian and Teutonic or Germanic races, it may be well to call attention here to the fact, now clearly ascertained, that these races are sprung from the same common family or human stock to which the Greeks and Romans belonged, and that at least certain ideas concerning the origin and primitive condition of the world are common to the mythologies of them all. From this it is reasonable to conclude that these ideas were arrived at previous to the separation of this great Indo-Germanic family, as it is called, and its development into distinct and isolated nations, as we find it at the dawn of historical times. From the Ganges to Iceland we meet with traces of a common early belief that the wild features of the earth had been produced by some long past convulsive conflict of Titanic beings, whom, though invisible, the stormy elements of nature still obeyed. We find that everywhere, within these limits of space and time, there existed among men the same sensitiveness to the phenomena of nature,—to light and darkness, to heat and cold, to rain and drought, to storms and peacefulness,—and the same readiness and power of imagining invisible beings of human form, but loftier attributes, as the cause of these phenomena. To these beings actions and habits of life were ascribed, such as were suggested by the phenomena which they were supposed to control; and in no case, it should be borne in mind, was any feeling of morality or immorality intended to be conveyed. For instance, when we find the natural process by which the clouds pour out their rain upon the earth, and are again filled from the sea, described as Hermes (the god of rain) stealing the cattle (clouds) of Apollo, we cannot attach to the story the idea of criminality which it at first suggests. Similar interpretations we must be prepared to seek throughout the mythologies of the Indo-Germanic races.

It may now be asked, from what source is this knowledge derived of the mythology of the ancients? To this we reply, from the works of ancient writers, poets, historians, philosophers, and others, to whom the religious belief of their countrymen was a subject of great importance, and whose writings have survived to our times; in the second place, from the representations of gods and mythological scenes on the immense number of ancient works of art that still exist, whether in the form of statues in marble and bronze, painted vases, engraved gems, or coins. These are the sources of our knowledge, and without becoming more or less familiar with them it is perhaps impossible to understand fully the spirit of these ancient myths; and contrariwise, to be able to appreciate at its real worth the beauty of ancient works, whether in literature or in art, it is necessary to become acquainted with the mythology and the religious spirit which guided their authors; and if that be not sufficient temptation to follow our descriptions of the various deities and heroes of ancient times, we can still appeal to this,—that a great part of our grandest modern poetry and works of art can only be intelligible to those who know the ancient mythology.

Drawing near, as we are now, to the details of our subject, we become anxious to guard against all feelings of impropriety in what we may have occasionally to relate. We would therefore remind the reader of the principle of interpretation which we have endeavoured to explain in the preceding pages. We would also repeat that we have here to do with a system of religious belief which, whatever its apparent or real shortcomings may have been, exercised enormous influence on the education of at least two of the most civilized nations of the earth.

THE CREATION OF THE WORLD.

IN thinking of the origin of the world in which they lived, the Greeks for the most part, it would appear, were satisfied with the explanation given by the poet Hesiod,—that in the beginning the world was a great shapeless mass or *chaos* out of which was fashioned first the spirit of love, **Eros** (Cupid), and the broad-chested earth, **Gaea**; then **Erebos,** darkness, and **Nyx,** night. From a union of the two latter sprang **Æther,** the clear sky, and **Hemera,** day. The earth, by virtue of the power by which it was fashioned, produced in turn, **Uranos,** the firmament which covered her with its vault of brass, as the poets called it, to describe its appearance of eternal duration, the mountains, and **Pontos,** the unfruitful sea. Thereupon Eros, the oldest and at the same time the youngest of the gods, began to agitate the earth and all things on it, bringing them together, and making pairs of them. First in importance of these pairs were Uranos and Gaea, heaven and earth, who peopled the earth with a host of beings, Titans, Giants, and Kyklopes, of far greater physical frame and energy than the races who succeeded them. It is a beautiful idea, that of love making order out of chaos, bringing opposite elements together, and preparing a world to receive mankind.

Another apparently older and certainly obscure notion, is that expressed by Homer, which ascribes the origin of the world to **Okeanos,** the ocean. How the earth and heavens

22

sprang from him, or whether they were conceived as co-exist-
ing with him from the beginning, we are not told. The
numerous ancient stories, however, concerning floods, after
which new generations of men sprang up, and the fact that
the innumerable fertilizing rivers and streams of the earth
were believed to come from the ocean, as they were seen to
return to it, and that all the river gods were accounted the
offspring of Okeanos, suggest the prevalence of such a form
of belief with regard to the origin of the world in times previous to Hesiod. We are told that the ocean encircled the
earth with a great stream, and was a region of wonders of all
kinds; that Okeanos lived there, with his wife **Tethys**; that
there were the islands of the blest, the gardens of the gods,
the sources of the nectar and ambrosia on which the gods
lived. Within this circle of water the earth lay spread out
like a disc with mountains rising from it, and the vault of
heaven appearing to rest on its outer edge all round. This
outer edge was supposed to be slightly raised, so that the
water might not rush in and overflow the land. The space
between the surface of the earth and the heavens was seen to
be occupied by air and clouds, and above the clouds was supposed to be pure ether, in which the sun, moon, and stars
moved. The sun rising in the eastern sky in the morning,
traversing the celestial arch during the day, and sinking at
evening in the west, was thought to be under the guidance of
a god in a chariot drawn by four splendid horses. After
sinking into Okeanos, it was supposed that he took ship and
sailed during the night round to the east, so as to be ready to
begin a new day.

In the region of air above the clouds moved the higher
order of gods; and when, for the sake of council or inter-

course they met together, the meeting place was the summit of one of those lofty mountains whose heads were hid in the clouds, but chief of all, the inaccessible Olympos in Thessaly. Round the highest point of it was the palace of Zeus, with the throne on which he sat in majesty to receive such visits as those of Thetis (Iliad i. 498) when she came to plead for her son. On plateaus or in ravines lower down were the mansions of the other gods, provided, as was thought, with the convenience of store-rooms, stabling, and all that was usual in the houses of princes on earth. The deities who thus inhabited Olympos, and for that reason were styled the Olympian deities, were twelve in number. We do not, it is true, always find this number composed of the same gods, but the following may be taken as having been the most usual; **Zeus** (Jupiter), **Hera** (Juno), **Poseidon** (Neptune), **Demeter** (Ceres), **Apollo, Artemis** (Diana), **Hephaestos** (Vulcan), **Pallas, Athene** (Minerva), **Ares** (Mars), **Aphrodite** (Venus), **Hermes** (Mercury), and **Hestia** (Vesta). Though allied to each other by various degrees of relationship, and worshipped in many places at altars dedicated to them as a united body, they did not always act together in harmony, a most memorable instance of their discord being that (Iliad viii. 13-27) in which Zeus threatened to hurl the others into Tartaros, and challenged them to move him from Olympos by letting themselves down with a golden chain and pulling with all their might. Should they try it, he said, he could easily draw them up with earth and sea to the bargain, fasten the chain to the top of Olympos, and let the whole hang in mid air. The name of Olympos was not confined to the Thessalian mountain, though it may have had the earliest, as in after times it had the principal, claim to the title, but was applied to no less than fourteen mountains in various parts of the Greek world, each of which appears to have been regarded as an occasional meeting place, if not a permanent seat of the gods. Finally, the word was used to designate a region above the visible sky, from which, to express its height, it was said that once a brazen anvil fell nine days and nine nights before it reached the earth. At an equal distance beneath the surface of the earth was Tartaros, a vast gloomy space walled in with brass, where the Titans lived in banishment.

The lower order of deities, having naturally no place in Olympos, were restricted to the localities on earth where they exercised their powers—as, for instance, the **Naiads,** or Nymphs of fountains, to the neighbourhood of fountains and springs; the **Oreads,** or mountain Nymphs, to the mountains and hills; and the **Dryads,** or Nymphs of trees, to trees. With regard to the place of residence of the heroes or semi-divine beings after their translation from earth, there existed considerable variety of opinion, of which we shall afterwards have occasion to speak.

Representations of the deities assembled in Olympos for a particular occasion—as at the birth of Athene from the head of her father Zeus—occur not unfrequently on the Greek painted vases. This was the subject chosen by Pheidias for the sculptures in one of the pediments of the Parthenon now in the British Museum. The loss, however, of many of the figures renders it impossible to say now who were the deities he selected, or whether he even adhered to the usual number of twelve. At one end of the pediment the sun rises in his chariot from the sea, at the other the moon rides away. The event must therefore have taken place at the break of day. The same fact is to be observed in the scene at the birth of Aphrodite, in presence of the assembled deities, with which Pheidias adorned the base of his statue of Zeus at Olympia, and of which we have still the description in Pausanias (v. 403.) At one end was the Sun stepping into his chariot, next to him Zeus and Hera, then Hephaestos (?) and Charis, then Hermes and Hestia. In the centre was Eros receiving Aphrodite as she rises from the sea, and Peitho crowning Aphrodite; then Apollo and Artemis, next Athene and Herakles, then Poseidon and Amphitrite, and lastly the Moon (Selene) riding away. The deities are thus grouped in pairs of male and female, those of greater importance being towards either end of the composition.

DEITIES OF THE HIGHEST ORDER.

URANOS

IS a personification of the sky as the ancients saw and understood its phenomena, and with him, according to the version of mythology usually accepted by the Greeks, commences the race of gods. Next succeeded **Kronos,** and lastly, **Zeus.** With regard to this triple succession of supreme rulers of the world, we should notice the different and progressive signification of their three names, Uranos signifying the heavens viewed as husband of the earth, and by his warmth and moisture producing life and vegetation everywhere on it; Kronos, his successor, being the god of harvest, who also ripened and matured every form of life; while in the person of Zeus, god of the light of heaven, as his name implies, culminated the organization and perfectly wise and just dispensation of the affairs of the universe. **Uranos,** as we have already observed, was a son of **Gaea** (the earth), whom he afterwards married, the fruit of that union being the **Titans,** the **Hekatoncheires,** and the **Kyklopes.**

The Hekatoncheires, or Centimani, beings each with a hundred hands, were three in number; **Kottos, Gyges** or **Gyes,** and **Briareus,** and represented the frightful crashing of waves and its resemblance to the convulsion of earthquakes. The Kyklopes also were three in number: **Brontes** with his

26

thunder, **Steröpes** with his lightning, and **Arges** with his stream of light. They were represented as having only one eye, which was placed at the juncture between nose and brow. It was, however, a large flashing eye, as became beings who were personifications of the storm-cloud, with its flashes of destructive lightning and peals of thunder. From a similarity observed between the phenomena of storms and those of volcanic eruptions, it was usually supposed that the Kyklopes lived in the heart of burning mountains, above all, in Mount Etna, in Sicily, where they acted as apprentices of **Hephaestos** (Vulcan), assisting him to make thunderbolts for **Zeus**, and in other works. Uranos, it was said, alarmed at their promise of fierceness and strength, had cast the Hekatoncheires and Kyklopes at their birth back into the womb of the earth from which they had sprung.

The Titans were, like the Olympian deities, twelve in number, and grouped for the most part in pairs: **Okeanos** and **Tethys, Hyperion** and **Theia, Kreios** and **Eurybia, Koios** and **Phœbe, Kronos** and **Rhea, Japetos** and **Themis.** Instead of Eurybia we find frequently **Mnemosyne.** Their names, though not in every case quite intelligible, show that they were personifications of those primary elements and forces of nature to the operations of which, in the first ages, the present configuration of the earth was supposed to be due. While Themis, Mnemosyne, and Japetos may be singled out as personifications of a civilizing force in· the nature of things, and as conspicuous for having offspring endowed with the same character, the other Titans appear to represent wild, powerful, and obstructive forces. In keeping with this character we find them rising in rebellion first against their father and afterwards against Zeus.

In the former experiment the result was that **Uranos,** as we learn from the poetic account of the myth, threw them into Tartaros, where he kept them bound. But **Gaea,** his wife, grieving at the hard fate of her offspring, provided the youngest son, **Kronos,** with a sickle or curved knife, which she had made of stubborn adamant, and told him how and when to wound his father with it irremediably. The enterprise succeeded, the Titans were set free, married their sisters, and begat a numerous family of divine beings, while others of the same class sprang from the blood of the wound of Uranos as it fell to the ground. Of these were the **Giants,** monsters with legs formed of serpents; the **Melian nymphs,** or nymphs of the oaks, from which the shafts used in war were fashioned; and the **Erinys,** or **Furiæ,** as the Romans called them,—**Tisiphone, Megæra,** and **Alekto,**—creatures whose function it was originally to avenge the shedding of a parent's blood. Their form was that of women, with hair of snakes and girdles of vipers. They were a terror to criminals, whom they pursued with unrelenting fury. The whole of these divine beings, however, with the exception of the **Erinys,** who were worshipped at Athens under the name of the "venerable deities," were excluded from the religion of the Greeks, and had a place only in the mythology, while among the Romans they were unknown till later times, and even then were only introduced as poetic fictions, with no hold upon the religious belief of the people.

I

Kronos.

Rhea.

KRONOS,

(PLATE I.,)

'The ripener, the harvest god,' was, as we have already remarked, a son of **Uranos**. That he continued for a long time
to be identified with the Roman deity, **Saturnus**, is a mistake which recent research has set right, and accordingly we
shall devote a separate chapter to each. **Uranos**, deposed
from the throne of the gods, was succeeded by **Kronos**, who
married his own sister **Rhea**, a daughter of **Gaea**, who bore
him **Pluto**, **Poseidon** (Neptune), and **Zeus** (Jupiter),
Hestia (Vesta), **Demeter** (Ceres), and **Hera** (Juno).   To
prevent the fulfilment of a prophecy which had been communicated to him by his parents, that, like his father, he too
would be dethroned by his youngest born, **Kronos** swallowed
his first five children apparently as each came into the world.
But when the sixth child appeared, Rhea, his wife, determined
to save it, and succeeded in duping her husband by giving
him a stone (perhaps rudely hewn into the figure of an infant)
wrapped in swaddling clothes, which he swallowed, believing
he had got rid of another danger.

While the husband was being deceived in this fashion, **Zeus,**
the newly-born child, was conveyed to the island of Crete,
and there concealed in a cave on Mount Ida.   The nymphs
Adrastea and Ida tended and nursed him, the goat Amalthea
supplied him with milk, bees gathered honey for him, and in
the meantime, lest his infantile cries should reach the ears of
Kronos, Rhea's servants, the **Kurētes**, were appointed to
keep up a continual noise and din in the neighbourhood by
dancing and clashing their swords and shields.

When Zeus had grown to manhood he succeeded by the aid of **Gaea**, or perhaps of **Metis**, in persuading Kronos to yield back into the light the sons whom he had swallowed and the stone which had been given him in deceit. The stone was placed at Delphi as a memorial for all time. The liberated gods joined their brethren in a league to drive their father from the throne and set Zeus in his place. This was done; but the change of government, though acquiesced in by the principal deities, was not to be brooked by the Titans, who with the exception of Okeanos proceeded to war. The seat of war was Thessaly, with its wild natural features suggestive of a conflict in which huge rocks had been torn from mountain sides and shattered by the violence with which they had been thrown in combat. The party of Zeus had its position on Mount Olympos, the Titans on Mount Othrys. The struggle lasted many years, all the might which the Olympians could bring to bear being useless until, on the advice of Gaea, Zeus set free the Kyklopes and Hekatoncheires, of whom the former fashioned thunderbolts for him, while the latter advanced on his side with force equal to the shock of an earthquake. The earth trembled down to lowest Tartaros as Zeus now appeared with his terrible weapon and new allies. Old Chaos thought his hour had come, as from a continuous blaze of thunderbolts the earth took fire and the waters seethed in the sea. The rebels were partly slain or consumed, and partly hurled into deep chasms, with rocks and hills reeling after them, and consigning them to a life beneath the surface of the earth. The cause of Kronos was thus lost for ever, and the right of Zeus to rule established for all time.

The island of Crete, where civilization appears to have dawned earlier than elsewhere in Greece, and where the story

of the secret up-bringing of Zeus was made the most of, was
the principal centre of the worship of Kronos. Here, however, and in Attica, as well as in several other districts of
Greece, it was less as the grim god who had devoured his children that he was worshipped than as the maturer and ripener,
the god of harvest, who sends riches and blessings, prosperity
and gladness. So it happened that his festivals in Greece, the
Kronia, and the corresponding **Saturnalia** in Italy, were
of that class which imposed no restraint on the mirth and
pleasure of those present, and seemed like a reminiscence of
an age when under the rule of Kronos there had been a perpetual harvest time on earth. As the devourer of his children
Kronos bears some resemblance to the Phœnician Moloch,
and it is highly probable that this phase of his character originated in Crete, where the influence of Phœnician settlers
had been felt from very remote times. It is also to be noted
that his wife Rhea enjoyed a very early and wide-spread worship in Asia Minor.

The scene where Rhea presents the stone carefully wrapped up to her husband as he sits on his throne, was the subject of a sculpture executed for Pla-
taeae by Praxiteles (Pausanias ix. 2, 7), from which it is possible that the
relief may have been made which is represented in Plate I, and is now in the
Capitoline Museum, Rome. The thoughtful attitude of Kronos, and especially the veiled head, seem to indicate a plotting mind, while the sickle in his
left hand is emblematical of his function as god of harvest, and at the same
time a memorial of the deed he wrought upon his father Uranos. The war
with the Titans (Titanomachia) was superseded in popular estimation as
early as the time of Euripides by the Gigantomachia, or war of Giants, which
will be described in connection with Zeus. Artists following the popular taste
neglected the former altogether as a source of subjects.

SATURNUS,

According to the popular belief of the Romans, made his
first appearance in Italy at a time when **Janus** was reigning

king of the fertile region that stretches along the banks of the
Tiber on either side. Presenting himself to Janus, and being
kindly received, he proceeded to instruct the subjects of the
latter in agriculture, gardening, and many other arts then
quite unknown to them: as, for example, how to train and
nurse the vine, and how to tend and cultivate fruit-trees.
By such means he at length raised the people from a rude
and comparatively barbarous condition to one of order and
peaceful occupations, in consequence of which he was everywhere held in high esteem, and in course of time was selected
by Janus to share with him the government of the kingdom,
which thereupon assumed the name of **Saturnia**, ' a land
of seed and fruit.' The period of Saturn's government was
in later times sung of by poets as a happy time when sorrows
and cares of life were unknown, when innocence, freedom,
and gladness reigned throughout the land, in such a degree
as to deserve the title of the golden age. Greek mythology
also has its golden age, said to have occurred during the
reign of **Kronos**, and this, perhaps, more than any other
circumstance, led to the identification of Saturnus and Kronos,
in spite of the real difference between the two deities. The
name of Saturn's wife was **Ops.**

Once a year, in the month of December, the Romans held
a festival called **Saturnalia** in his honour. It lasted from
five to seven days, and was accompanied by amusements of
all kinds. During those days the ordinary distinctions were
done away with between master and servant or slave. No
assemblies were held to discuss public affairs, and no punishments for crime were inflicted. Servants or slaves went about
dressed like their masters, and received from them costly
presents   Children received from their parents or relatives

II.

Rhea.

Zeus, or Jupiter.

presents of pictures, probably of a gaudy type, purchased in the street where the picture dealers lived.

There was a temple of Saturn in Rome, at the foot of the Capitoline Hill, containing a figure of him with his feet wrapped round with pieces of woollen cloth, which could only be removed during the festival of the Saturnalia. In one hand he held a curved garden-knife, as a sign of his having been the first to teach the people how to trim the vine and olive. In this temple were preserved the state chest and the standards of the army.

RHEA.

(PLATES I. AND II.)

As Uranos, the representative of the fertilizing force in nature, was superseded by Kronos the representative of a ripening force, so Gaea, the primitive goddess of the earth with its productive plains gave way to Rhea, a goddess of the earth with its mountains and forests. Gaea had been the mother of the powerful Titans. Rhea was the mother of gods less given to feats of strength, but more highly gifted: **Pluto, Poseidon,** and **Zeus, Hera, Demeter,** and **Hestia.** Her titles—as for example, **Dindumene** and **Berekuntia**—were derived for the most part from the names of mountains in Asia Minor, particularly those of Phrygia and Lydia, her worship having been intimately associated with the early civilization of these countries. There her name was **Kybelē** or **Kybēbē,** which also, from its being employed to designate her sanctuaries (Kybela) in caves or mountain sides, points to her character as a mountain goddess.

3

The lofty hills of Asia Minor, while sheltering on their cavernous sides wild animals, such as the panther and lion, which it was her delight to tame, also looked down on many flourishing cities which it was her duty to protect. In this latter capacity she wore a mural crown, and was styled **Mater turrita.** But though herself identified with peaceful civilization, her worship was always distinguished by wild and fantastic excitement, her priests and devotees rushing through the woods at night with torches burning, maiming and wounding each other, and producing all the din that was possible from the clashing of cymbals, the shrill notes of pipes, and the frantic voice of song. To account for this peculiarity of her worship, which must have been intended to commemorate some great sorrow, the story was told of how she had loved the young Phrygian shepherd, **Attis,** whose extraordinary beauty had also won the heart of the king's daughter of Pessinus; how he was destined to marry the princess, and how the goddess, suddenly appearing, spread terror and consternation among the marriage guests. Attis escaped to the mountains, maimed himself, and died beside a pine tree, into which his soul transmigrated, while from his blood sprang violets like a wreath round the tree. The goddess implored Zeus to restore her lover. This could not be. But so much was granted that his body should never decay, that his hair should always grow, and that his little finger should always move. The pine was a symbol of winter and sadness, the violet of spring and its hopeful beauty.

The first priests of Rhea-Kybele were the Kuretes and Korybantes, for whom it was also claimed that they had been the first beings of mere human form and capacity that had appeared on the earth, having sprung from the mountain side

III

Zeus, or Jupiter.

like trees. The great centre of her worship was always at Pessinus in Phrygia, under the shadow of Mount Dindymon, on which was a cave containing what was believed to be the oldest of her sanctuaries. Within this sanctuary was the tomb of Attis, and an ancient image of the goddess in the shape of a stone, which was said to have fallen from heaven. The first temple at Pessinus had been erected, it was said, by King Midas. Successive rulers of Phrygia maintained and endowed it so liberally that it continued to be a place of importance long after Phrygian civilization had sunk. Spreading from this centre, the worship of Kybele took hold first in the neighbouring towns of Sardis, Magnesia, Smyrna, Ephesus, Lampsakos, and Kyzikos; thence to Athens, and in later times to the mountainous district of Arcadia, where it was locally believed that Zeus had been born and that the creation of mankind had taken place.

In Plate II. Rhea is represented as Mater turrita, or turrigera. In Plate I. she appears as the goddess of mountain tops, riding on a lion, and holding a sceptre in one hand and a cymbal in the other; beside her the moon and a star. At other times she is seated on a throne with a lion in her lap, or with a lion at each side, or in a chariot drawn by lions or panthers.

ZEUS or JUPITER.

(PLATES II. AND III.)

THIRD and last on the throne of the highest god sat **Zeus.** The fertile imagination of early times had, as we have seen, placed his abode on Mount Olympos in Thessaly. But a later and more practical age usually conceived him as inhabiting a region above the sky, where the source of all light was supposed to be. He was god of the broad light of day,

as his name implies, had control of all the phenomena of the
heavens, and accordingly sudden changes of weather, the
gathering of clouds, and, more than all, the burst of a thun-
der-storm made his presence felt as a supernatural being in-
terested in the affairs of mankind. Hence such titles as
'cloud-gatherer,' 'god of the murky cloud,' 'thunderer,' and
'mighty thunderer,' were those by which he was most frequently invoked. On the other hand, the serenity and bound-
less extent of the sky over which he ruled, combined with the
never-failing recurrence of day, led him to be regarded as an
everlasting god: 'Zeus who was and is and shall be.' To indicate this feature of his character he was styled **Kronides**
or **Kronion**, a title which, though apparently derived from
his father Kronos, must have assumed even at a very early
time a special significance ; otherwise we should expect to
find it applied also to his two brothers, Poseidon and Hades.

The eagle soaring beyond vision seemed to benefit by its
approach to Zeus, and came to be looked on as sacred to him.
Similarly high mountain peaks derived a sanctity from their
nearness to the region of light, and were everywhere in
Greece associated with his worship, many of them furnishing
titles by which he was locally known—as, for instance, **Aet-
naeos**, a title derived from Mount Ætna in Sicily, or **Ata-
byrios**, from a mountain in Rhodes. Altars to him and
even temples were erected on hill tops, to reach which by
long toiling, and then to see the earth spread out small beneath, was perhaps the best preparation for approaching him
in a proper spirit. In contrast with this, and as testimony to
the saying of Hesiod that Zeus Kronides lived not only in
the pure air but also at the roots of the earth and in men,
we find the low ground of **Dodona** in Epiros viewed with

peculiar solemnity as a spot where direct communion was to be enjoyed with him. A wind was heard to rustle in the branches of a sacred oak when the god had any communication to make, the task of interpreting it devolving on a priesthood called **Selli**. A spring rose at the foot of the oak, and sacred pigeons rested among its leaves, the story being that they had first drawn attention to the oracular powers of the tree. It should here be noted that the real importance of this worship of Zeus at Dodona belonged to exceedingly early times, and that in the primitive religion of the Italian, German, and Celtic nations the oak was regarded with similar reverence.

As the highest god, and throughout Greece worshipped as such, he was styled the father of gods and men, the ruler and preserver of the world. He was believed to be possessed of every form of power, endued with wisdom, and in his dominion over the human race partial to justice, and with no limit to his goodness and love. Zeus orders the alternation of day and night, the seasons succeed at his command, the winds obey him, now he gathers, now scatters the clouds, and bids the gentle rain fall to fertilize the fields and meadows. He watches over the administration of law and justice in the state, lends majesty to kings, and protects them in the exercise of their sovereignty. He observes attentively the general intercourse and dealings of men—everywhere demanding and rewarding uprightness, truth, faithfulness, and kindness; everywhere punishing wrong, falseness, faithlessness, and cruelty. As the eternal father of men, he was believed to be kindly at the call of the poorest and most forsaken. The homeless beggar looked to him as a merciful guardian who punished the heartless, and delighted to reward pity and sympathy. To illustrate his rule on earth we would here give a familiar story.

Philemon and **Baukis,** an aged couple of the poorer class, were living peacefully and full of piety towards the gods in their cottage in Phrygia, when Zeus, who often visited the earth, disguised, to inquire into the behaviour of men, paid a visit, in passing through Phrygia on such a journey, to these poor old people, and was received by them very kindly as a weary traveller, which he pretended to be. Bidding him welcome to the house, they set about preparing for their guest, who was accompanied by Hermes, as excellent a meal as they could afford, and for this purpose were about to kill the only goose they had left, when Zeus interfered; for he was touched by their kindliness and genuine piety, and that all the more because he had observed among the other inhabitants of the district nothing but cruelty of disposition and a habit of reproaching and despising the gods. To punish this conduct he determined to visit the country with a destroying flood, but to save from it Philemon and Baukis, the good aged couple, and to reward them in a striking manner. To this end he revealed himself to them before opening the gates of the great flood, transformed their poor cottage on the hill into a splendid temple, installed the aged pair as his priest and priestess, and granted their prayer that they might both die together. When after many years death overtook them they were changed into two trees, that grew side by side in the neighborhood—an oak and a linden.

While in adventures of this kind the highest god of the Greeks appears on the whole in a character worthy of admiration, it will be seen that many other narratives represent him as labouring under human weaknesses and error. The first wife of Zeus was **Metis** (Cleverness), a daughter of the friendly Titan Okeanos. But as **Fate**, a dark and omnıscient being, had predicted that Metis would bear Zeus a son who should surpass his father in power, Zeus followed in a manner the example of his father Kronos, by swallowing Metis before she was delivered of her child, and then from his own head gave birth to the goddess of wisdom, Pallas Athene (Minerva). Next he married, it is said, but only for a time, **Themis** (Justice), and became the father of **Astraea** and the **Horae.** His chief love was, however, always for **Hera** (Juno,) with her many charms, who, after withstanding his entreaties for a time, at length gave way, and the divine marriage took place amid great rejoicing, not on the part of the gods of heaven alone, for those other deities also, to whom the management of the world had been in various departments delegated, had been invited, and went gladly to the splendid ceremony.

Hera became the mother of **Hebe, Ares** (Mars), and **Hephæstos** (Vulcan). Zeus did not, however, remain constant and true to the marriage with his sister, but secretly indulged a passion for other goddesses, and often, under the disguise of various forms and shapes, approached even the daughters of men. Hera gave way to indignation when she found out such doings. From secret intercourse of this kind **Demeter** (Ceres) bore him **Persephone** (Proserpina); **Leto** (Latona) became the mother of **Apollo** and **Artemis** (Diana); **Dione,** the mother of **Aphrodite** (Venus); **Mnemosyne,** of the **Muses; Eurynome,** of the **Charites** (Graces); **Semelē,** of **Dionysos** (Bacchus); **Maia,** of **Hermes** (Mercury); **Alkmene,** of **Herakles** (Hercules); several of the demigods, of whom we shall afterwards speak being sons of Zeus by other and different mothers.

These numerous love passages of Zeus (and other gods as well), related by ancient poets, appear to us, as it is known they appeared to the right-thinking men amongst the ancients themselves, unbecoming of the great ruler of the universe. The wonder is how such stories came into existence; unless indeed this be accepted as a satisfactory explanation of their origin,—that they are simply the different versions of one great myth of the marriage of Zeus, peculiar in early times to the different districts of Greece, each version representing him as having but one wife, and being constant to her. Her name and the stories connected with their married life would be more or less different in each case. In after-time, when the various tribes of the Greeks became united into one people, and the various myths that had sprung up independently concerning Zeus came, through the influence of poets and by other means, to be known to the whole nation, we may imagine that the only way that presented itself of uniting them all into one consistent narrative was by degrading all the wives, except Hera, to the position of temporary acquaintances. It is, however, unfortunate that we cannot now trace every one of his acquaintances of this sort back to a primitive position of sufficiently great local importance. At the same time, enough is known to justify this principle of interpretation, not only with regard to the apparent improprieties in the conduct of Zeus, but also of the other deities wherever they occur. Properly Zeus could have but one wife, such being the limit of marriage among the Greeks.

Of the several localities in Greece where the worship of Zeus was conducted with unusual ceremony and devotion, the two most deserving of attention are Athens and Olympia. In Athens the change of season acting on the temperament of

the people seemed to produce a change in their feelings towards the god.   For from early spring and throughout the
summer they called him the friendly god (**Zeus Meilichios**),
offered public sacrifices at his altars, and on three occasions
held high festival in his honour.   But as the approach of winter made itself felt, thoughts of his anger returned, he was
called the cruel god (**Zeus Maemaktes**), and an endeavour
was made to propitiate him by a festival called **Maemakteria**.
At Olympia, in Elis, a festival, which from an early period
had assumed national importance, was held in his honour in
the month of July (**Hekatombaeon**) every fifth year, that
is, after the lapse of four clear years.   It lasted at least five
and perhaps seven days, commencing with sacrifice at the
great altar of Zeus, in which the deputies from the various
states, with their splendid retinues, took part.   This ceremony
over, a series of competitions took place in foot-racing, leaping from a raised platform with weights (*halteres*) in the hands
to give impetus, throwing the disk (a circular plate of metal
or stone weighing about 8 lb.), boxing with leather thongs
twisted round the arm and sometimes with metal rings in the
hands, horse-racing, chariot-racing with two or four horses,
and lastly, a competition of musicians and poets.   The lists
were open to all free-born Greeks, except such as had been
convicted of crime, or such as had entailed in former contests
the penalty of a fine and had refused to pay it.   Intending
competitors were required to give sureties that they had gone
through a proper course of training, and that they would abide
by the decision of the judges.   Slaves and foreigners might
look on, but the presence of married women was forbidden.
The entire management of the festival was in the hands of a
board elected from their own number by the people of Elis.

The plain of Olympia, where this national meeting in honour
of Zeus was held, is now a waste ; but some idea may still be
gathered from the description of Pausanias of its magnificent
temple and the vast number of statues that studded the sacred
grove.   Within the temple was a statue of the god, in gold
and ivory, the work of Pheidias, the most renowned of an
cient sculptors.   It was forty feet in height, and for its beauty
and grandeur was reckoned one of the **Seven Wonders***
of the ancient world.

As some would have it, these games had been established
by Zeus himself to commemorate his victory over the Titans,
and even the gods in early times are said to have taken part
in the contests.   The people of Elis maintained that the festival had been founded by **Pelops,** while others ascribed that
honour to **Herakles.**   The usual method of reckoning time
was by the interval between these festivals, one **Olympiad**
being equal to four years.   The first festival from which the
reckoning started, as ours does from the birth of Christ, occurred in the year 776 B. C.

The birth and early life of Zeus, up to the period, when,
after a long and fierce war around Olympos, he defeated the
Titans and established his right to reign in the place of his
father Kronos, has already been related.   That his two

---

* The seven wonders of the ancient world were—(1) The Pyramids of
Egypt; (2) The Walls of Babylon; (3) The Hanging Gardens of Babylon;
(4) The Temple of Diana at Ephesus; (5) The Statue of Zeus at Olympia;
(6) The Mausoleum at Halicarnassus; (7) The Colossus at Rhodes; all
monuments of art of extraordinary beauty or stupendous dimensions.   In
statues of gold and ivory, such as that of Zeus at Olympia, and many others,
the face and nude parts of the body were made of ivory, while the hair and
drapery were reproduced in gold, richly worked in parts with enamel.   We
obtain an idea of the expense of such splendid statues, from the statement that
a single lock of the hair of Zeus at Olympia cost about £250 of our money.

brothers, to whose assistance he had been greatly indebted during the war, might have a share in the management of the world, lots were cast; and to Poseidon fell the control of the sea and rivers, while Hades obtained the government of the world under the earth. Opposition, however, on the part of the kindred of Kronos had not yet ceased, and the new dynasty of gods had to encounter a fresh outbreak of war even more terrible than had been that of the Titans, the enemy being in this case the **Giants**, a race of beings sprung from the blood of Uranos. The Giants took up their position on the peninsula of Pallene, which is separated from Mount Olympos by a bay. Their king and leader was **Porphyrion**, their most powerful combatant **Alkyoneus**, against whom Zeus and Athene took up arms in vain. Their mother Earth had made the Giants proof against all the weapons of the gods— not, however, against the weapons of mortals; and knowing this Athene brought **Herakles** on the scene. Sun and moon ceased to shine at the command of Zeus, and the herb was cut down which had furnished the giants with a charm against wounds. The huge Alkyoneus, who had hurled great rocks at the Olympians, fell by the arrows of Herakles; and Porphyrion while in the act of seizing Hera, was overpowered. Of the others, **Pallas** and **Enkelados** were slain by Athene, the boisterous **Polybotes** fled, but on reaching the island of Kos was overtaken by a rock hurled at him by Poseidon and buried under it, while **Ephialtes** had to yield to Apollo, **Rhoetos** to Dionysos and **Klytios** to Hecate or Hephaestos. To the popular mind this war with the Giants had a greater interest than the Titanomachia. Ultimately the two were confounded with each other.

These wars over, there succeeded a period which was called

the **Silver Age** on earth.   Men were rich then, as in the **Golden Age** under the rule of Kronos, and lived in plenty; but still they wanted the innocence and contentment which were the true sources of human happiness in the former age; and, accordingly, while living in luxury and delicacy, they became overbearing in their manners to the highest degree, were never satisfied, and forgot the gods, to whom, in their confidence of prosperity and comfort, they denied the reverence they owed.   To punish them, and as a warning against such habits, Zeus swept them away and concealed them under the earth, where they continued to live as dæmons or spirits, not so powerful as the spirits of the men of the Golden Age, but yet respected by those who came after them.

Then followed the **Bronze Age**, a period of constant quarrelling and deeds of violence.   Instead of cultivated lands and a life of peaceful occupations and orderly habits, there came a day when everywhere might was right; and men, big and powerful as they were, became physically worn out, and sank into the lower world without leaving a trace of their having existed, and without a claim to a future spiritual life.

Finally came the **Iron Age**, in which enfeebled mankind had to toil for bread with their hands, and, bent on gain, did their best to overreach each other.   **Dike** or **Astræa**, the goddess of justice and good faith, modesty and truth, turned her back on such scenes, and retired to Olympos, while Zeus determined to destroy the human race by a great flood.   The whole of Greece lay under water, and none but **Deukalion** and his wife **Pyrrha** were saved. Leaving the summit of **Parnassos**, where they had escaped the flood, they were commanded by the gods to become the founders of a new race of men—that is, the present race.   To this end, it is said,

they cast around them as they advanced stones, which presently assumed the forms of men, who, when the flood had
quite disappeared, commenced to cultivate the land again and
spread themselves in all directions; but being little better
than the race that had been destroyed, they, too, often drew
down the displeasure of Zeus and suffered at his hands.

Among the Romans **Jupiter** held a place of honour corresponding in some degree to that held by Zeus among the
Greeks. His favorite title was Optimus Maximus. His name
being of the same derivation as that of Zeus, indicates his
function as god of the broad light of day and armed with the
weapon of lightning. Temples and altars were erected for
the purposes of his worship, statues were raised, and public
festivals held in his honour. As to sacrifice, both he and
Zeus delighted most in bulls. To both the eagle, the oak,
and the olive were sacred.

The growth of religious feeling precedes the development of artistic faculty
in man, and accordingly we find that in the earliest ages the presence of a god
was symbolized only by some natural object. In the case of Zeus this was an
oak-tree, while in the case of Rhea-Kybele it was, as we have seen, a stone
which was believed to have fallen from heaven. The first artistic efforts to
reproduce the image of a god were called **xoana,** and consisted of a pillar
rudely shaped like a human figure seen at a distance, the artist's attention
being mostly directed to the head. Of this kind was the figure of Zeus
Labrandeus as represented on the coins of Caria, the figure of Zeus with three
eyes at Argos, and the figure of him without ears at Crete. Piety caused these
rude and strange images to be retained till long after the art of sculpture had
become equal to the production of imposing figures The gold and ivory
statue of Zeus at Olympia, of which mention has already been made, represented him seated on his throne, and some small idea may still be gained of it
from what is no doubt a copy of it on the coins of Elis. The bust of plate iii.,
known as the Zeus of Otricoli, is perhaps the best existing example of the face
of Zeus as conceived by the Greek sculptors. The attributes of Zeus are the
eagle, a sceptre, a thunderbolt, and, in the case of an ancient image in Caria,
an axe. He is represented sometimes with Hera by his side, sometimes with

Athene, or with both, or with Athene and Herakles. When he leaves his throne it is generally to rise in might against an enemy such as the Giants, and in these cases he is always armed with the thunderbolt, and either stands in the act of hurling it, or drives in a chariot attended by other gods, as he is frequently to be seen on the ancient painted vases. Another favourite subject on these vases is the birth of Athene from the head of Zeus. In works of art no distinction is made between Zeus and Jupiter, for this reason, that Rome had no distinctive sculpture of its own. Plate vii. represents the infancy of Zeus in Crete.

HERA, or JUNO,

(PLATES IV. AND V.),

WAS a divine personification of what may be called the female power of the heavens—that is, the atmosphere, with its fickle and yet fertilizing properties; while **Zeus** represented those properties of the heavens that appeared to be of a male order. To their marriage was traced all the blessings of nature, and when they met, as on Mount Ida in a golden cloud, sweet fragrant flowers sprang up around them. A tree with golden apples grew up at their marriage feast, and streams of ambrosia flowed past their couch in the happy island of the west. That marriage ceremony took place, it was believed, in spring, and to keep up a recollection of it, an annual festival was held at that season in her honour. Like the sudden and violent storms, however, which in certain seasons break the peacefulness of the sky of Greece, the meetings of this divine pair often resulted in temporary quarrels and wrangling, the blame of which was usually traced to Hera; poets, and most of all Homer, in the Iliad, describing her as frequently jealous, angry, and quarrelsome, her character as lofty and proud, cold, and not free from bitterness. Of these scenes of discord we have several instances, as when (Iliad i. 586) Zeus actually

IV

Hera, or Juno.

beat her, and threw her son Hephætos out of Olympos; or (Iliad xv. 18) when, vexed at her plotting against Herakles, he hung her out of Olympos with two great weights (earth and sea) attached to her feet, and her arms bound by golden fetters—an illustration of how all the phenomena of the visible sky were thought to hang dependent on the highest god of heaven; or again (Iliad i. 396) when Hera, with Poseidon and Athene, attempted to chain down Zeus, and would have succeeded had not Thetis brought to his aid the sea giant Aegaeon. As goddess of storms, Hera was consistently described as the mother of Ares, herself taking part in war occasionally, as against the Trojans, and enjoying the honour of festivals, accompanied by warlike contests, as at Argos, where the prize was a sacred shield.

Her favourite companions, in periods of peace, were the **Charites** (Graces) and the **Horae** (Seasons), of which the latter are also found in company of her husband. Her constant attendant was **Iris,** goddess of the rainbow. The peacock, in its pride and gorgeous array, and the cuckoo as herald of the spring, were sacred to her. In the spring-time occurred her principal festival, at which the ceremony consisted of an imitation of a wedding, a figure of the goddess being decked out in bridal attire, and placed on a couch of willow branches, while wreaths and garlands of flowers were scattered about, because she loved them. Another singular festival was held in her honour every fifth year at Olympia in Elis, the ceremony consisting in the presentation of a splendidly embroidered mantle (*peplos*) to the goddess, and races in which only girls and unmarried women took part, running with their hair streaming down, and wearing short dresses,—the judges on the occasion being sixteen married women.

The character, however, in which Hera was most generally viewed was that of queen of heaven, and as the faithful wife of Zeus claiming the highest conceivable respect and honour. Herself the ideal of womanly virtues, she made it a principal duty to protect them among mortals, punishing with severity all trespassers against her moral law—but, naturally, none so much as those who had been objects of her husband's affections—as, for instance, **Semele,** the mother of Dionysos, or **Alkmene,** the mother of Herakles. Her worship was restricted for the most part to women, who, according to the various stages of womanhood, regarded her in a different light: some as a bride, styling her **Parthenia;** others as a wife, with the title of **Gamelia, Zygia** or **Teleia;** and others again in the character of **Eileithyia,** as helpful at childbirth. Of these phases of her life that of bride was obviously associable with the phenomena of the heavens in the springtime, when the return of dazzling light and warmth spread everywhere affectionate gaiety and the blooming of new life. As queen of heaven and wife of Zeus she will be found, in connection with the legends of Argos and its neighbourhood, possessed, from motives of jealousy, of a hatred towards the nocturnal phenomena of the sky, and especially the moon, as personified by the wandering Io, whom she placed under the surveillance of Argos, a being with innumerable eyes, and apparently a personification of the starry system.

The town of Argos, with its ancient legends, which clearly betray some powerful sensitiveness to the phenomena of light, was the oldest and always the chief centre of this worship of Hera. There was her principal temple, and within it a statue of the goddess, by Polykleitos, which almost rivalled in grandeur and beauty the Zeus at Olympia, by Pheidias. Next came Samos, with its splendid temple erected for her by Poly-krates. In Corinth also, in Eubœa, Bœotia, Crete, and even in Lakinion, in Italy, she had temples and devotees.

Juno, the Roman equivalent of Hera, was mostly regarded from the maternal point of view, and in accordance with that frequently styled **Lucina,** the helper at child-birth. Temples were erected and festivals held in her honour—of the festivals that called **Matronalia** being the chief. It was held on the 1st of March of each year, and could only be participated in by women, who went with girdles loose, and on the occasion received presents from husbands, lovers, or friends, making presents in turn to their servants. The spirits that guarded over women were called in early times **Junones.**

The image of Hera is said to have consisted at first of a long pillar, as in Argos, and in Samos of a plank, and to have assumed a human form only in comparatively late times. The statue of her by Polykleitos, mentioned above, was of gold and ivory and of colossal size. It represented her seated on a throne, holding in one hand a pomegranate, the symbol of marriage, and in the other a sceptre on which sat a cuckoo. On her head was a crown orna-mented with figures of the Charites (Graces) and Horae. We can still in some measure recall the appearance of the statue from the marble head known as the Juno Ludovisi (on plate iv.), from the coins of Argos, and from several ancient heads in marble of great beauty. Praxiteles made a colossal statue of her in the character of the protectress of marriage rites, and also a group of her seated, with Athene and Hebe standing beside her. On the painted vases the scene in which she most frequently occurs is that where she appears before Paris to be judged of her beauty.

4

POSEIDON, or NEPTUNE.

(PLATE V.)

IT has already been told how, when all the resources had
failed which the Titans could bring to bear for the restoration of Kronos to the throne, the. government of the world
was divided by lot among his three sons, **Zeus, Poseidon,
Hades.** To Zeus fell, besides a general supremacy, the control of the heavens; and we have seen how he and his con-
sort Hera, representing the phenomena of that region, were
conceived as divine persons possessed of a character and performing actions such as were suggested by those phenomena.
To Poseidon fell the control of the element of water, and he
in like manner was conceived as a god, in whose character
and actions were reflected the phenomena of that element,
whether as the broad navigable sea, or as the cloud which
gives fertility to the earth, growth to the grain and vine, or
as the fountain which refreshes man, cattle, and horses. A
suitable symbol of his power, therefore, was the horse, admirably adapted as it is both for labour and battle, whilst its
swift springing movement compares finely with the advance
of a foaming wave of the sea. " He yokes to the chariot,"
sings Homer in the Iliad, " his swift steeds, with feet of brass
and manes of gold, and himself, clad in gold, drives over the
waves. The beasts of the sea sport round him, leaving their
lurking places, for they know him to be their lord. The sea
rejoices and makes way for him. His horses speed lightly,
and never a drop touches the brazen axle."

It may have been to illustrate a tendency of the sea to en-
croach in many places on the coast, as well as to show the

V

Hera, or Juno.

Poseidon, or Neptune.

importance attached to a good supply of water, that the myth originated which tells us of the dispute between Poseidon and **Athene** for the sovereignty of the soil of Attika. To settle the dispute, it was agreed by the gods that whichever of the two should perform the greatest wonder, and at the same time confer the most useful gift on the land, should be entitled to rule over it. With a stroke of his trident Poseidon caused a brackish spring to well up on the Acropolis of Athens, a rock 400 feet high, and previously altogether without water. But Athene in her turn caused the first olive tree to grow from the same bare rock, and since that was deemed the greatest benefit that could be bestowed, obtained for all time sovereignty of the land, which Poseidon thereupon spitefully inundated.

A similar dispute, and ending also unfavourably for him, was that which he had with **Hera** concerning the district of Argos. But in this case his indignation took the opposite course of causing a perpetual drought. Other incidents of the same nature were his disputes with **Helios** for the possession of Corinth, with **Zeus** for Ægina, with **Dionysos** for Naxos, and with **Apollo** for Delphi. The most obvious illustrations, however, of the encroaching tendency of the sea are the monsters which Poseidon sent to lay waste coast lands, such as those which **Hesione** and **Andromeda** were offered to appease.

In the Iliad Poseidon appears only in his capacity of ruler of the sea, inhabiting a brilliant palace in its depths, traversing its surface in a chariot, or stirring the powerful billows till the earth shakes as they crash upon the shore. This limitation of his functions, though possibly to be accounted for by the nature of the poem, is remarkable for this reason, that among the earliest myths associated with his worship are those

in which he is represented in connection with well-watered
plains and valleys. In the neighbourhood of Lerna, in the
parched district of Argos, he had struck the earth with his
trident, and caused three springs to well up for love of
Amymone, whom he found in distress, because she could
not obtain the water which her father **Danaos** had sent her
to fetch. In Thessaly a stroke of his trident had broken
through the high mountains, which formerly shut in the whole
country and caused it to be frequently flooded with water.
By that stroke he formed the pleasant vale of **Tempe,** through
which the water collecting from the hills might flow away.
A district well supplied with water was favourable to pasture
and the rearing of horses, and in this way the horse came to
be doubly his symbol, as god of the water of the sea and on
the land. In Arcadia, with its mountainous land and fine
streams and valleys, he was worshipped side by side with
Demeter, with whom, it was believed, he begat that winged
and wonderfully fleet horse **Arion.** In Bœotia, where he
was also worshipped, the mother of Arion was said to have
been **Erinys,** to whom he had appeared in the form of a
horse. With **Medusa** he became the father of the winged
horse **Pegasos,** which was watered at springs by Nymphs,
and appeared to poets as the symbol of poetic inspiration.
And again, as an instance of his double capacity as god of the
sea and pasture streams, the ram, with the golden fleece for
which the Argonauts sailed, was said to have been his offspring
by **Theophane,** who had been changed into a lamb. Chief
among his other offspring were, on the one hand, the giant
Antaeos, who derived from his mother Earth a strength
which made him invincible, till Herakles lifting him in the
air overpowered him, and the Kyklops, **Polyphemos :** on

the other hand, **Pelias,** who sent out the Argonauts, and **Neleus** the father of **Nestor.**

To return to the instances of rebellious conduct on the part of Poseidon, it appears that after the conclusion of the war with the Giants a disagreement arose between him and Zeus, the result of which was that Poseidon was suspended for the period of a year from the control of the sea, and was further obliged during the time to serve, along with Apollo, **Laomedon** the King of Troy, and to help to build the walls of that city. Some say that the building of the walls was voluntary on the part of both gods, and was done to test the character of Laomedon, who afterwards refused to give Poseidon the reward agreed upon. Angry at this, the god devastated the land by a flood, and sent a sea-monster, to appease which Laomedon was driven to offer his daughter **Hesione** as a sacrifice. **Herakles,** however, set the maiden free and slew the monster. Thus defeated, Poseidon relented none of his indignation towards the Trojans, and would have done them much injury in after times, when they were at war with the Greeks, but for the interference of Zeus.

Though worshipped generally throughout Greece, it was in the seaport towns that the most remarkable zeal was displayed to obtain his favour. Temples in his honour, sanctuaries, and public rejoicings were to be met with in Thessaly, Bœotia, Arcadia, at Aegae, and Helike, on the coast of Achaea, at Pylos in Messenia, at Elis, in the island of Samos, at Corinth, Nauplia, Troezen, in the islands of Kalauria, Eubœa, Skyros, and Tenos, at Mycale, Taenarum, Athens, and on the Isthmus —that belt of land which connects Peloponnesos with the rest of Greece. In the island of Tenos an annual festival was held in his honour, at which he was worshipped in the character of a physician. People crowded to the festival from neighbouring islands, and spent the time in banquets, sacrifice, and common counsel. But chief of all the gatherings in his honour was that held on the Isthmus of Corinth in the autumn, twice in each Olympiad—a festival which had been established by **Theseus**, and in reputation stood next to the Olympian games, like them also serving the purpose of maintaining among the Greeks of distant regions the consciousness of their common origin. The Corinthians had the right of arranging and managing them, the Athenians having also certain privileges. It was in his double capacity of ruler of the sea and as the first to train and employ horses that the honours of this festival were paid to him. His temple, with other sanctuaries, stood in a pine grove, a wreath from which was the prize awarded to the victors. The prize had originally been a wreath of parsley. In this sacred pine grove was to be seen the **Argo,** the ship of the **Argonauts,** dedicated to **Poseidon** as a memorial of the earliest enterprise at sea; and there also stood the colossal bronze statue of the god, which the Greeks raised to commemorate the splendid naval victory gained over the Persians at Salamis. Horses and bulls were sacrificed to him, the method of performing the sacrifice being to throw them into the sea. It was the practice of fortunate survivors of shipwreck to hang up some memento of their safety in one of his temples.

The Romans, living mostly as herdsmen and farmers in early times, had little occasion to propitiate the god of the sea, and it was probably, therefore, rather as the father of streams that they erected a temple to **Neptunus** in the Campus Martius, and held a festival in his honour attended with games, feasting, and enjoyment like that of a fair.

Between Zeus and Poseidon there is, in works of art, such likeness as would be expected between two brothers. But Poseidon is by far the more powerful of the two physically—his build, like that of Herakles, expressing the greatest conceivable strength. But unlike Herakles, his attitudes and especially his head, are those of a god, not of an athlete. His features, one by one, resemble those of Zeus, but his hair, instead of springing from his brow, falls in thick masses over the temples, and is matted from the water. His attributes are a trident and dolphin. Possibly the sacred figures of him in his temples represented him seated on a throne, and clad in the Ionian chiton. But in the colossal statues of him erected on promontories and in harbours, to secure his favour, he was always standing wearing only a slight scarf, which concealed none of his powerful form, holding out a dolphin in his left, and the trident in his right hand, often with one foot raised on the prow of a vessel. In works of art not connected directly with his worship he was figured (as on plate v.), traversing the sea in a car drawn by Hippocamps, or other fabulous creatures of the sea. In one of the pediments of the Parthenon the dispute between him and Athene was represented.

AMPHITRITE,

THE rightful wife of Poseidon, was the goddess of the sea, had the care of its creatures, could stir the great waves, and hurl them against rocks and cliffs. She was a daughter of **Okeanos** and **Tethys,** or, according to another report, of **Nereus** and **Doris.** Usually she was represented with flowing hair and the toes of a crab protruding from her temples; sometimes seated on the back of a triton or other creature of the deep, alone among sea-animals and seaweed, or accompanying Poseidon. She may be compared with the sea-goddess of the Romans, **Salacia, Neverita,** and **Venilia.**

HADES, or PLUTO.

(PLATE VI.)

WE have seen how Zeus, Hera, and Poseidon came to be conceived as the three great deities who between them controlled
the elements of heavens, sky, and sea, and how a character
came to be ascribed to each of them such as was most naturally suggested by the phenomena of the provinces of the
world in which they respectively ruled. But there still remained a region which could not escape the observation of
people like the Greeks, gifted with so keen a sense of the various operations of nature. That region was, however, itself
invisible, being under the surface of the earth. The growth
of vegetation was seen to be steadily upward, as if impelled
by some divine force below. The metals which experience
showed to be most precious to mankind could only be obtained by digging into that dark region under the earth. Thither returned, after its day on earth was spent, every form of
life. In conceiving a god who should be supreme in the
management of this region, it was necessary to attribute a
double character to him: first, as the source of all the treasures and wealth of the earth, as expressed in his name **Plu-
ton**; and secondly, as monarch of the dark realm inhabited
by the invisible shades of the dead, as expressed in his name
of **Aïdes**.

While by virtue of his power of giving fertility to vegetation, of swelling the seed cast into the furrows of the earth,
and of yielding treasures of precious metal, he was justly
viewed as a benevolent deity and a true friend of man, there
was another and very grim side to his character, in which he

VI.

Pluto and Proserpina.

Demeter, or Ceres.   Hestia, or Vesta.

appears as the implacable, relentless god, whom no cost of sacrifice could persuade to permit any one who had once passed his gates ever to return. For this reason, to die, to go to Hades' house, to pass out of sight, to be lost in the darkness of the lower world, was looked forward to as the dismal inevitable fate awaiting all men. Yet there must have been some consolation in the belief that the life thus claimed by him had been originally his gift, as were the means of comfort and pleasure in life thus cut off. In later times, when the benevolent side of his character came more into view, assuring hopes arose concerning a future happy life that robbed death of its terrors. To impart such hopes was the purpose of the **Eleusinian Mysteries.**

It seems to have been to make this union of two such opposite powers in the person of one god more explicit that the myth concerning his marriage with **Persephone** originated, she being, as we shall afterwards see, a personification of young blooming life. The grim god of the dead carries off by force a young goddess full of life. But no new life issues from the marriage. Yet she loved him, it would seem ; for when her mother, **Demeter** (Ceres), implored her to come back to earth, her answer was that she had accepted from her husband the half of a pomegranate, or apple of love as it was called, and had eaten it. It is apparently in reference to this that both Hades and Persephone are represented in works of art holding each a fruit.

Hades, being a son of **Rhea** and **Kronos,** was entitled, after the dethronement of the latter, to a share along with his two brothers, **Zeus** and **Poseidon,** in the management of the world. They cast lots, and to Hades fell the dominion over the lower world. The importance assigned to his dominion may be judged from the fact of its monarch being a brother of Zeus, and styled, too, sometimes, " **Zeus** of the lower world."

With regard to the region where the realm of Hades was to be looked for we find the ancient authorities at variance, some representing it as in the under-world proper—that is, under the crust of the earth, others in the remote west, in Okeanos, where were the gloomy groves of Persephone.   It was entered from the upper world by any spot of sufficiently sombre or wild natural aspect, particularly chasms with dark waters such as inspire terror.   The most celebrated place of this kind was Lake **Avernus**, at Cumae in Italy, of which it was said, as of the Dead Sea, that no bird tried to fly across it but fell lifeless in its waters.   Beyond these entrances was an open gate through which all comers had to pass, and having passed could not as a rule retrace a step.   Exceptions to the rule were made in favour of heroes such as **Herakles** and **Orpheus**, who were permitted to visit the home of the dead, and return alive.   The entrance was guarded by the dog of Hades, the dreaded **Cerberus**, a monster with three heads and a serpent's tail, fawning on those who entered, but showing his horrible teeth to those who tried to pass out.   But besides by this gateway, the lower was separated from the upper world by rivers with impetuous torrents, of which the most famous was the **Styx**, a stream of such terrible aspect that even the highest gods invoked it as witness of the truth of their oaths.   Across this river the departed were conveyed by an aged ferryman appointed by the gods, and called **Charon**, but not until their bodies had been buried in the earth above with all due ceremony of sacrifice and marks of affection.   Till this was done, the souls of the departed had to

wander listlessly about the farther bank of the Styx, a prospect which was greatly dreaded by the ancients. For the
ferry Charon exacted a toll (*naulon*), to pay which a piece of
money (*danake*) was placed in the mouth of the dead at burial.

The other rivers of the under-world were named **Achĕ-
ron**, that is, the river of " eternal woe "; **Pyriphlĕge-
thon**, the stream of " fire "; and **Kokytos**, the river of
" weeping and wailing." To these is added, by a later myth,
Lethe, the river of " forgetfulness "—so called because its
waters were believed to possess the property of causing the
departed who drank of them to forget altogether their former
circumstances in the upper world. The purport of this myth
was to explain and establish the idea that the dead could not
take with them into the realm of everlasting peace the consciousness of the pains and sorrows of their lot on earth. In
the waters of Lethe they drank a happy oblivion of all past
suffering, wants, and troubles,—an idea of the means of for-
getting sorrow which later poets have made frequent use of.

In the last book of the Odyssey the souls of the slain
suitors, conceived as small winged beings, are described as
being conducted to the realm of Hades by Hermes in his capacity of **Psychopompos** (see Plate VI). The way is dark
and gloomy. They pass the streams of Okeanos, the white
rock, the gates of Helios, the people of dreams, and at last
reach the Asphodel meadow, where the spirits of the dead
inhabit subterranean caves.

With regard to the condition of the dead under the dominion of Hades, the belief was that they led a shadowy sort
of apparent life, in which, as mere reflections of their former
selves, they continued as in a dream, at any rate without dis-

tinct consciousness, to perform the labours and carry on the occupations to which they had been accustomed on earth. It was only to favoured individuals like the Theban seer, **Teiresias,** of whom we have more to say afterwards, that the privilege of complete consciousness was granted. Such was the sad condition of the dead; and how they bore it may be guessed from the complaint of **Achilles** to **Odysseus,** in the Odyssey: "I would rather toil as a day-labourer on the earth than reign here a prince of dead multitudes." Occasionally the shades of the dead were permitted to appear to their friends on earth. It was also possible to summon them by a sacrifice, the blood of which, when they had drunk of it, restored consciousness and speech, so as to enable them to communicate with the living.

We must, however, clearly distinguish between this underworld as the abiding place of the great mass of the dead, and two other regions where spirits of the departed were to be found,—the one **Elysion** (the Elysian Fields), with the islands of the blest, and the other **Tartaros.** The former region was most commonly placed in the remotest West, and the latter as far below the earth as the heavens are above it. In early times it appears to have been believed that **Elysion** and the happy islands were reserved less for the virtuous and good than for certain favourites of the gods. There, under the sovereignty of **Kronos,** they lived again a kind of second golden age of perpetual duration. But in later times there spread more and more the belief in a happy immortality reserved for all the good, and particularly for those who had been initiated into the Eleusinian Mysteries (see below). **Tartaros,** on the other hand, was the region where those were condemned to punishment who had committed any crime against the gods while on earth. What was the misery of their condition we shall be able to judge from the following account of a few of the best known of those condemned to such punishment,—as **Tantalos, Ixion, Sisyphos, Tityos,** and the **Danaïdes.**

Tantalos, once a king of Phrygia, had given offence to the gods by his overbearing and treachery, as well as by the cruelty which he had practised on his own son. For this he was doomed to Tartaros, and there to suffer from an unceasing dread of being crushed by a great rock that hung above his head, he the while standing up to the throat in water, yet possessed of a terrible thirst which he could never quench, and a gnawing hunger which he tried in vain to allay with the tempting fruits that hung over his head but withdrew at every approach he made.

Ixion, once a sovereign of Thessaly, had, like Tantalos, outraged the gods, and was in consequence sentenced to Tartaros, there to be lashed with serpents to a wheel which a strong wind drove continually round and round.

Sisyphos, once king of Corinth, had by treachery and hostility incurred the anger of the gods in a high degree, and was punished in Tartaros by having to roll a huge stone up a height, which he had no sooner done, by means of his utmost exertion, than it rolled down again.

Tityos, a giant who once lived in Euboea, had misused his strength to outrage **Leto** (the mother of **Apollo** and **Artemis**), and was condemned by Zeus to Tartaros, where two enormous vultures gnawed continually his liver, which always grew again.

The **Danaïdes,** daughters of **Danaos,** king of Argos (of whom see below), were sentenced to Tartaros for the murder of their husbands. The punishment prescribed for them was to carry water, and continue to pour it into a broken cistern or vase, the labour being all in vain, and going on for ever.

Hades and **Persephone,** however, were not only rulers over the souls of the departed, but were also believed to exercise the function of judges of mankind after death. In this task they were assisted by three heroes who while on earth had been conspicuous for wisdom and justice,—**Minos, Rhadamanthys,** and **Æakos,** the last being also, apart from this, the gate-keeper of the lower region, according to a later opinion.

Both among the Greeks and Romans the worship of **Pluton-Hades** was wide-spread, and the honours paid him great. In Greece his principal temples were at Pylos, Athens, and Olympia in Elis. The cypress, narcissus, and boxwood were sacred to him. In Rome a great festival was held in his honour in the month of February, at which sacrifices (*februationes*) of black bulls and goats were offered, and the officiating priests wore wreaths of cypress, the whole ceremony extending over twelve nights. The **Sæcular Games,** which were held once in a century, were in his honour, and as a tribute to the dead.

In works of art Hades is represented as having inherited the same type of face as his brothers Zeus and Poseidon, differing only in a certain grimness of expression. His hair shades his brow in heavy masses. In attitude he is either seated on a throne with Persephone by his side (as on plate vi.), or standing in a chariot and carrying her off. His attributes are a sceptre like that of Zeus, and a helmet, which, like the cloud cap of Siegfried in German mythology, made its wearer invisible. His attendant is the three-headed dog Cerberus. On the painted vases scenes of torment in Tartaros are not unfrequent—such, for example, as the Danaïdes pouring water into the broken vase, or Ixion bound to the wheel, or Sisyphos pushing up the stone : Herakles carrying off Cerberus, and Orpheus on his memorable visit to bring back Eurydike, are also represented on the vases.

PERSEPHONE, or PROSERPINA,

(PLATE VI.,)

Or **Persephoneia**, also called **Kora** by the Greeks, and by the Romans **Libera**, was a daughter of **Zeus** and **Demeter**, and the wife of **Aïdes**, the marriage being childless. Struck with the charms of her virgin beauty, Hades had obtained the sanction of his brother Zeus to carry her off by force; and for this purpose, as the myth relates, he suddenly rose up from a dark hole in the earth near to where she was wandering in a flowery meadow not far from Ætna in Sicily, plucking and gathering the narcissus, seized the lovely flower-gatherer, and made off with her to the under-world in a chariot drawn by four swift horses, Hermes leading the way. Persephone resisted, begged and implored gods and men to help her; but Zeus approving the transaction let it pass. In vain Demeter searched for her daughter, traversing every land, or, as other myths say, pursuing the escaped Hades with her yoke of winged serpents, till she learned what had taken place from the all-seeing and all-hearing god of the sun. Then she entreated with tears the gods to give her daughter back, and this they promised to do provided she had not as yet tasted of anything in the under-world. But by the time that Hermes, who had been sent by Zeus to ascertain this, reached the under-world, she had eaten the half of a pomegranate which Hades had given her as an expression of love. For this reason the return of Persephone to the upper world for good became impossible. She must remain the wife of Hades. An arrangement was however come to, by which she was to be allowed to stay with her mother half the year on earth and among the gods of Olympos, while the other half of the year was to be spent with her husband below.

In this myth of **Persephone-Kora,** daughter of Zeus, the god of the heavens, which by their warmth and rain produce fertility, and of Demeter, the maternal goddess of the fertile earth, we see that she was conceived as a divine personification of the process of vegetation—in summer appearing beside her mother in the light of the upper world, but in the autumn disappearing, and in winter passing her time, like the seed, under the earth with the god of the lower world. The decay observed throughout Nature in autumn, the suspension of vegetation in winter, impressed the ancients, as it impresses us and strikes modern poets, as a moral of the transitoriness of all earthly life; and hence the carrying off of Persephone appeared to be simply a symbol of death. But the myth at the same time suggests hope, and proclaims the belief that out of death springs a new life, but apparently not a productive life, and that men carried off by the god of the under-world will not for ever remain in the unsubstantial region of the shades. This at least appears to have been the sense in which the myth of Persephone and her mother was presented to those initiated into the Eleusinian Mysteries, which, as we have remarked before, held out assuring hopes of the imperishableness of human existence, and of an eternal real life to follow after death.

As queen of the shades Persephone had control over the various dreaded beings whose occupation, like that of the **Sirens,** was to beguile men to their death, or like that of the **Erinys,** to avenge murder and all base crimes. She shared the honours paid to her husband in Greece, lower Italy, and especially in the island of Sicily. Temples of great beauty were erected for her in the Greek Locri, and at Kyzikos on the Propontis.

The principal festivals held in her honour in Greece occurred in the autumn or in spring, the visitors at the former appearing dressed in mourning to commemorate her being carried off by Pluto, while at the spring festival all wore holiday garments to commemorate her return.

There remains, however, the important phase of her character in which she returns to the upper world and is associated with her mother Demeter. But this it will be more convenient to consider in the next chapter. The attributes of Persephone were ears of corn and poppies. Her attribute as the wife of Hades was a pomegranate ; her sacrifice consisted of cows and pigs. In works of art she has a more youthful appearance, but otherwise closely resembles her mother Demeter. The Roman **Proserpina**, though the name is clearly the same as Persephone, appears to have had no hold on the religious belief of the Roman nation, their goddess of the shades being **Libitina,** or **Lubentina.**

DEMETER, or CERES,

(PLATE VI.,)

A daughter of **Kronos** and **Rhea**, was the goddess of the earth in its capacity of bringing forth countless fruits, the all-nourishing mother, and above all the divine being who watched over the growth of grain, and the various products of vegetation most important to man. The first and grand thought in her worship was the mysterious evolution of life out of the seed which is cast into the ground and suffered to rot—a process of nature which both St. Paul (1 Corinthians xv. 35) and St. John (xii. 24) compare with the attainment of a new life through Christ. The seed left to rot in the ground was in the

5

keeping of her daughter Persephone, the goddess of the lower world, the new life which sprang from it was the gift of Demeter herself; and from this point of view the two goddesses, mother and daughter, were inseparable.   They were regarded as "two in one," and styled "the great deities."

From being conceived as the cause of growth in the grain Demeter next came to be looked on as having first introduced the art of agriculture, and as being the source of the wealth and blessings which attended the diligent practice of that art.

When Hades carried off her young loved daughter, Demeter, with a mother's sorrow, lit her torch, and mounting her car drawn by winged snakes, drove through all lands searching for her, leaving, wherever she rested and was hospitably received, traces of her blessing in the form of instruction in the art of agriculture.   But nowhere in Greece did her blessing descend so richly as in the district of Attica; for there **Keleos**, of Eleusis, a spot not far from Athens, had received her with most cordial hospitality.   In return for this she taught him the use of the plough, and before departing presented to his son, **Triptolemos**, whom she had nursed, the seed of the barley along with her snake-drawn car, in order that he might traverse all lands, teaching by the way mankind how to sow and to utilize the grain, a task which Triptolemos performed faithfully, and so extended the art of agriculture to most distant lands.

In Arcadia, Crete, and Samothrace we find her associated with a mythical hero called **Jasion**, reputed to have been the first sower of grain, to whom she bore a child, whose name of **Plutos** shows him to be a personification of the wealth derived from the cultivation of grain.   In Thessaly there was a legend of her hostility to a hero sometimes called **Erysichton,** 'the earth upturner' or 'the ploughman,' and some-

times **Aethon**, a personification of famine.   Again we find a
reference to her function as goddess of agriculture in the story
that once, when Poseidon threatened with his superior strength
to mishandle her, Demeter took the form of a horse and fled
from him; but the god, taking the same shape, pursued and
overtook her, the result being that she afterwards bore him
Arion, a wonderful black horse of incredible speed, and
gifted with intelligence and speech like a man.   Pain and
shame at the birth of such a creature drove her to hide for a
long time in a cave, till at last she was purified by a bath in
the river **Ladon,** and again appeared among the other
deities.   From the necessities of agriculture originated the
custom of living in settled communities.   It was Demeter
who first inspired mankind with an interest in property and
the ownership of land, who created the feeling of patriotism
and the maintenance of law and order.

   The next phase of her character was that which came into
prominence at harvest time, when the bare stubble fields re-
minded her worshippers of the loss of her daughter Persephone.   At that time two kinds of festivals were held in her
honour, the one kind called **Haloa** or **Thalysia**, being apparently mere harvest festivals, the other called **Thesmo-
phoria**.   Of the latter, as conducted in the village of Hali-
mus in Attica, we know that it was held from the 9th to the
13th of October each year, that it could only be participated
in by married women, that at one stage of the proceedings
Demeter was hailed as the mother of the beautiful child, and
that this joy afterwards gave way to expressions of the deepest grief at her loss of her daughter.   At night orgies were
held at which mysterious ceremonies were mixed with boisterous amusements of all sorts.   The Thesmoi or 'institu-

tions' from which she derived the title of Thesmophoros appear to have referred to married life.

We have no means of knowing to what extent the ancient
Greeks based their belief in a happy existence hereafter on
the mysterious evolution of life from the seed rotting in the
ground, which the early Christians adopted as an illustration
of the grand change to which they looked forward. But that
the myth of the carrying off of Persephone, her gloomy existence under the ground, and her cheerful return, originated in
the contemplation of this natural process, is clear from the
fact that at Eleusis Demeter and Persephone always retained
the character of seed goddesses, side by side with their more
conspicuous character as deities in whose story were reflected
the various scenes through which those mortals would have to
pass who were initiated into the **Mysteries of Eleusis**.
These mysteries had been instituted by Demeter herself, and
whatever rites they may have consisted in, we know from the
testimony of men like Pindar and Aeschylos, who had been
initiated, that they were well calculated to awaken most profound feelings of piety and a cheerful hope of better life in
future. It is believed that the ceremony of initiation consisted, not in instruction as to what to believe or how to act
to be worthy of her favour, but in elaborate and prolonged
representations of the various scenes and acts on earth and
under it connected with the myth of the carrying off of Persephone. The ceremony took place at night, and it is probable that advantage was taken of the darkness to make the
scenes in the lower world more hideous and impressive. Probably these representations were reserved for the **Epoptae** or
persons in the final stage of initiation. Those in the earlier
stages were called **Mystae.** Associated with Demeter and

Persephone in the worship at Eleusis was Dionysos in his youthful character and under the name of **Jacchos**. But at what time this first took place, whether it was due to some affinity in the orgiastic nature of his worship, or rather to his local connection with Attica as god of the vine, is not known.

Two festivals of this kind, **Eleusinia**, were held annually, —the lesser in spring, when the earliest flowers appeared, and the greater in the month of September. The latter occupied nine days, commencing on the night of the 20th with a torch-light procession. Though similar festivals existed in various parts of Greece and even of Italy, those of Eleusis in Attica continued to retain something like national importance, and from the immense concourse of people who came to take part in them, were among the principal attractions of Athens. The duties of high priest were vested in the family of Eumolpidae, whose ancestor Eumolpos, according to one account, had been installed in the office by Demeter herself. The festival was brought to a close by games, among which was that of bull-baiting.

In Italy a festival founded on the Eleusinian Mysteries and conducted in the Greek manner was held in honour of **Bacchus** and **Ceres**, or **Liber** and **Libera** as they were called. It appears, however, to have never commanded the same respect as the original. For we find Romans who had visited Greece, and like Cicero been initiated at Eleusis, returning with a strong desire to see the Eleusinian ceremonies transplanted to Rome. Altogether it is probable that the Roman Ceres was but a weak counterpart of the Greek Demeter.

The attributes of Demeter, like those of Persephone, were ears of corn and poppies; on her head she wore a modius or

corn measure as a symbol of the fertility of the earth. Her
sacrifice consisted of cows and pigs.

Statues that can positively be assigned to Demeter are very rare, the best by
far being that found at Cnidus and now in the British Museum, which represents her seated, draped, and with a veil falling from the back of her head.
On her head is neither the modius nor the crown which she also wears sometimes. On the painted vases, however, figures of her are less rare. On a vase
in the British Museum she appears beside Triptolemos, who is seated in the
winged car which she gave him. On another vase, also in the national collec-
tion, we find the scene at the institution of the Eleusinian Mysteries. In the
centre is Triptolemos seated in the car; before him Persephone (here called
Pherophatta, a more ancient form of her name), and a figure called Eleusis;
behind him Demeter and Eumolpos; on the other side of the vase are Zeus,
Dionysos, Poseidon, and Amphitrite. A marble relief, found at Eleusis, represents, it is believed, Demeter, Persephone, and the youthful Jacchos.

HECATE,

(PLATE VII.,)

Though, properly speaking, not one of the supreme order of
deities, is entitled to be placed here on account of a resemblance to Persephone in her mysterious functions both in the
upper and lower world. She is a goddess of Titanic origin,
daughter of **Tartaros** and **Night,** or of **Perses** and **Aste-
ria** (Starry-Night), the sister of **Leto,** according to other
accounts. The stories current among the ancients concerning her vary greatly, and often confuse her with other deities,
especially those of the night, such as **Sēlēne** or **Luna,** the
goddess of the moon, while standing to Persephone in the relation of servant or companion. She belongs to the class of
torch-bearing deities, like **Artemis,** and was conceived as
carrying a burning torch, to suit the belief that she was the
nocturnal goddess of the moon, and a huntress who knew her

VII.

Hecate.

Kuretes Keeping Guard over Infant Zeus.

way also in the realm of spirits. All the secret powers of
Nature were at her command, it was thought. She had a
control over birth, life, and death, and enjoyed great honour
among the gods of Olympos as well as in the under-world.
To express her power in the three regions of nature, heaven,
earth, and the under-world, she was represented as of triple
form, and named **Triformis.** Dogs were sacred to her. Her
character being originally that of a mysterious deity, it happened that more prominence was always given in the conception of her to her gloomy and appalling features, her chief
function being held to be that of goddess of the nether world,
of night and darkness, mistress of all the witchcraft and black
arts which were believed in as much in antiquity as in the
middle ages. Accordingly her festivals were held at night,
worship was paid her by torchlight, and sacrifices of black
lambs presented with many strange ceremonies. Her presence
was mostly felt at lonely cross-roads, whence she derived the
name of **Trivia.**

A mysterious festival was held in her honour every year in
the island of Ægina, in the Saronic Gulf. Beside the lake of
Avernus, in lower Italy, was a dark grove sacred to her.

HESTIA, or VESTA,

(PLATE VI.,)

Sister of Demeter, and daughter of **Kronos** and **Rhea,** was
worshipped both by Greeks and Romans as the goddess of the
home-fire, or hearth, the name of which was identical with her
own. She was properly, therefore, the guardian of family
life ; her altars were everywhere, the hearth of every house
being her sanctuary, and when the family gathered round it

daily it was with feelings of regard for that goddess. Every meal prepared on the fire at home revived a grateful sense of the common enjoyments of family life. In every building of public resort she had a sanctuary in the shape of a fire; and when in Greece a body of colonists were about to emigrate to new and distant homes, one of their chief considerations was to take with them some portion of fire sacred to Hestia, in order to carry with them the favour of the goddess; for the Greeks looked upon the state as a great family, with an altar of Hestia as its central point: and thus, by taking with them to their new homes a portion of the fire from that altar, or state hearth, the colony retained its interest and participation in the public affairs of their parent state. No enterprise was commenced without sacrifice and prayer at her altar; and when the fire of one of those holy places chanced to be extinguished, it could only be rekindled by a light from some other sanctuary, not by ordinary and impure fire.

As the goddess of a pure element, **Hestia** despised love, and, though pressed to consent both by **Poseidon** and **Apollo**, obtained from **Zeus** the privilege she prayed for, of remaining in a single state. Her spotless purity fitted her peculiarly to be the guardian of virgin modesty.

Though zealously worshipped throughout Greece, there was no temple specially devoted to her. Her proper sanctuary was, as we have said, by the fire of every house where people gathered together. She had a share in all the sacrifices offered at the temples of other gods, and at every burnt-offering her presence was recognised as goddess of the sacred hearth and altar flame, as it was also in the libations of water, wine, and oil, and in the prayers addressed to her. At the same time she had her own peculiar sacrifices, consisting of young shoots of grain, the first-fruits of the harvest, and young cows. Her priestesses had to remain virgins.

In Rome, however, there was a temple to **Vesta** that had been built by **Numa Pompilius.** It was of a round shape, and contained in its centre her symbol of an altar, with a fire that was never allowed to go out. This temple, which stood open by day but was closed by night, contained, besides other very old figures of deities, the **Palladium,** a small wooden image of **Minerva** (Pallas-Athene), which, according to the myth, originally fell from heaven upon the citadel of Troy, and was carried thence to Greece, and afterwards to Rome. Upon the preservation of this figure depended, the people believed, the safety and existence of the Roman empire. Her priestesses, six in number, were called vestal virgins, their duty being to feed the sacred flame of her temple, and to present sacrifices and prayers for the welfare of the state. To this office they were chosen by the high-priest, who was styled Pontifex maximus. They wore robes of white, with a fillet round the hair, and a veil, additional ornaments being permitted in later times. It was necessary that the girls selected for this service should be between six and ten years of age, and that they should take a vow of chastity, and serve in the temple for thirty years. After that period they were permitted to leave it, and even to marry, though neither proceeding was viewed with pleasure by the public, who feared the goddess to whom they had been devoted might take offence in either case. While engaged in the services of the temple the vestal virgins enjoyed great esteem and important privileges. Their person was inviolable, they were free from paternal control, and had the right of disposing of their own property. In their festal processions through the streets of

Rome they were preceded by lictors (or officers of justice), who carried with them the *fasces*, that is, a number of twigs tied together into a bundle, out of which an axe projected as a symbol of sovereign power,—an honour which, besides them, only the consuls or highest magistrates of Rome were entitled to. And in the course of the procession, should they meet a criminal on his way to expiate his crime by death, they had the prerogative of ordering him to be set free.

With all this respect and esteem, they were very severely dealt with when guilty of neglect of duty, such as permitting the sacred flame of the altar of **Vesta** to die out, which could only be rekindled by means of a burning glass held up to the rays of the sun. A priestess guilty of this was condemned by the high-priest of the goddess to a dark chamber, and there flogged. For the crime of forfeiting her chastity she was conveyed to a place called the Campus Sceleratus, or " criminals' field," and there placed in a subterranean chamber provided with a bed, a lighted lamp, and some bread and water. The chamber was then closed upon her, the earth thrown over it and made smooth, and the unfortunate priestess left to die a most agonizing death. Her seducer was publicly scourged to death. The whole city was sorrowful, and sacrifice and long earnest prayers were offered up to appease the injured goddess. The procession, in which the condemned priestess was carried to her crypt, tied down on a litter, and so closely covered up that even her screams could not be heard, was a spectacle that raised a shudder, and caused that day to be remembered as one of the greatest pain and grief throughout the city.

At first there were only two vestal virgins, this number being afterwards increased to four, and again by King Servius to six. They were chosen always from the noblest families of Rome. If the legend concerning the foundation of the city of Rome be true, even **Romulus** and **Remus,** the founders of that city, were sons of a vestal priestess named **Rhea Sylvia** and **Mars.**

The sacred fire on the hearth of the goddess, and the laurel that shaded it, were renewed on the 1st of March of each year; on the 15th of June her temple was cleaned and repaired. But previous to this, on the 9th of June, a festival was held in her honour, called the **Vestalia,** only women being admitted to the temple, and these barefooted, and in the character of pilgrims.

ARES, or MARS,

(PLATES VIII. AND XXVIII.,)

A son of **Zeus** and **Hera,** according to the belief of the Greeks, was originally god of the storm and tempest, and more particularly of the hurricane; but this his natural meaning was lost sight of at an earlier period, and more completely than in the case of most of the other gods, the character in which he appears to us being exclusively that of " god of the turmoil and storms in human affairs," in other words, " god of dreadful war," or more correctly, " of the wild confusion and strife of battle." Of all the upper gods he was the most fierce and terrible, taking pleasure in slaughter and massacre.

In this respect he forms a striking contrast to **Pallas-Athene,** the goddess of well-matched chivalrous fights, whom we often find opposed to him in mythical narratives. When fighting she was invulnerable, and always on the side of the victor; while Ares being not only god of battle but also a personification of war, with its double issue of victory and defeat, was sometimes wounded, and even taken prisoner. When assisting the Trojans in their war with the Greeks, in the course of which he took under his special protection their leader, Hector, he was wounded by the Greek hero Diomedes, aided by the goddess Athene. He fell—so Homer describes the event in the Iliad (v. 853)—with a thundering crash to the ground, like the noise of nine or ten thousand warriors engaged in battle. Again (Iliad xxi. 400) he was wounded by Athene and fell, his armour clanking, and his body covering with his fall seven acres of ground,—an obvious reference to the roar and destruction attending a great storm. He was once captured by Otos and Ephialtes, the giant sons of Aloeus the planter, and kept imprisoned in a great bronze vase (Iliad v. 385) for thirteen months—a space of time which, when we remember that the names of the two heroes are derived from husbandry, seems to indicate a full year of peaceful agriculture. Like himself, his offspring were distinguished for their prowess or delight in strife; as, for example, **Meleager,** the prince of Kalydon, who speared the Kalydonian boar (see below); **Kyknos,** whom Herakles slew, and for this would have been avenged by Ares had not Zeus stopped the conflict of his two powerful sons by a flash of lightning; then **Parthenŏpæos,** one of the seven leaders in the assault on the town of Thebes (see below); **Oenomæos,** and others. The expression, " a son or offshoot of Ares," frequently applied to other heroes, must not be understood literally, but merely as indicating physical strength and valour, equal to that of his actual descendants.

Eris, the personification of fatal strife, was usually by his side, Dread and Alarm (Deimos and Phobos) attended on his steps. On the other hand we find him, even in the Iliad (v. 355 and xxi. 416), where his general character is that of a huge fierce combatant, associated with Aphrodite, the goddess of love. In the Odyssey (viii. 266) the story is told of his secret visit to her, when he was detected by **Helios,** who informed Hephæstos of the fact, whereupon the latter devised a cunning net, and catching the two together under it exhibited them to the gods of Olympos, and called upon Zeus to bring them to trial. This relation of Ares to Aphrodite, who was even worshipped as his proper wife in Thebes, indicates very probably the peace and rest that follow the turmoil of war.

It is true that **Ares** was worshipped in Greece, but not as a great protecting deity, such as he was deemed by the Romans. In Athens the **Areopagos,** or "Mars' Hill," on which was held a court of justice for the decision of cases involving life and death, derived its name from him, the story being that he had once appeared before it in a cause against Poseidon. The warlike people of Tegea, the Spartans, who had a very ancient temple in his honour, the Athenians, for whom Alkamenes the sculptor, a contemporary and rival of Pheidias, made a statue of him, and the Eleans, all worshipped him with more or less zeal. But the real home and centre of his worship was Thrace, with its wild warlike population and its stormy tempestuous sky. It was in Rome, however, with its conquests and pride of military power, that he enjoyed under the name of **Mars** the highest honour, ranking next to **Jupiter** as guardian of the state. The Romans considered themselves to be actual descendants of Mars, on the ground of his having been, as was believed, the father of Romulus and Remus, styling him **Marspiter,** that is, Mars Pater, their father **Mars.** At Reate, in Italy, he had even an oracle. In Rome there was a field consecrated to him, and named the "Field of Mars," where military exercises and manœuvres took place, athletic competitions, called "martial games," were held, and public assemblies were summoned to consider important questions of the state. The race course and the temples of the god were there; and there every four years were held the census and muster of citizens liable to be called into the field in the event of war. On this occasion a sacrifice was presented to him, consisting of a bull, a ram, and a goat, which, before being slain, were led three times round the assembled crowd, while during the ceremony a prayer was offered up that the immortal gods might still enlarge and ennoble the Roman empire more and more, or as it was expressed in later times, that they might give stability and endurance to the Roman state. Chariot-races were held there twice a year, at the beginning of March and in October; the ceremony of sacrificing to Mars the off-horse of the bigá that won the race—the October horse as it was called—being performed at the latter. In the "Field of Mars" was dedicated the booty brought back from campaigns, and no Roman general went to war without first proceeding to the temple of **Mars,** to swing the sacred shield and spear, adding the words, "Watch over us, O Mars!" This shield (**ancile**) was believed to have fallen from heaven at the time when Numa Pompilius was king of Rome, and, like the Palladium in the temple of Vesta, was looked on with veneration. Both it and a sacred spear were preserved in the temple of Mars, under the custody of priests, who were called Salii, and whose duty it was every year to celebrate a festival of thanksgiving for this important present from the gods. In the earliest times the sacrifices offered to Mars consisted of human beings, particularly those who had been taken prisoners in

VIII.

Hephæstos, or Vulcan

Ares, or Mars.   Aphrodite, or Venus.

battle; but in later times this custom was abandoned, and horses, rams, dogs, and a portion of the booty captured from enemies, offered instead. Besides these animals, the wolf, cock, and woodpecker were sacred to him.

The attributes of Ares were a spear and a burning torch, such as, according to ancient custom, his priests carried when they advanced to give the sign of battle to opposing armies. The animals chosen as his symbols were the dog and the vulture, the constant visitants of battle-fields.

In works of art Ares is represented generally as of a youthful but very powerful build, armed with helmet, shield, and spear. At other times he is bearded and heavily armed. A favourite subject was his meeting with Aphrodite, as on plate xxviii.

HEPHAESTOS, or VULCAN,

(PLATE VIII.,)

Was the divine personification of the fire that burns within the earth and bursts forth in volcanic eruptions—fire which has no connection with the sun or the lightning of heaven; and such being his character, we can readily understand the mutual dislike which existed between him and the god of the light of heaven. He was indeed the son of **Zeus** and **Hera**, the supreme deities of heaven; but he was born to be a cause of quarrel between them, and alternately at enmity with both. Once, when he took his mother's part, Zeus seized him by the heels and tossed him out of Olympos (Iliad i. 560). Through the air he fell for one whole day; at evening, as the sun went down, reaching the island of Lemnos, where he was found by some Sintian people, and taken under friendly care. The place where he was found, and where in after times was the principal centre of his worship, was the neighbourhood of the burning mountain Mosychlos.

Another version of the myth has it that **Hera**, ashamed of the decrepit form which he presented at his birth, threw him with her own hands from Olympos.   Falling into the sea, he was picked up by **Thetis** and **Eurynome**, was cared for by them, remained for nine years in the abode of the sea-gods, none but they knowing his whereabouts, and executed there many wonderfully clever examples of handiwork.   It may be that this belief originated in observing the nearness of volcanic mountains to the sea-shore, and the fact of whole islands, like the modern Santorin, being suddenly thrown up from the sea by volcanic force.   Among the works which he fashioned in the palace of the sea-gods was a cunningly devised throne, which he presented to Hera, as a punishment for casting him out of heaven, knowing that when she sat down on it she would be locked within its secret chains so firmly that no power but his could free her.   This happened, and **Ares** went to bring him by force to her assistance, but was compelled to retreat in fear of the fire brand with which Hephaestos assailed him.   At last **Dionysos**, the god of wine, succeeded by his soft conciliatory speech in restoring friendship between mother and son, and her bonds were forthwith undone.   Perhaps it is from this intimacy with Dionysos that he is said to have once appeared as cup-bearer in Olympos, on which occasion the ·assembled deities could not contain themselves with laughter at the droll figure limping from couch to couch.   It seems to be the unsteady flicker of flame that is represented in the lameness of the fire-god, and it may have been the genial influence of the hearth which was the source of the quaint stories about him.

From being originally god of fire, Hephaestos naturally developed into god of those arts and industries dependent on fire, especially the arts of pottery and working in metal. He was the artist god who worked in a smoky smithy down in the heart of burning mountains, and produced clever works of dazzling beauty, which he gave freely away to gods and to favourite heroes. For Zeus he made the dreaded ægis and a sceptre; for **Achilles** and **Memnon** their armour; for himself two wonderful handmaidens of gold, who, like living beings, would move about and assist him as he walked; and when Homer has to describe any bronze work of great beauty, his highest praise is always that it was the work of Hephaestos. The throne which he made for Hera, and the net in which he caught Aphrodite and Ares, have already been mentioned.

From being god of the warmth within the earth—of volcanic fire, Hephaestos came also, when the fertility of a volcanic soil became known by experience, to be looked on as one who aided the spread of vegetation, this function of his being recognized most in the spread of the vine, which thrives and bears its best fruit on volcanic soil. It was from knowledge of this fact, no doubt, that the idea arose of the close friendship between him and the wine-god **Dionysos**, which we find exemplified partly in the joint worship of these two deities, and partly in the story already told, of how Dionysos led Hephaestos back to Olympos, and smoothed his differences with the other gods.

His worship was traceable back to the earliest times, Lemnos being always the place most sacred to him. There, at the foot of the burning mountain Mosychlos, which is now extinct, stood a very ancient temple of the god—on the very spot, it was said, where **Prometheus** stole the heavenly fire,

6

and for the theft was taken away among the Caucasus mountains, there nailed alive to a rock by Hephaestos, and compelled to suffer every day an eagle sent by Zeus to gnaw his
liver, which daily grew afresh. A somewhat gloomy ceremony of expiating this theft of fire took place annually in the
island, all fires being put out, and forbidden to be relit until
the return of the ship that had been despatched to the sacred
island of Delos to fetch new fire. Then, after being nine
days extinguished, all the fires in dwelling-houses and in
work-shops were rekindled by the new flame.

Next to Lemnos, perhaps the most important seat of his
worship was Athens, where the unusually large number of
persons employed in the potteries and in metal-working recognized him as their patron god, and associating him with
Athene, held annually in October a festival called **Chalkeia,**
in honour of both. In the same month occurred the festival
Apaturia, at which, by the side of Zeus and Athene a prominent place was assigned to Hephaestos in his capacity of
god of the hearth, and protector of the domestic life which
gathered round it. On this occasion sacrifices were offered
at the hearth, and a public procession took place of men clad
in festival garments, carrying lighted torches and singing
songs in his praise. Again, the torch race, which formed part
of the Panathenaic games, was intended to commemorate the
theft of fire by **Prometheus.** In connection with this community of worship existing between Athene and Hephaestos
at Athens, it was said that he once endeavoured to obtain the
love of the goddess, and that even though this failed she had
devoted special care to Erichthonios, the offspring of his intercourse with **Gaea,** the goddess of the earth.

In Sicily Hephaestos had a temple on Mount Etna, which

was watched by dogs possessed of the faculty of distinguishing the pious from the impious and profane, whose approach they fiercely resisted. His worship had also spread to lower Italy and the Campania.

In Rome it was said that **Vulcan** had a temple as early as the time of Romulus, who, in fact, caused it to be erected, and instituted the festival called **Vulcanalia,** which was wont to be held on the 23d of August, the ceremony consisting of a sacrifice for the purpose of averting all the mishaps that arise from the use of fire and lights; for the days were then beginning to be noticeably shorter, and the necessity of light to work by in the evenings to be felt.

The wife of Hephaestos, according to the Iliad, was **Charis,** but the popular belief of later times assigned that place to **Aphrodite.** By neither had he any children.

In works of art Hephaestos is represented as an aged bearded man, with serious furrowed face, wearing a short *chiton* or *exomis* and a pointed cap or *pilos*, the mark of workmen or fishermen (which Odysseus also wears), hammering at an anvil, his attitude showing the lameness of which the myth speaks. On the early coins of Lemnos he appears without a beard. One of the favourite subjects both of poets and artists was the story of his catching Hera in the throne which he gave her, the ludicrousness of it making it an attractive subject for the ancient comedy. On a painted vase in the British Museum is a scene from a comedy in which Hera appears seated on the throne, while Ares and Hephaestos are engaged in combat before her. Another scene which frequently occurs on the painted vases is that in which Hephaestos appears on his way back to Olympos in a state of intoxication, riding on a mule, or walking, and accompanied by Dionysos, Sileni, and nymphs. At the birth of Athene it was he who split open the head of Zeus to let the goddess come forth, and in the frequent representations of this scene on the vases he appears hammer in hand. At other times we find him fashioning the armour of Achilles or fastening Prometheus to the rock.

APHRODITE, or VENUS,

(PLATES VIII., IX., AND XXVIII.,)

Was the goddess of love in that wide sense of the word which in early times embraced also the love of animals, and the love which was thought to be the cause of productiveness throughout nature. Accordingly we find in her character, side by side with what is beautiful and noble, much that is coarse and unworthy. In the best times of Greece the refined and beautiful features of her worship were kept in prominence, both in poetry and art ; but these, when times of luxury succeeded, had to give way to impurities of many kinds.

The feelings awakened by observing the productive power of nature had, it would seem, given rise to a divine personification of love in very remote early times among the nations of the East. The Phœnicians called this personification **Astarte**, and carried her worship with them wherever they established factories or markets in Greece, in the islands of the Mediterranean, and on to Italy. The early Greeks coming in contact with these traders, and obtaining from them a knowledge of coinage, weights, measures, and other necessaries of commerce and trade—including, it is said, a system of writing—appear to have transferred some of the functions of the oriental goddess to their own Aphrodite, as, for instance, the function of protecting commerce. The earliest known Greek coins—those of Ægina—the weights of which correspond accurately with the oriental standard, have the figure of a tortoise, the well-known symbol of Aphrodite.

How much else of the character of their goddess the Greeks may have derived from the Phœnicians it would be impossi-

Aphrodite, or Venus.

ble to say. But the extraordinary zeal with which she continued to be worshipped in Cyprus, Cytherea, Corinth, Car-
thage, Sicily, and wherever in early times the Phœnicians had
made settlements, may signify that others of her functions
besides that of protecting commerce had been borrowed from
the oriental goddess. The older Aphrodite worshipped in
Greece previous to the introduction of Phœnician elements in
her character is described as a daughter of **Zeus** (Iliad v.
312) and **Dione**, and through her mother was associated with
the ancient worship at Dodona.

The younger goddess, on the other hand, is described
(Hesiod, Theogony, 188-206) as the offspring of **Uranos,**
born among the foam of the sea, first stepping on land in
Cyprus, and styled **Anadyomene,** or "she who came out of
the sea." Under the title of **Urania** she was regarded as a
personification of that power of love which was thought to
unite heaven, earth, and sea into one harmonious system, and
as such was distinguished from **Aphrodite Pandemos,** the
personification of love among men. As the goddess born of
the foam of the sea, she naturally came to be held in veneration by the fishermen and sailors on the coast as the goddess
of the smiling sea, and the cause of prosperous voyages.
Hence it was the custom in the island of Ægina to follow up
the sacrifice and banquet in honour of Poseidon with a festival
of great rejoicing and excitement in honour of Aphrodite.
In Knidos she was styled and worshipped as goddess of the
peaceful sea; a character which is symbolized by the dolphin
frequently given her as an attribute. The island of Cytherea
(Cerigo) derived its name from one of her titles, Cythere,
the belief being that she had appeared there before landing
on Cyprus.

The earlier and pure Greek phase of her character, in which she is called a daughter of Zeus and Dione, was that of a goddess who presides over human love; she is described as accompanied by her son **Eros** (**Amor** or **Cupid**), the **Charites** (Graces), the **Horæ, Himeros** (God of the desire of love), **Pothos** (God of the anxieties of love), and **Peitho** (Suadela, or the soft speech of love).   But her special favourite was the young rosy shepherd **Adonis ;** her grief at his death, which was caused by a wild boar, being so great that she would not allow the lifeless body to be taken from her arms until the gods consoled her by decreeing that her lover might continue to live half the year, during the spring and summer, on the earth, while she might spend the other half with him in the lower world, beside **Persephone** (Proserpina); a reference to the change of seasons, which finds its explanation in the fact of Aphrodite being also goddess of gardens and flowers.   Her presence in nature was felt in spring, her absence in winter. This change of the seasons was further observed and celebrated by a festival in honour of Adonis, in the course of which a figure of him was produced, and the ceremony of burial, with weeping and songs of wailing, gone through; after which a joyful shout was raised, " Adonis lives, and is risen again !"   She was called **Adōnaia** and **Adōnias,** with reference to this love passage.   Next to him her chief favourite was **Anchises,** to whom she bore **Æneas,** who through his son **Ascanius,** or **Julius,** became, as story goes, the founder of the great Julian family in Rome.   With regard to the story of **Pygmalion,** the Adonis of Cyprus, into whose statue of her she breathed life on the occasion of one of her festivals, perhaps the same meaning is intended to be conveyed as in the alternate life and death of Adonis—that is, the alternate fervour and coldness of love, or the alternate bloom and frost of nature.

The husband of Aphrodite was Hephaestos (Vulcan), whose manner of punishing her when he found her in the company of Ares has already been related. Among her children, but not by Hephaestos, were **Eros** (Amor), and **Anteros, Hymen,** and **Hermaphroditus.**

But if she had favours for some she had strong antipathies for others, and proved this spirit on **Hippolytos,** whom she slew; on **Polyphontē,** whom she changed into an owl; on **Arsinoë** whom she turned to stone; and **Myrrha,** whom she transformed into a myrtle tree. Of her strife and competition with Hera and Athene for the prize of beauty, which the Trojan prince, Paris, awarded to her, we shall give an account later on, in connection with the narrative of the Trojan war.

As a result of her power to unite by means of love all beings, whether in heaven, or earth, or in blackest Tartaros, she came to be viewed as a goddess presiding over married life and marriage ceremonies. She had a number of temples in the island of Cyprus, but none of them so splendidly decorated as that in the town of Paphos, whither thousands of visitors streamed to take part in the annual festival and rejoicings in her honour. There also she had an oracle, and, as **Urania,** was worshipped jointly with **Ares** (Mars); the latter fact showing that her connection with this god was founded in the religious belief of the people. At times, and particularly in her very ancient sanctuary in the island of Cythere, as also in Sparta, Argos, and on the Acropolis of Corinth, she was represented armed.

The worship of **Venus** did not become general in Rome till later times. A festival, called **Veneralia,** was held in her honour every year, a great part of the ceremony consisting of nocturnal dances and passionate enjoyment in gardens and among blooming arbours.   She had a temple on the Capitol, and one of the Colline gates was consecrated to her.   The month of April was held sacred to her, for then the flowers bud and plants shoot; or, as the Greek myth expresses it, Adonis comes back from the under-world.

The symbols of Aphrodite were the dove, ram, hare, dolphin, swan, and tortoise, with the rose as a flower, the myrtle tree, and other beautiful plants, the apple, and fruits of various kinds.

In Paphos the earliest form or image under which she was worshipped was that of a ball or a pyramid, surrounded with burning torches or candelabra, as is to be seen on the coins of Cyprus; but gradually, as art advanced, she took a finer form, fresh charms being continually added, till all the resources of expressing imperious overpowering beauty were exhausted.   In the best days of art she was always represented draped, in later times nude, and in various attitudes.   The scene of her birth from the sea was represented by Pheidias, on the base of the statue of Zeus at Olympia, as taking place in presence of the gods of Olympos, she being received first by Eros, who elsewhere is called her son.   One of the most famous pictures of Apelles represented her as rising out of the sea.   To indicate her connection with Ares she was represented as Venus Victrix, standing with one foot on a helmet and with both arms raising a shield.   Of this type are the Venus of Capua and the Venus of Milo.   In a temple erected to her as Euploia or goddess of prosperous voyages, in Knidos, was a statue of her by Praxiteles, which was celebrated above all her other statues in ancient times; and of which the so-called Medicean Venus is believed to be a free copy.

PALLAS-ATHENE, or MINERVA,

(PLATES XI. AND XII.,)

Called also **Tritogeneia** or **Tritonia** and **Athenæa**, is usually described, in the myths concerning her birth, as having

XI

Pallas-Athene, or Minerva.

Apollo.

Helios, or Sol.

sprung into life, fully armed, from the head of **Zeus,** with its thick black locks, all heaven and earth shaking meanwhile, the sea tossing in great billows, and the light of day being extin- guished. Zeus, it was said, had previously swallowed his wife **Metis** (Intelligence), to prevent her giving birth to a son. The operation of laying his head open, that Pallas might come forth, was performed by **Hephæstos** (Vulcan), or, according to other versions of the story, **Prometheus.** There is, however, another myth, which ascribes her origin to a connection of **Poseidon** (Neptune) with the nymph **Tritonis,** adding that Zeus merely adopted her as his daughter. But this seems to have had no foundation in the general belief of the people, and to have been only an invention of later times, when her name, Tritogeneia, or Tritonia, had become unintelligible.

No being connected with the earth, whether deity or mortal, had a part in her birth. She was altogether the issue only of her father,-the god of heaven, who, as the myth very plainly characterizes it, brought her into being out of the black tem- pest-cloud, and amidst the roar and crash of a storm. Her character must therefore be regarded as forming in some way a complement to his. The purpose for which she was brought into existence must have been that she might do what he would plan, but as the supreme and impartial god, could not carry out. She is at once fearful and powerful as a storm, and in turn, gentle and pure as the warmth of the sky when a storm has sunk to rest and an air of new life moves over the fresh- ened fields.

To express both these sides of her character—terrible and mighty as compared with open, gentle, and pure—she had the double name of **Pallas-Athēnē :** the former was applied to her function of goddess of storms—she who carried the ægis or storm-shield of her father. And further, as Pallas, she became the goddess of battle—valiant, conquering, frightening with the sight of her ægis whole crowds of heroes when they vexed her, and even driving **Ares** before her with her lightning spear. At the same time the soft, gentle, and heavenly side of her character took from her functions, as goddess of battle, that desire of confused slaughter and massacre which distinguished Ares, and formed the contrast we have already mentioned between the two deities of war. **Pallas** presides over battles, but only to lead on to victory, and through victory, to peace and prosperity.

When the war has been fought out, and that peace established which—whether it be amid the political life of nations here on earth, or whether it be amid the passions of individual men—is always the result of conflict and war, then it is that the goddess Athene reigns in all gentleness and purity, teaching mankind to enjoy peace, and instructing them in all that gives beauty to human life, in wisdom and art. If we observe and keep clearly before our minds these two sides of her character, the inseparable union of both, and their action and reaction upon each other, we shall see that this goddess, **Pallas-Athēnē**, is one of the most profound conceptions of a deep religious feeling—a being into whose hands the pious Greek could, with due reverence, commit his keeping.

The mutual relation of these two sides of her character is sufficiently obvious in the various myths relating to the goddess. The principal of these we shall proceed to narrate. But, first, we must call attention to this point, that **Athēnē** is represented in the myths as for ever remaining a virgin, scorning the affections which are said to have been frequently offered to her. Instead of suggesting her liability, in the smallest degree, to earthly passions and foibles, the myth shows admirably that she was a divine personification of mind, always unfettered in its movements ; a personification, at the same time, of the origin of mind from the brain of the supreme Divine Being : a proof that mind is neither of a male nor of a female order, but a single and independent power at work throughout the whole of nature.

In the course of the war with the Giants **Pallas** rendered most valuable assistance to Zeus, both by advice and deed ; being, in fact, the cause of his calling in the aid of **Herakles,** and thus completing successfully the subjugation of the rebels. Single-handed she overpowered the terrible giant **Enkelados ;** but when Zeus' rule was at last firmly established, she took up the task of assisting and protecting those heroes on earth whom she found engaged in destroying the grim creatures and monsters upon it. In this capacity she was the constant friend of **Herakles** in all his hardships and adventures (see below), and of **Perseus,** whom she helped to slay the Gorgon Medusa, whose head she afterwards wore upon her ægis, and for this reason obtained the name of **Gorgophone,** or Gorgon slayer. Along with Hera she protected the **Argonauts,** while to her assistance was due the success with which **Theseus** (see below) overcame and slew monsters of all kinds. She stood by the Greeks in their war against Troy, which we shall describe afterwards, and devised the scheme by which, after ten years' duration, it was brought to a close.

But, in times of peace, her power as goddess in all kinds of skill and handicraft, of clearness like that of the sky, and of mental activity, was uniformly exercised, as has been said, for the general good and prosperity. The arts of spinning

and weaving were described as of her invention.   She taught
how to tend and nurse newly-born infants; and even the heal•
ing art was traced back to her among other gods.   The flute,
too, was her invention.   As became the goddess of war, it
was her duty to instruct men in the art of taming horses, of
bridling and yoking them to the war-chariot—a task which we
find her performing in the story of **Bellerophon,** for whom
she bridled the winged horse Pegasos; and in the story of
Erichthonios, at Athens, the first mortal who learned from
her how to harness horses to chariots.   In a word, she was the
protectress of all persons employed in art and industry, of
those whose business it was on earth to instruct and educate
mankind, and therefore to help forward the general happiness.

The principal scene of her influence and actions was Attica,
that district of Greece which, according to the myth related
above, she obtained as her special and peculiar province, after
a contest for it with **Poseidon,** the god of the sea.   There
her worship and honour surpassed that of all other deities, and
from her was named the chief town of the land.   The visible
proof and testimony of her guardianship of Attica was the
olive on the Acropolis of Athens, which she created in the
contest with **Poseidon,** and from which the Athenians believed all the olive trees of Attica to have spread.   In the
produce of the olives consisted the chief wealth of the land.
Ancient writers relate a touching story concerning this olive
tree on the Acropolis, which reveals how firmly the belief of
their goddess was rooted in the minds of her people.   When
the Persians advanced with their overwhelming forces against
Greece, it is said that Athene presented herself at the throne
of her father, and begged for the preservation of her city.   But
fate had otherwise decreed: Athens must perish, in order that

a better and nobler city might rise from its ruins, and accordingly Zeus was obliged to refuse the prayer of his beloved daughter.   The Athenians took to their fleet, abandoning altogether the city, which the Persians then entered, and destroyed utterly with fire and sword, not even sparing the sacred olive of the goddess.   But, lo! as a sign that she had not forsaken her city even in ruins, there sprang suddenly from the root which remained a new shoot, which, with wonderful quickness, grew to a length of three yards, and was looked on as an emblem of the regeneration of the city.   With the aid of their goddess the Athenians fought foremost of all the Greeks in the famous sea-fight that ensued at Salamis, in which the Persian fleet, though vastly superior in numbers, was wholly destroyed, while the troops on the mainland were compelled to escape with shame and immense losses from Greece.

Among the great variety of her titles, some derived from her functions as a goddess, and others from the localities where her worship had a special hold on the people, we find Athene at Elis styled "mother," in consequence of her care over the nursing of children; in Athens and several other places, **Polias**, the "protectress of cities"; **Sōteira**, the "saviour"; **Glaukopis**, "blue-eyed goddess"; **Parthenos**, "the virgin"; **Hippia**, "tamer of horses"; **Ergane**, "mistress of industry", **Nike**, the "victorious"; and **Mechănitis**, "ingenious."   Every year a festival lasting several days, and called **Panathenaea**, was held in her honour at Athens, to commemorate the part she had taken in the war against the Giants: every fourth year—that is, every third year of the current Olympiad—it was celebrated with redoubled splendour.   This festival is said to have been instituted by Theseus, or at least to have first derived its importance from him; in

any case it was a festival of very great antiquity.   Festal processions were formed, athletic games were held, while sacrifices
and banquets took place on a large scale—all the Athenians,
whether at home or abroad in colonies, having the privilege
of taking part.   The prizes in the games consisted of large
painted earthenware vases filled with pure olive oil, the pro-
duct of the tree sacred to **Athene.**   Of these vases a small
number have been preserved down to our times.   On one side
is painted a figure of the goddess striding forward in the attitude of hurling her spear, with a column on each side of her,
to indicate the race course.   On the reverse side is a view of
the contest in which a particular vase was won.   But perhaps
the chief attraction of the festival was the procession in which
a new robe or peplos, woven and embroidered for the goddess
by a select number of women and girls in Athens, was carried
through the town spread like a sail on a mast, placed on a
wagon in the form of a ship.   In this procession it appears
as if the whole population of Attica took part, the youth of
the nobility on horseback or in chariots, the soldiery in arms,
and the burgesses with their wives and daughters in holiday
attire.   The new robe was destined for the very ancient statue
of Athene which was preserved in the Erechtheum.   This
custom of placing actual drapery on statues appears to have
been handed down from remote times, when the art of sculpture was unequal to the task of imitating the human figure,
and it is not improbable that the statue of Athene, of which
we are speaking, dated from that early time.   The magistrates
of Athens offered sacrifices to her at the commencement of
spring.   The services of her sanctuary were conducted by two
virgins elected for the period of one year.

   In Rome the worship of **Minerva** was conducted with as

much zeal as that of **Athene** at Athens, her character as god‧ dess of wisdom and serious thought being admirably calculated to attract a people like the Romans. She was the protectress of their arts and industries, of the domestic operations of spinning and weaving and embroidering, just as she was among the Greeks. In Rome she had several temples, one of the oldest of them being that on the Capitol. A festival which lasted from March 19th to 23d was annually held in her honour. But the object connected with her, which the Romans venerated above all things else, was the **Palladium,** or an‑ cient figure of the goddess, the story of which was that it had originally fallen from heaven, and had thereupon become the property of the royal family of Troy, the possession of it being from that time always considered an assurance of the safety of that city. But in the course of the war between the Greeks and Trojans it was secretly carried off by **Diomedes** and **Odysseus,** upon which followed the capture of the town by means of the wooden horse. Another version of the story has it that **Æneas** took it with him when he fled from the city; and in consequence of this inconsistency in the story it happened in later times that more than one city claimed the pos‑ session of the real Palladium—as, for example, Argos, Athens, and Rome. Wherever it was believed to be, there the firm conviction existed that the endurance of the city depended on the possession of the image, and so it happened afterwards that the expression Palladium was employed in a wider sense to objects thought to be of similar importance; and when, for instance, we hear of the "Palladium of Freedom being carried off," we understand that the principal provision and security of freedom has been lost. The symbols of Athene were the owl, the cock, the snake, and the olive tree.

In works of art Athene generally appears as a virgin of serious aspect, armed with helmet, shield, and spear, wearing long full drapery, and on her breas' the ægis, with a border of snakes, and the face of Medusa in the centre. She is often accompanied by an owl. Of the many statues of her, the two most famous in antiquity as works of art were those by the sculptor Pheidias : the one of gold and ivory stood in her great temple at Athens, the Parthenon. Some idea is given of it by Plate XII., which represents a restoration from a presumed copy of the original.

The other was of bronze (Plate XI.), colossal in size, and stood on the Acropolis, towering above the temple just named, the crest of her helmet and point of her spear being visible from the sea as far away as Cape Sunium, the most southern point of Attica. Her attitude was that of preparing to hurl her spear, and the title she bore, that of **Promachos,** or "Van of Battle." A representation of the statue is to be seen on the coins of Athens on which a view of the Acropolis is given.

The last record we have of the statue of gold and ivory is in the year 375 A. D., how and when it perished remaining still a mystery. The attitude of the bronze statue exists, it is believed, in several small statuettes, of which there is one in the British Museum, which was found in Athens. On the painted vases we find many representations of her birth, of her contest with the Giants, of her assisting heroes, such as Perseus and Herakles, in their exploits. The subjects of the sculptures, now in the British Museum, which decorated the pediments of the Parthenon, were, in the front, her birth, and at the back, her contest with Poseidon. In the Erechtheum at Athens was an ancient figure of the goddess, believed to have fallen from heaven ; while another ancient figure of her, the Palladium properly so called, was preserved in the city under the care of a priestly family named Byzigi. It also was believed to have fallen from heaven. In its presence was held a court for the trial of cases of bloodshed.

PHŒBOS-APOLLO AND HELIOS, OR SOL.

(PLATE XI.)

From the sun comes our physical light, but that light is at the same time an emblem of all mental illumination, of knowledge, truth, and right, of all moral purity; and in this respect a distinction was made between it as a mental and a physical phenomenon—a distinction which placed **Phœbos-Apollo**

XII

Pallas-Athene, by Pheidias.

on one side and **Helios** on the other.   Accordingly Phœbos-Apollo is the oracular god who throws light on the dark ways of the future, who slays the **Python,** that monster of darkness which made the oracle at Delphi inaccessible.   He is the god of music and song, which are only heard where light and security reign, and the possession of herds is free from danger. Helios, on the other hand, is the physical phenomenon of light, the orb of the sun, which, summer and winter, rises and sets in the sky.   His power of bringing secrets to light has been already seen in the story of Vulcan and Venus.

The myth of **Apollo** is, like that of **Aphrodite,** one of the oldest in the Greek system, but, unlike the latter, which is at least partly traceable to oriental influence, is a pure growth of the Greek mind.   No doubt certain oriental nations had deities of the sun and of light similar in some points to Apollo, but this only proves the simple fact that they viewed the movements of the sun and the operations of light in a general way similarly to the Greeks.   We have seen in the preceding chapters how the sky, earth, sea, and lower world were personified by divine beings of a high order, while in the same way other forces and powers in nature were imagined as beings.   In the myth of Apollo we shall find represented the various operations of the eternal light of the sun.

It is the sun's rays, or the arrows of **Apollo,** that everywhere, as the fields, and gardens teach us, quicken life, and foster it towards ripeness; through them a new life springs all around, and in the warmth of their soft, kindly light the jubilant voice of nature is heard and awakens an echo in the human soul.   At the same time these arrows destroy the life of plants and animals; even man falls under them in southern climates, such as Greece.   Their light penetrates to dark

7

corners, and is capable of reaching to inmost recesses.   All these ideas are represented in the myth of **Apollo**, who is therefore conceived in various ways corresponding to the genial radiance of the sun, with all its friendly influences: (1) as the personification of youth and beauty; (2) as god of earthly blessings; (3) as god of the herds that graze on the fields which are warmed by him,—a character in which he appeared herding the cattle of **Laomedon**, which multiplied largely under his care, and when alone piping on his flute, till the wild beasts were attracted from their dens; (4) as god of medicine, who provided for the growth of healing plants; (5) as god of music, for everywhere were heard happy, joyful sounds, when his kindly beams spread light and warmth over nature; (6) as god of oracles which reveal the secrets of the future, as the light of heaven dispels all darkness, and detests nocturnal gloom.

The sun appears ever young and powerful in the heavens, and so also must eternal youth, strength, and endurance be ascribed to **Apollo**.   For this reason he came to be a protector of youth when engaged in athletic contests, as well as in war.   But summer heat produces plagues, and so it was necessary to view **Apollo** as the cause of the same, as the god of death, whose unerring arrows carry destruction with them.   In this latter phase of his character we find him styled **Karneios**, and worshipped with particular zeal in Sparta, a festival being held annually in his honour in the month of August, the entire population withdrawing from the town and for several days encamping in tents in the neighbourhood, like a besieging army—the object being, by living in tents, to avoid the injurious effects of the intense heat of the dog-days. The name of this festival was **Karneia**.   As a religious ceremony, the intention of it was to appease the dreaded god, and accordingly it was attended with great reverence in Sparta, and from thence transplanted to Kyrene, a Greek colony on the north coast of Africa, to the islands of Rhodes and Sicily, and to the Greek cities in lower Italy—such as Tarentum and Sybaris. The finest of the temples in honour of this Apollo was at Amyklæ.

Another phase of his character, in which his destroying power is combined with his function as god of youth and blooming vegetation, is represented in the myth from which he derived the title of **Hyakinthios**, and enjoyed a form of worship which was for the most part peculiar to the Peloponnesos, the modern Morea, extending over the whole of the south coast of it, to Sikyon, Messenia, Amyklæ, and Sparta. It was accompanied by laments sung from place to place, and by poetic competitions, the idea to be conveyed in the whole ceremony being the transitoriness of nature, and the return of life again in course of time. In this spirit the festival of the **Hyakinthia** was celebrated annually at Sparta in July, and lasted nine days, commencing with sadness and expressions of grief, and concluding with joyous excitement.

The myth to which this festival related tells how **Apollo** accidentally killed, in throwing his disc, the beautiful **Hyakinthos**, whom he dearly loved, the youngest son of **Amyklas**; or, in another version, how **Zephyros**, the wind-god, who also loved the boy, hurled back the disc at the head of Hyakinthos, out of jealousy towards Apollo. The sorrow at the beginning of the festival of the Hyakinthia was to commemorate his death, while the belief that he had been transformed into the flower which sprang up where his blood fell, and bears his name, gave occasion afterwards to happy feelings of confidence in his return. Clearly the object of the

myth, like that of **Persephone,** was to point to the alter‑
nating decay and return of life in nature, which in this in‑
stance is conceived under the form of a youth, the disc of
Apollo being equally clearly a symbol of the sun, which
scorches up vegetation.

A similar idea seems to run through the story which relates
how Apollo and Artemis, taking offence at **Niobe** because,
with a mother's pride, she had boasted herself higher than
Leto as the mother of beautiful children, shot down her
children,—Apollo the sons, and Artemis the daughters.
When one after another had fallen before the angry deities,
all but the youngest daughter, Niobe, with the child cling‑
ing to her, implored them in anguish to spare the last of her
many children, but could not avert the fatal shaft.   When it
struck, her mother's heart became like a stone, and she refused
to murmur or complain.   She was transformed, it was said,
into a rugged rock, down which tears trickled silently (see
plate XIII.).

While bringing sometimes a pleasant death with his arrows,
Apollo at other times, as during the Trojan war, when he took
part against the Greeks, appears to exercise his destroying
power with irresistible fury.   Whole ranks of fighting men
fall dead when he shakes his ægis, and the walls raised by the
Greeks tumble like structures of sand made by children at play.

As god of the sun in its friendly influence upon the face of
nature, we find Apollo styled **Thargelios,** and a festival
called **Thargelia,** being held in his honour at Athens in the
month of May, to celebrate the ripening of the fruits of the
field under the warmth of the sun, and at the same time to
serve as a festival of expiation in memory of the human sacri‑
fices of ancient days.   In August occurred another festival at

XIII

Niobe.

Athens, called **Metageitnia,** at which Apollo, as god of harvest and plenty, was thought of as entertaining the other gods and encouraging neighbourly feelings among his wor‑ shippers. In October the first fruits of the field were presented to him as a sacrifice, and in September was held a festival at which he was invoked as a helper in battle.   Under the title of **Nomios** he was regarded by herdsmen as their patron god. But the genial influence of the sun is felt on the sea as well as on land, and for this reason he was styled **Delphinios,** and in this capacity worshipped, among other places, at Athens, where his temple, called the **Delphinion,** was in early times a place of refuge and a court for the trial of capital crimes. An annual festival was held in May, called **Delphinia,** to commemorate the tribute of seven boys and seven girls, whom Athens had been compelled in remote times to send every year to Crete to be offered as sacrifices to the Minotaur.

As a god of the sun in its annual course, Apollo was thought to spend the winter away in a northern region among a mythical people called Hyperboreans, to whom it was always light.   As the winter approached poets sang farewell to him. At his birth Zeus had given him a mitra (or cap), a lyre, and a car drawn by swans, in which he was to proceed to Delphi, but the swans carried him off to the bright land of the Hyper‑ boreans.   When the summer came the priests of Delphi hailed his return in festal songs.   The voice of the nightingale wel‑ comed him back.   A peculiar festival, the **Daphnephoria,** was held at Thebes every eighth year in honour of Apollo **Ismenios,** the ceremony consisting of a procession in which was carried a branch of olive hung with wreaths and represen‑ tations of the sun, moon, stars, and planets, and called the **Kopo.**   From the statement that the number of wreaths was

365, to indicate the days of the year, it may be gathered that the festival as we know it was not of very high antiquity, symbols so obvious as this being usually of late origin.   On the other hand, it may be supposed, from the character of Apollo as sun-god, that the ceremony had existed in a simpler form in early times.   The number *seven* was sacred to him. Sacred swans made a circle seven times round the island of Delos at his birth, which occurred on the seventh day of the month.   From this he took the title of **Hebdomeios.**

One of the oldest forms of his worship appears to have been that in which he was regarded simply as god of light, and styled **Lykios,** the original centre of this worship being Lycia in the south-west of Asia Minor.

Turning now to that phase of his character in which he represents the light of the sun as the symbol of an all-seeing and all-knowing power, we find Apollo regarded as the great god of oracles, with Delphi as the principal centre of his activity.   His oracles were there communicated through a priestess, with the title of **Pythia,** who sat aloft on a sacred tripod of gold which stood above the opening of a chasm in the rock.   Out of this chasm rose a continuous stream of cold vapour, which drove the priestess into a state of frenzy when she sat above it.   Her method of prophesying was by uttering in her frenzy single words or sounds, which persons educated for the purpose caught up and put into verse, generally in such a cunning way as to have, instead of a clear incontrovertible meaning, a double and easily mistaken import.

To give one example: the oracle, when consulted by the Athenians for advice as to how to meet best the approach of the Persian force, returned as its answer, "Trust to your citadel of wood."   This the Athenian sages misunderstood, and proceeded to have the Acropolis protected with wooden bulwarks, which naturally could not for a moment resist the enemy.   Themistocles, however, and the younger men of the day declared that the words referred to the fleet, and succeeded in persuading the people to take to the ships, the result of which was the glorious victory of Salamis.   Had the interpretation of the sages been accepted generally, the oracle would have had the answer ready, that it meant the fleet.   It was only by such tricks that the oracle of Delphi, clever and far-seeing as the priests were, could have maintained its reputation for unerringness and its vast influence.

Of the same nature, but apparently older, were the oracles of Apollo in Asia Minor; as for instance those of Colophon and Didymi near Miletus, the latter of which was in the hands of the priestly family of the Branchidæ.   Sometimes the god exercised the power of communicating the prophetic gift to mortals, as he did to **Cassandra,** and to **Deiphobe, a** daughter of Glaukos.   The latter lived in a grotto beside the town of Cumæ, in the Campania of Italy, and was known by the name of the **Cumæan Sibyl.**   It was from her that Tarquin the Proud, the last king of Rome, acquired the three Sibylline books which contained important prophecies concerning the fate of Rome, and were held in great reverence by the Romans.   They were preserved carefully in the Capitol down to the time of Sulla, when they perished in a fire.   In Greece also was a famous seer or prophet, and favourite of **Apollo Epimenides,** of whom the myth reports that when a herdsman he fell asleep in a grotto, slept for fifty-six years, and on awakening found himself endowed with the prophetic gift in a high degree.

Connected with his gift of prophecy was his power of music.

For not only were the oracles expressed in verse, but the strains of music, when spontaneous, were thought to originate in an inspired foresight into the future. As god of music he was leader of the Muses, **Musagetes** ; and himself played on a wonderful lyre which Hermes had made for him.

At Delphi he was styled Apollo **Pythios,** and enjoyed several annual festivals, such as the **Theophania,** to celebrate his return from the Hyperboreans, and the **Theoxenia,** at which, it being harvest time, he was supposed to receive the other gods at his hospitable table. The principal festival, however, was that at which the **Pythian Games** were held. The games had been instituted to commemorate the victory of Apollo over the dragon Python, which resisted his entrance upon his duties as oracular god at Delphi. They were held at first every seventh, afterwards every ninth, and latterly every fifth year.

As being himself possessed of eternal youth, and of the finest conceivable athletic form, Apollo came to be regarded as a patron of the athletic contests of youth, and in this capacity ranked with Herakles and Hermes. He was the god also to whom persons polluted either with disease or crime turned for purification, and on this account his high power was brought home frequently and seriously to a great part of the people. He was, therefore, properly viewed as the father of Asklepios, the god of medicine.

The story of the birth of Apollo is that he, with his twin sister **Artemis,** was a son of **Zeus** and **Leto** (or Latona) ; that Leto, after wandering long hither and thither, pursued by the jealous **Hera,** at last found shelter in the island of Delos, in the Egean sea, and there was delivered. It was said that hitherto that island had been only a waste rock driven about in the sea, but that it became fixed in its present position on the occasion of the birth of Apollo and Artemis, an event which was celebrated by a blaze of golden light shed over the island, while sacred swans flew round encircling it seven times. This was in May, and for that reason his festival at Delos, the **Delia**, was held in that month. But Leto was compelled, through the pursuit of Hera, to abandon her children. They were entrusted to **Themis**, a name which signifies "justice," and indicates here the indisputable sense of right present with Apollo from his birth. By her he was fed on ambrosia and nectar, upon which he grew so strong, and that, too, so quickly, that within only a few hours after his birth he was a youth of dazzling appearance, and escaped his divine nurse, proclaiming that his destiny was to be a bowman, a player on the lyre and to give truthful oracles to mankind.

To accomplish the end of his ambition he set out at once on a pilgrimage to search for a suitable place for an oracle, neither too public nor too retired. After searching through many districts of Greece he arrived at the quiet rocky valley of **Delphi**, or Pytho, which he recognized as the desired spot, on account of its peaceful position in the heart of Greece. Moreover there had been an oracle of **Themis** there from a remote early time, and she was willing to hand over her duties to the young god. A terrible dragon, however, called Python, stood in the way, refused entrance, and tried to repel him; but in vain, for the young god, confident in the unerring aim of his arrows, attacked the monster, and slew it after a short combat. In this way he acquired his world-famed oracle, and from his victory over the dragon obtained the title of **Pythios**.

From that time forward, with one exception, Apollo remained in undisputed possession of the sacred tripod and oracle at Delphi, and that was when he had to take up their defence against **Herakles,** who, because the acting priestess did not prophesy as he wished, offered her violence and carried off the tripod. Apollo hastened to the aid of his priestess, and Zeus had to settle the quarrel between his two sons, who thereafter lived in the closest friendship.

Amongst the other incidents of his life, it is related that Apollo once incurred the severe displeasure of Zeus, and was driven for a time out of Olympos, through having shot at some of the Kyklopes in revenge for Zeus having struck **Asklepios** (Æsculapius), a son of Apollo, with a thunderbolt. During his exile on earth, he acted as a herdsman to his friend **Admetos,** the king of Pheræ, in Thessaly, and again in the same capacity to Laomedon, prince of Troy. In vexation at his banishment he joined with Poseidon in an attempt to dethrone Zeus. But the scheme failed, and both deities were in consequence sentenced to assist in building the walls of Troy. **Laomedon** refused to give them the payment agreed on for the service, and Apollo revenged himself by sending a dreadful pestilence which depopulated the town and neighbourhood of Troy. During the time of his servitude he had also a quarrel with **Pan,** who insisted that the flute was a better instrument than the lyre. The decision, which was left to **Midas,** a king of Lydia, was given in favour of Pan, for which Apollo punished Midas by causing his ears to grow long like those of an ass. **Marsyas,** too, had boasted that he could surpass Apollo in the art of playing on the flute, and for this had to suffer the cruel punishment of being flayed alive.

In Rome the worship of Apollo was not established till 320

B. C., a temple being raised to him in that year in consequence
of a pestilence that had visited the city.   Afterwards a second
temple to him was erected on the Palatine hill.   The **Apolli-
narian Games** were instituted during the second Punic war.

No distinction was made by the Greek poets of later times
between Apollo and the sun-god, **Helios**.   As little did the
Romans distinguish between Apollo and Sol.   In both cases
the confusion arose from the fact that the fundamental idea of
both deities was that of sun-gods.   The title of Phœbos plainly
designated Apollo as god of pure streaming light, particularly
of the light of heaven, and this phase of his character was
made more conspicuous by the fact of his mother's name being
Leto, "darkness," strictly "goddess of the dark night."   But
this, his original signification, came in time to be lost sight of
in the variety of other functions which he assumed.   Helios,
or Hyperion, on the contrary, remained, properly speaking,
only the orb of the sun which is visible in the heavens by day,
and disappears by night in a regular course.   That was the
only signification he had.   The number *seven* was sacred to
him, as it was to Apollo, and in the island of Trinakia, supposed to be Sicily, it was said, he had seven herds of cows
and seven herds of lambs, fifty in each herd, which never increased or diminished in numbers.   It was one of his pleasures
to see them grazing when he rose in the morning and when he
descended in the evening.

Of the sons of Helios the most famous is Phaëthon, of
whom it is said that he once had a dispute about his origin
with **Epaphos**, a son of **Zeus** and **Io**, and in consequence
begged Helios, if he really was his father, to prove himself
such by granting one request ; upon which Helios called the
river Styx to witness that he would not refuse to grant it.

The request was, that he, Phaëthon, should be permitted for one day to drive the chariot of the sun. Helios, astonished at the boldness of the request, and alarmed at the danger that threatened his son in such an undertaking, endeavoured to move him from his determination. But Phaëthon only clung to the bargain all the more firmly, and Helios, finding himself bound by his oath, instructed his son how to drive and manage the horses, and handed over to him the task for one day. The youth, however, through being unused to the work, and unacquainted with the right way, soon became confused, and lost his strength and his senses. The spirited horses wheeled out of the right course, and brought the chariot of the sun so near to the earth that in some places the latter took fire, fountains were dried up, rivers began to boil, and part of the human race became black in colour. Zeus, alarmed at the unexpected danger in which both heaven and earth were thus placed, slew Phaëthon with a stroke of lightning, and cast him from the chariot of the sun down into the river Eridanos. The three sisters of Phaëthon, **Heliades**, as they were called —that is, daughters of Helios, **Phaëthusa**, **Ægle**, and **Lampetia**, wept for him a long time, and finally became transformed into larch trees, that overhang the river's banks, the tears that continually flowed from them being changed by the sun into amber (*elektron*.) Phaëthon's friend **Kyknos** mourned his loss deeply, and was transformed into a swan, while Helios was so grieved at his son's death that only the entreaties of the gods could prevail on him to resume the reins of the chariot of the sun.

The symbols of Helios were horses' heads, a crown of seven rays, a cornucopia, and a ripened fruit. The symbols of Apollo were the wolf, swan, raven, stag, dolphin, laurel, and lyre.

XIV

Artemis, or Diana.

Dionysos, or Bacchus.

In works of art Apollo is usually represented as having the figure of a youthful athlete—perhaps the finest existing statue of him being the Apollo Belvidere of the Vatican.   His hair is long, and usually tied, like that of his sister Artemis, in a large knot above his forehead.   In the character of Musagetes he wears long ample drapery girt at the waist, a diadem round his head, and long tresses falling on his shoulders.   Though the general representation of him is that in which he is engaged in playing on the lyre, or resting from doing so, as in plate xi., we find him also with bow and arrows, as Sauroktonos, killing a lizard, holding forth his ægis to destroy his enemies, and present at the flaying of Marsyas.

ARTEMIS, or DIANA; AND SELENE or LUNA.

(PLATES XIV. AND XV.)

Originally **Artemis** was the divine personification of the moon, just as her brother **Apollo** was originally god of the sun.   But by degrees, as the moon came to be viewed like the sun, on the one hand as a mere illuminating orb, and on the other as possessing a real or apparent and generally believed influence upon vegetation, and on human as well as animal life, there grew up a distinction between moon-goddesses of two kinds, corresponding to the sun-gods of two kinds.   The one was **Selēnē,** or **Luna,** whose signification was merely that of goddess of the orb of night, as Helios, the sun, was of the orb of day.   The other was **Artemis, or Diana,** who embraced in her character all the other functions exercised by the moon on earthly life, and accordingly, like Apollo, became the subject of a largely developed religious belief; while the myth of Selēnē, on the contrary, like that of Helios, was but little and sparingly improved upon.

Great as was the variety of the real and fancied influences of the moon upon natural life, proportionately great was the variety in the myth of Artemis—a locality of worship some

times, at other times a particular point of view of her character determining the phase of it. And further, it should be
observed that many peculiar features in the myths of **Artemis**
are traceable to the fact of her being twin-sister of **Apollo,**
whose inner and spiritual qualities she was believed to share.

It was observed that the vegetation of warm southern lands
spread and flourished most under the quickening influence of
the coolness of night and the fall of dew, which often for
whole months was a substitute for the missing rains. It was
known by experience that the fall of dew is most copious when
the sky is clear and the moon sheds her pure light—and hence
to **Artemis** was ascribed the cause of fertility in this direction. Hence she was believed to roam by night through woods
and groves, over hills and valleys, accompanied by the nymphs
of the fountains; beside rivers, fountains, and marshes her
presence was felt. But the presence of the moon in the heavens gave security to travellers and to herds, especially from
the attacks of wild animals, whose enemy Artemis was therefore thought to be. Under the title of **Agrotora** she was the
patron goddess of huntsmen, her favourite hunting-ground being Arcadia, with its many heights and glens well-wooded and
well-watered. Here she was worshipped under the form of a
bear, and called **Kalliste,** the Arcadians, or bear-people,
boasting their descent from her. On the other hand, the regularly recurring absence of the moon from the heavens, which
could only have been regarded as due to a voluntary act on
the part of the goddess, showed that though opposed to wild
animals, she could also employ them for the purpose of punishing men, and to illustrate this, the story was told of her having
sent among the Ætolians the so-called Kalydonian boar, which
laid waste their fields, till after a great hunt it was slain by

Meleager and **Atalanta.** As a huntress her favourite animal was the stag, because its swiftness gave the best opportunity for her method of capture, which was by bow and speed of foot. As an instance of how severely she would punish the wanton slaying of the stag, there is the story of how for such a crime on the part of **Agamemnon** she detained the Greek fleet, on its way to Troy, in the harbour of Aulis, and exacted from him the sacrifice of his daughter, **Iphigeneia. Aktaeon,** the huntsman, had seen the goddess bathing, and for this offence to her modesty was transformed into a stag, and devoured by his own hounds—a story which appears to illustrate the destructive influence of the dog-star, **Sirius.** Another hunter whom she slew with her sweet arrows was **Orion,** a personification of the bright constellation, which at the beginning of summer is seen in early morning in the east, where it remains until extinguished by the morning light. To express this in the form of a myth, Orion was said to have been too pressing in his advances towards **Eos,** the morning, and for this the goddess of the moon slew him.

From the coincidence observed between the courses of the moon and the ebb and flow of tides, Artemis came to be viewed as a goddess who protected the occupation of the fishermen, not only on the shore and on arms of the sea, but also on lakes and rivers. In this character she bore the name of **Diktynna,** or **Britomartis,** and was worshipped with zeal among other places in the island of Crete, where, to account for the former of her two names, the story was told of her having, to escape the pursuit of Minos, thrown herself from a rock into the sea, upon which she was caught in a fisherman's net.

From the joyous feelings awakened by calm moonlight, and perhaps partly from her relationship to Apollo, she was described as fond of music and the dance—a view of her character which appears to have presented itself in a strong light to the people of Arcadia.

By whatever process the belief was arrived at, whether from some comparison which suggested itself between the life of man and the waxing and waning of the moon, or whether because mankind at birth seemed to come out of night into the light of day, we find Artemis represented as the guardian and helper of child-birth, with the title of **Eileithyia, Ilithyia,*** or **Eleutho.** She was throughout looked upon as a goddess of the female productive power in nature, and accordingly the care and nursing of children through their illness were placed under her supervision.   A festival, accompanied by the dancing of young girls, was held in her honour as the goddess of youth, in Messenia, Lakonia, Elis, and elsewhere in Greece.   Similarly, from the notion that mankind after death seems to sink into night again, she came to be viewed as goddess of death, particularly of that manner of death which could not be assigned to a known cause—it being said of those who were stricken suddenly, without an ostensible cause, such as an injury or wound, that Apollo or Artemis had laid them low with a kindly arrow: and in these cases the death of men was ascribed to Apollo, and of women to Artemis, as a rule.

From the fact that the moon, with its pure serene light, naturally suggested, as it does to us also, the idea of a modest pure virgin, Artemis, as her name implies, the "modest, spotless goddess," came to be looked on as a virgin, and as having under her special care all shy and modest youths, whether boys

---

* Both names are also assigned to **Hera,** while **Eileithyia** herself is described as a daughter of **Zeus** and **Hera.**

or girls, from whom she received presents of wreaths of flowers in the spring-time. When girls had reached an age at which her care was no longer necessary, it was customary for them to dedicate their girdles to the goddess. Young girls were sometimes called "bears," in allusion to their patron goddess, and her symbol of a bear. She was worshipped in Athens, Corinth, and Thebes as goddess of strict upbringing, of good fame, of upright mind, and of sensibility in the affairs of ordinary life. She chased and fired her arrows at all wild and unchecked creatures and actions.

When only a maiden of tender age she resolved, and obtained **Zeus'** consent, to remain always in a single state, and, like **Athēnē**, continued constant and true to her resolve, punishing with great severity every offence against this principle on the part of the nymphs who accompanied her, as we see in the examples of **Daphnē**, whom she transformed into a laurel tree, and **Kallisto** into a bear.

It may have been from the same motive which assigned the bear as a symbol, that in early times her worship was attended with human sacrifice. Of this kind was the worship of the **Tauric Artemis**, at first peculiar to the countries on the shores of the Black Sea, the Crimea being the principal centre of it. From the Crimea, it is said, Orestes brought an image of the goddess, and transplanted her worship to Greece, where it took root, among other places, at Sparta. There she was styled **Orthia** or **Orthosia**. The sacrifices of human beings were however, in later times, commuted for the well-known ceremony of flogging youths at her altar, said to have been introduced by the Spartan legislator Lykurgos.

As goddess of marshes she was styled **Limnaia**, and as a river goddess **Potamia**. In this latter capacity she took under
8

her protection the nymphs of fountains, as, for example, **Are-thusa,** whose beauty had attracted the river-god Alpheios, and made her the object of his constant pursuit, till Artemis to elude him, caused the water of the spring which she repre- sented to flow under-ground. As **Munychia,** or moon-god- dess, she was worshipped at the harbour of Athens, and en- joyed an annual festival, at which cakes of the shape of a full moon, with lights stuck in them, were presented to her. As **Brauronia,** with the symbol of a bear, she had a sanctuary on the Acropolis of Athens. In Eubœa she was styled **Am-arynthia,** and was worshipped with great ceremony.

Selene, or **Luna,** it has already been said, stood as god- dess of the moon, in the same relation to Artemis as did Helios to Phœbos-Apollo, inasmuch as she merely represented the orb of the moon, while Artemis represented the influence exercised on nature by night, the symbol of which was the moon, as the sun was symbol of day. Accordingly, as com- pared with **Helios,** the rising star of day, **Selene** represents evening and night, carrying a torch, and clad in long heavy robes, with a veil covering the back of her head. On her brow she wears a half-moon (less frequently horns), and leans forward, as if moving with speed, in a chariot drawn by two horses ; or she rides on a mule. The story of her love for the beautiful young **Endymion,** whom she found asleep on a hill-side, and, enamoured of his loveliness, descended to him, is the best known of the myths concerning her, and may be taken as a symbolical representation of the gentle influence of the goddess of night, who watches the slumbers of unconscious creatures. Among the Romans **Luna** had a handsome tem- ple, founded by King Servius Tullius, on the Aventine hill, another on the Capitol, and a third on the Palatine.

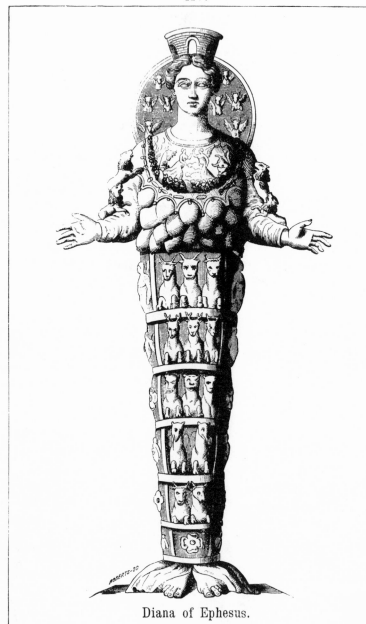

XV

Diana of Ephesus.

Compared with the Artemis whom we have up to now been describing, the so-called Ephesian Artemis, or **Diana of Ephesus**, presents (Plate XV.) so very different and strange an aspect, that at first sight we are completely at a loss to understand how by any possibility the term of a virgin could be applied to her.   Her appearance altogether wants the simplicity, humanity, and truth to nature which characterized the Greek deities, and, what is more, bears the most obvious signs of maternity. . It would seem that the Greeks, who settled as colonists in very early times on the coast of Asia Minor, found this goddess being worshipped by the native population of that land, and adopted her in the place of Artemis, who, leaving out the fact of her being a virgin, was probably identical with the Asiatic goddess in respect of her divine power over fertility, childbirth, the moon, and hunting.

The worship of **Diana of Ephesus** extended throughout the part of Asia Minor colonized by Greeks, and thence spread to other places—never, however, obtaining a firm footing in Greece Proper.   At Ephesus she had a temple, which, for the grandeur of its architecture, its size, splendour, and wealth, was reckoned one of the seven wonders of the ancient world. On the night on which Alexander the Great was born it was set fire to and almost completely destroyed by a man named Herostratos, whose object, being simply to hand down his name in history, was gained.   Afterwards, when Alexander had acquired renown by his extraordinary conquests in Asia, this coincidence was remarked, and accepted as having been an omen of his future fame.   Whether he himself believed so or not, he gladly assisted in the rebuilding of the temple, so that when finished it was more magnificent than before. Diana was still being worshipped zealously when the Apostle Paul

went to Ephesus to preach Christianity, and accordingly he
was received with hostility, especially by the silversmiths and
goldsmiths, whose trade consisted largely in the production of
small shrines, or representations of the front of the temple of
Diana, to be sold among her worshippers and devotees. Feeling that the success of Paul's preaching would ruin their trade,
they raised so great an opposition to him and his followers that
they were obliged to leave the town. Nevertheless the new
religion found converts, who from that time forward formed a
Christian community there. This Artemis was also worshipped
under the title of **Leukophryne** in Asia Minor, and as such
had a splendid temple at Magnesia on the Mæander.

Among the Romans the worship of Diana appears to have
been of native growth, and not, as was the case with that of
many of the other deities, imported from Greece. A temple
had been erected to her in Rome on the Aventine hill as early
as the time of King Servius Tullius. Her sacrifices consisted
of oxen and deer; and these, as well as the fruit presented to
her, had to be perfectly clean and faultless, as became offerings to a virgin goddess. Stags, dogs, and the first-fruits of
the fields were sacred to her.

In works of art Artemis was usually represented as a huntress, either in the
act of running with speed in pursuit of her game, or resting, and presenting
the picture of a young virgin, fleet of foot, her dress girt high, and unencum-
bered except by bow and arrows. In type of face she resembles her brother
Apollo so closely that, from the face alone, it is sometimes difficult to distinguish them. Her hair, like his, is gathered into a large knot above the forehead. The most celebrated of the statues of her that have come down to us is
the so-called Diana of Versailles. In early works of art, and in some of the
later—as, for example, a marble statue in the British Museum—her drapery
reaches to her feet, but in these cases also she is represented as in active movement, like the moon hastening through the clouds. Of the incidents in which
she figured we find that of Aktaeon being transformed into a stag and devoured

by his hounds, in a sculptured group, on a painted vase, and on the fragment of a cameo in the British Museum. The hunt of the Kalydonian boar
occurs on painted vases.

The Ephesian Artemis was represented (plate xv.) with a mural crown on
her head. Behind the crown is a disc, as symbol of the full moon; on her
breast, like a necklace, a garland of flowers, as a sign of her influence in spring
time, while above it are figures of maidens, to indicate her patronage of young
girls; lions cling to her arms; as mother of wild beasts, she has many breasts;
her legs are closely bandaged and ornamented with figures of bulls, stags, lions
and gryphons; at the sides are flowers and bees. How far this figure may
have resembled the original image of the goddess which had fallen from heaven,
it is impossible to say.

Selēnē or Luna is represented as riding on a mule or a horse; on the pediment of the Parthenon it is a horse. On a painted vase in the British Museum
there occurs a representation of sunrise; Helios is seen rising in his chariot,
the stars, in the form of youths, dive headlong into the sea, and the moon (Selēnē) rides away over the hill-tops on a horse, and as she departs is bayed at
by a dog.

DIONYSOS, or BACCHUS,

(PLATE XIV.,)

Having more titles than any of the other deities, was styled, to
increase their number, "God of the many names," of these the
most familiar being, **Bromios, Lyaeos, Dithyrambos,**
and **Bakchos.** The belief in the existence and powers of
this god appears to have been borrowed by the Greeks in its
primitive form from oriental mythology, to have been developed by them, and in later times communicated to the
Romans. His original signification was that of a divine being
whose power might be noticed operating in the sap of vegetation ; and, accordingly, spring was a season of gladness and joy
for him, and winter a season of sorrow. From this sprung his
double character of god of the vintage and its gay accompani-
ments, and god of the ecstatic and mystic ceremonies in which

his sufferings during winter were deplored. As time went on
he came to be viewed chiefly as the source of the happiness and
mirth which arise from the enjoyment of the noble fruit of the
vine; while afterwards, from the fact that his festivals in spring
and summer, with their gaiety and mirth, gave occasion to
the first attempts at dramatic performances, he added the
function of god of the theatre to that of god of the vine.

He was born, it was commonly believed, at Thebes, and
was a son of **Zeus** and **Semele,** a daughter of **Kadmos,**
the founder of that town, a son of **Agenor,** and grandson
of **Poseidon.** Of his birth poets relate how **Hera,** indignant at this rival in her husband's affections, determined to
get rid of her; and to this end, assuming a disguise, went to
Thebes, and presented herself to Semele; how she succeeded
in winning her confidence, and thereupon took occasion to
propose that she should ask Zeus to visit her for once in all
the plenitude of his majesty as a god of thunder, how Zeus,
who, without waiting to listen, had hastily sworn "by the
black waters of the Styx," to grant whatever she should ask,
was vexed when he heard the foolish request, from granting
which no power could absolve him; how one day he appeared
before the luckless Semele with a display of thunder and
lightning which caused her death. So far the desire of vengeance on the part of Hera was satisfied. But Semele, at the
moment of her death, gave birth to a male child, whose life
Zeus fortunately restored. That was the child **Bakchos.**
To prevent its suffering at the hands of Hera, Hermes, the
messenger of the gods, was secretly despatched with the infant
to a place called Nysa, where were certain nymphs, to whom,
along with **Silenos,** the charge of bringing up the child was
entrusted. His title of **Dithyrambos,** it is said, means

"twice born," and refers to the incident of his life being restored by Zeus. In after times it was applied to a species of song in honour of the god of wine, of which Arion of Methymna was the reputed originator.

The childhood of **Dionysos** was spent in innocence and happiness among the nymphs, satyrs, sileni, herdsmen, and vine-tenders of Nysa. But when he arrived at manhood he set out on a journey through all known countries, even into the remotest parts of India, instructing the people, as he proceeded, how to tend the vine, and how to practise many other arts of peace, besides teaching them the value of just and honourable dealings. He was praised everywhere as the greatest benefactor of mankind. At the same time, it is said, apparently with reference to the fierce and stubborn mood which in some cases follows copious indulgence in wine, that he met occasionally with great resistance on his journey, but always overcame it and punished those who opposed him most severely. As an instance of this, we will take **Lykurgos**, the king of Thrace, whom, for his resistance, Dionysos drove mad, and caused to fell his son, mistaking him for a vine-plant, and afterwards to kill himself in despair. Or, again, **Pentheus**, a king of Thebes, whom he caused to be torn to pieces by his own mother and her following of women, because he had dared to look on at their orgiastic rites.

Nowhere was the knowledge of how to utilize the vine appreciated more than in Attica, where the god had communicated it to Ikaros, whose first attempt to extend the benefit of it to others brought about his own death, an event which was deeply grieved for afterwards. In December a festival, with all manner of rustic enjoyments, was held in honour of Dionysos in the country round Athens. In January, a festival called **Lenaea** was held in his honour in the town, at which one of the principal features was a nocturnal and orgiastic procession of women. Then followed in February the **Anthesteria**, the first day of which was called 'cask-opening day,' and the second 'pouring day.' Lastly came the great festival of the year, the **Great Dionysia**, which was held in the town of Athens, and lasted from the ninth to the fifteenth of March, the religious part of the ceremony consisting of a procession in which an ancient wooden image of the god was carried through the streets from one sanctuary to another, accompanied by excited songs. The theatre of Dionysos was daily the scene of splendid dramatic performances, and the whole town was astir and gay.

His worship extended to Lemnos, Thasos, and Naxos, where the story was told of his turning the Tyrrhenian pirates into dolphins, and where he found the beautiful **Ariadne**, when she had been abandoned by Theseus. It spread to Crete, the home of Ariadne, and into Asia Minor. In Phrygia he was worshipped with wild ceremonies, called **Sabazia**, and in Thrace and Macedonia, called **Kottytia**. As the god who had advanced through Asia Minor and on to India, accompanied by his wild and clamorous following, he was styled the Indian Dionysos, and in this character was represented as advanced in years.

The sufferings which the god was supposed to endure in winter led him to be associated with Demeter in the mysteries of Eleusis, the purpose of which was, as has been said, to celebrate the grief of the goddess in winter, and her prospects of joy in the coming spring.

The vine, ivy, and pomegranate were sacred to this god ; his sacrifices consisted of goats and pigs.

XVI.

Ariadne.

In works of art **Dionysos** was represented under a variety of forms; of these, however, two are to be specially noticed. The one called the "Indian Bakchos" represents him as a man of years, with worthy aspect, a long beard, a diadem on his brow, and long drapery sweeping to his feet. In the other figure he is represented as a beautiful youth with an almost feminine appearance (plate xiv.), beardless, his hair falling in long tresses, and adorned with a wreath of ivy or vine tendrils, sometimes wearing the skin of a stag over his shoulders, or with small horns on his brow, and often in a car drawn by panthers or lions, or riding on one of these beasts.

At other times he appears as a child, and that sometimes when he is being handed over by Hermes to the care of Silenos and the nymphs of Nysa. The youthful Dionysos is frequently represented in the company of Ariadne, while the elder Dionysos is usually accompanied by Sileni and Satyrs, as when he visited Ikaros and taught him the use of the vine, a scene which occurs on several ancient reliefs, of which two are in the British Museum. On his journey to India he rides on a camel, and on other occasions he is attended by panthers. His staff is a *thyrsus*—a rod with a pine cone at the top. In his hand is often a drinking cup. The movement and excitement of the persons who were associated with Dionysos was a great attraction to Praxiteles and the sculptors of his time, and it is probable that the many sculptures of Dionysiac subjects which we now possess come from that school either as originals or direct imitations.

HERMES, or MERCURY,

(PLATES X. AND XVII.,)

A son of **Zeus** and **Maia,** a daughter of **Atlas,** was regarded in the first instance as the special deity to whom was due the prolificness and welfare of the animal kingdom. In consequence, however, of the fact that in early times the chief source of wealth consisted in herds of cattle, the prolificness of which was traced to him, it came to pass in time that he was considered generally to be the first cause of all wealth, come whence it might. But as civilization advanced, and it became known by experience that there was no means of acquiring wealth so rapidly as by trade his province was extended to trade, and the protection of traders.   Again, since the main condition of prosperity in trade was peace and undisturbed commerce by land and sea, he came to be viewed as guardian of commerce.   And, further, assuming that all who took part in trade were qualified to look after their own interests, shrewd and prudent, the function of protecting prudence, shrewdness, and even cunning, was assigned to him.   In certain aspects of trade, if not in the best, it was reckoned a great point to talk over and cajole purchasers, and from his protection of this ·method of doing business, **Hermes** came to be god of "persuasive speech" or oratory.   Finally, it being only a short step from this to cunning and roguery, we must not be surprised to find him described as protector of thieves and rascals, though no doubt this task was assigned him more in joke than in earnest.

His office of messenger and herald of the gods, in particular of **Zeus**, appears to have originated partly in the duty assigned to him of protecting commerce, the success of which depends largely on the messengers and envoys employed in it, and partly in other functions of his which would lead us too far to explain.   As messenger and envoy of **Zeus**, Hermes conducts the intercourse between heaven and earth, announcing the will of the gods to men, and from this office was further derived his character of a god of oracles.   In the capacity of messenger or herald he had access even to the under-world, whither, under the title of **Psychopompos**, he guided the souls of the departed, crossing in Charon's bark, and placing them before the throne of the deities below. (Plate VI.) From the shadowy world of spirits to that of sleep and dreams is a short step for the imagination, and accordingly we find Hermes described as **Oneiropompos**, guide of dreams.   As the swift messenger of the gods he readily came to be looked on as a model for the youth practising in the palæstra, in which capacity he had the title of **Enagonios.**

In proportion to the variety of the tasks which he had to perform was the variety of mythical stories about his actions and life, some of them, taking us back to the very day of his birth. For it was not an uncommon practice in the early myth-making age to ascribe to the infancy of a god some instance of the peculiar qualities by which he was afterwards distinguished. So it happened with Hermes.

His birth having taken place on the fourth of the month, that day became sacred to him. Born, as it was believed, during the darkness of night, in an unfrequented, lonesome cave on Mount Kyllene, in Arcadia, and on this account styled **Kyllenios,** he was only a day old when a remarkable example of his cunning and knavery occurred. Slipping out of the couch in the cave where he was left asleep as was supposed, the night being dark and cloudy, he found a herd of cattle belonging to his brother Apollo (as sun-god), and stole a number of them. When the morning came Apollo searched in vain for the missing cattle; for the infant god had cleverly succeeded in obliterating all traces of them by fastening bunches of broom to their hoofs, and in this condition driving them backwards into a cave at Pylos, so as to produce the impression that they had left instead of entered the cave. After this adventure he slunk back to his couch, and feigned to be asleep. He had, however, been observed by a rustic named Battos, who informed against him, whereupon Apollo, angry at such a daring piece of robbery, dragged him out of his couch, and took him off to the throne of **Zeus** to be punished and made an example of. But **Hermes** was irrepressible, took up a lyre which he had made the day before out of the shell of a tortoise, and proceeded to play on it, to the amuse-ment and delight of both Zeus and Apollo, and further in-gratiated himself with his brother by giving him the lyre, in-venting for his own use a shepherd's pipe. The cattle of the sun-god were the clouds, and Hermes was a god who presided over the fertility of nature. The signification of the story of his stealing some of these cattle on a dark night would there-fore seem to be simply that of clouds discharging fertilizing showers by night.

The two brothers having thus made their peace, continued from that time forward on the best of terms, Apollo attesting his good disposition towards Hermes by giving him in return for the lyre a present of a golden divining-rod, and also the power of prophecy. This condition, however, was attached to the gift, that he was not to communicate his revelations of the future by words as did Apollo, but by signs and occur-rences. That is to say, that persons revolving some under-taking in their mind were to be guided by certain unexpected sights, accidents, or incidents, and were to recognize in them the favour or displeasure of the gods with reference to the enterprise in question,—a method of proceeding common enough in modern superstition. These signs and incidents were believed to be sent by Hermes, whose counsel in other cases of doubt, as to whether to do or not do a thing, was sought for by recourse to dice, the belief being that a high throw signified his approval, and a low throw the reverse.

The cunning and adroitness, the same good humour and ready answer which he gave proof of in the first days of his infancy, were often afterwards and with like success displayed by him—as, for example, when he stole the sceptre of **Zeus,**

Hephæstos, or Vulcan.

Hermes, or Mercury.

Aphrodite's girdle, **Poseidon's** trident, the sword of
Ares, the tongs of **Hephæstos**, or **Apollo's** bow and arrows, in each case managing to make up matters, and smooth
away the indignation of his victims.   But the most celebrated
instance in which his brilliant talents were fully displayed was
the affair of **Argos** with the hundred eyes, whom **Hera** had
appointed to watch over **Io**, one of the favourites of **Zeus**,
whom the latter, that she might escape the vengeance of the
jealous **Hera**, had transformed into a cow, a trick which the
goddess had perceived.

Well, Hermes being commanded by Zeus to release **Io** from
the surveillance of **Argos**, and in doing so to use no force,
found the task no easy matter, seeing that the watchman had
a hundred eyes, of which, when in his deepest sleep, only fifty
were closed. Hermes succeeded, however, and in this fashion.
Presenting himself to Argos, he commenced to amuse him by
telling all kinds of tales, and having by these means fairly
gained the watchman's confidence, he next produced a
shepherd's pipe, and played on it various tunes of such sweetness that they gradually lulled Argos into so deep a sleep that
one by one all his hundred eyes closed. The moment the last
eyelid drooped Hermes slew him, and at once released Io, and
led her away.   For this service he rose high in the estimation
of Zeus, and from that time the name of " Argos-slayer,"
Argeiphontes, was the proudest title which he bore.   As a
memorial of Argos, Hera, it was said, set his eyes in the tail
of her favourite bird, the peacock.   But these and such-like
instances of his knavery and cunning do not by any means
express the whole character of **Hermes**; for his skill was also
directed frequently to purposes of useful invention. It was he,
for example, who invented **Apollo's** lyre, as well as that one

by which the Theban musician, **Amphion,** did such wonders; and it was he who taught **Palamedes** to express words in writing. And, besides, wherever danger that required skill and dexterity as much as courage presented itself, he was always present to assist. He acted as guide to heroes in their dangerous enterprises, and in that capacity frequently, as in the case of **Herakles,** was associated with **Athene.** To travellers who had lost their way he was a ready guide, and to exiles a constant and willing helper in strange lands and among ill-disposed people.

In the primitive form of his worship Hermes was, as has been said, the god who gives prolificness to flocks and herds. In this character we find him in what appears to have been the oldest centre of his worship in Greece, that is in Samothrace and the neighbouring islands of Imbros and Lemnos, where he bore the title of **Kadmilos** or **Kasmilos.** His usual title among herdsmen was either **Nomios** or **Epimelios.**

A messenger himself, it became his office to aid human messengers and travellers, and to this end it was he who inspired the idea of erecting sign-posts at cross-roads with directions as to whither each road led. These sign-posts took the form of statues, if they may be so called, consisting of a pillar running narrower towards the foot, and surmounted by a head of Hermes, and called **Hermæ.** It was the duty of travellers on passing one of them to place a stone beside it, a custom which not only largely helped towards clearing the fields of stones, but also led to improvement in the roads themselves, and hence to increased facilities for commerce. If more than two roads crossed, a corresponding number of heads were placed on the pillar, one facing each way. Similar figures were also found outside houses in Athens for the purpose of cheering parting travellers

Themis.

Leto, or Latona.

The attributes of Hermes were the *caduceus* or *kerykeion,* that is, a short staff with a pair of wings and a knotted snake attached to it, and the *petasos* or winged cap. Beside him sometimes is a cock or a goat. For sacrifice he delighted in the tongues of animals, a suitable sacrifice to the god of oratory.

The Roman **Mercurius** appears to have possessed in common with Hermes only the character of god of trade and oratory. Roman traders held a festival to him on the 25th of May.

In the earlier works of art Hermes appears bearded and about middle age, frequently carrying a sheep or a kid over his shoulders. His form is athletic. In more recent works we find him of a youthful figure, such as became his office as messenger of the gods. He wears the *petasos*, and sometimes wings at his heels, carries the *caduceus*, and sometimes, as god of trade, a purse. Among the incidents of his life, one which occurs frequently on the painted vases is that in which he appears presenting the three goddesses to Paris, who had to decide their claims as to which of them was the most beautiful. Sometimes he is represented in sculptures as a mere boy. Many of the Hermæ described above have come down to our times.

THEMIS,

(PLATE XVIII.,)

A daughter of **Uranos** and **Gaea,** was the personification of that divine law of right which ought to control all human affairs, of that highest and noblest sense of right which is subject to no human influences. In this capacity she came to be viewed also as goddess of the rites of hospitality. She was a personification of divine will as it bore upon the affairs of the world, and accordingly the Delphic oracle had been under her control before it was yielded to **Apollo,** to whom, as her successor, she communicated the prophetic art. A long time

passed before **Zeus** could persuade her to become his wife—
his first wife, as some myths have it; his second, according to
others, which say that **Metis** was his first. To him she bore
the **Horæ, Mœræ** or **Parcæ,** and **Astræa,** the goddess of
justice, of whom we have already told how she forsook the
earth during the Bronze Age. The proper home of Themis
was Olympos, and hence she was styled **Urania.** But during
the war with the Titans she descended to earth, and there,
throughout the Golden Age, taught mankind the exercise of
right and moderation. When, afterwards, the human race
sank into degradation, she returned again to Olympos.

In consequence of the profound wisdom and open truthful-
ness which formed the essential features of the character of
Themis, even the supreme gods consulted and acted on her
advice; as, for example, did **Zeus,** when he declined to
marry **Thetis,** because of the prediction of Themis, that a
son would be the issue of the marriage, who would excel even
his father in might. We shall afterwards have to relate how
Thetis was given in marriage to **Peleus,** a mortal, in order
that her son might not be a source of danger to the gods.
The worship of Themis extended to many districts of Greece,
where temples, altars, and statues were raised in her honour.
The principal centres of it, however, were Athens, Trœzene,
the island of Ægina, Thebes, and Olympia.

Ancient artists represented her as a woman of mature age,
with large open eyes; while modern artists—and they alone,
it must be observed—figure her as in Plate XVIII.

She is further represented holding a sword and chain in
one hand and a balance in the other, to indicate the severity
and the accuracy with which justice is to be meted out and
administered.

II. INFERIOR DEITIES.

HITHERTO our descriptions have been confined to those deities of the Greeks and Romans, who, because their functions were subordinate to no god but **Zeus**, were styled of the superior order, or Olympian deities, **Hades** and **Persephone** being included, though their realm was the underworld, not Olympos. We proceed now to the inferior order, such as occupied subordinate positions in the system of gods, but were nevertheless worshipped independently, if not so universally as the others.

We begin with the

HORÆ,

(PLATE XXV.,)

The goddesses of the "seasons," daughters of **Zeus** and **Themis**. Their number was variously estimated according to the variety of the divisions of the year into periods,—winter, however, not being reckoned as one, because it was the season of sleep and death in nature. Thus we find the worship of only two goddesses of seasons in Athens, the one called **Thallo**, or goddess of "blossoming," and the other **Karpo**, or goddess of "harvest and fruit." But elsewhere in Greece the

9

usual number was three, and as such they were represented in
works of art (see Plate XXV.), with the attributes of the seasons: Spring with its flowers, Summer with its grain, and
Autumn with its grapes and fruit.

Occasionally we find a fourth season, that of Winter, represented in the act of returning with booty from the chase;
but, unlike her sisters, she is nameless.

As deities of the kindly seasons which bring about the bud-
ding and growth of nature, they were directly under the control of the superior deities, especially of Zeus and Hera.   At
times they are to be seen along with the **Charites** (Graces)
in the company of Aphrodite, and sometimes along with the
Muses in the company of Apollo; for it is in the happy seasons of the year that the joyous voice of nature is heard.

In the capacity of goddesses who watched over the blessings
of the fields, it became their duty, further, to regulate changes
of the weather, now opening and now shutting the gates of
heaven, alternately sending rain and sunshine as suited best
the increase of vegetation.   Tender and gladsome, moving in
mazy dances, with crowns of gold and of flowers, they were
always good and faithful to mankind, and, though sometimes
seeming to be impatient to come late, always bringing with
them something sweet and beautiful, never proving untrue or
deceitful.

The figure (in Plate XXXI.) represents a **Hora** dancing,
with a wreath of palm-leaves on her head.   The dish of fruit
in her left hand probably indicates that she is the Hora of
Autumn.

Such were their functions in nature.   In consequence, however, of the great and plenteous blessings that were observed
to flow from the unchangeable and orderly succession of the

seasons, the Horæ were also supposed to watch over good order and propriety in human life and morality—a task which seems to have given rise to the belief that they were daughters of **Themis.** Their names, in the cases where the three appear together, have been admirably chosen to suit this metaphorical notion of their character: as, **Eunomia** (wise legislation), **Dikē** (justice), and **Eirēnē** (peace). Eunomia's services were mostly directed to political life, the results being warmly praised by poets, and her worship never neglected by the State. Dikē's sphere of operations was more among the incidents of the lives of individuals, informing, it was said, her father **Zeus,** of every injustice done on earth. Eirēnē, finally being the most cheerful of the three sisters, was said to have been the mother of **Plutos**—that is, of riches, the gay companion of **Dionysos,** and guardian goddess of songs and festivities.

The goddess of spring was also especially worshipped as a Hora (plate XXI.) under the title of **Chloris,** which corresponds to the Roman **Flora.** She was the goddess of buds and flowers, of whom **Boreas,** the north winter wind, and **Zephyros,** the west spring wind, were rival lovers. She chose the latter, and became his faithful wife.

POMONA

Was goddess of garden fruits, and was represented wearing a wreath composed of such, or holding in her hand a horn of plenty full of them, with a dog by her side. Her appearance was that of a virgin in rustic garments. It was said that she had been originally a **Hamadryad,** but had yielded her affections to **Vertumnus.** Her worship was confined to the

Romans.   She had a priest, styled **flamen pomonalis**, specially devoted to her service.

VERTUMNUS,

The husband of **Pomona**, was worshipped by the Romans as
a deity of the second order, who watched over the seasons as
well as the garden fruits, and was represented with attributes
similar to those of Pomona.   In October an annual festival,
resembling a harvest thanksgiving, was held in his honour,
the offerings brought him on that occasion consisting of first-
fruits from the garden, and wreaths of flowers of all kinds.
Like Pomona, he, too, had a priest of his own.   At times he
was represented, like **Saturn**, with a pruning-knife in his
hand, and a wreath composed of ears of corn on his head.
Originally he was worshipped under the form of a rough
wooden post, but had afterwards a beautiful bronze statue
made by a Roman artist.

JANUS,

(PLATE XVII.,)

Was a deity unknown to the Greeks, but from the earliest
times held in high estimation by the Romans, who placed him
on almost an equal footing with **Jupiter**, even giving his
name precedence in their prayers, and invoking the aid of
both deities previous to every undertaking.   To him they ascribed the origin of all things, the introduction of the system
of years, the change of season, the ups and downs of fortune,
and the civilization of the human race by means of agriculture, industry, arts, and religion.   According to the popular

Janus.

Hermes, or Mercury.

belief, Janus was an ancient king who had come in remote early times from Greece to Latium, there instituted the worship of the gods and the erection of temples, and himself deserved high honours like a god, for this reason, that he had conferred the greatest boon upon mankind by his instructions in many important ways. In some of the stories he is confounded with **Saturn**. In others it is said that Saturn, driven out of Greece, took refuge with Janus in Latium, and shared the government with him.

It is easy to explain the great honour paid to Janus by a people like the Romans, who, as a rule, had this peculiarity of pondering well the prospects of an undertaking before entering upon it. The beginning of everything was a matter of great importance to them, and Janus was the god of a " good beginning." It is in this spirit that the Roman poet, Ovid, makes Janus say, " Everything depends on the beginning." Even when Jupiter had consented to an enterprise, prosperity in carrying it out was believed to be under the control of Janus, and, accordingly, great stress was laid on the circumstances attending the commencement of any project. Janus opened and closed all things. He sat, not only on the confines of the earth, but also at the gates of heaven. Air, sea, and land were in the hollow of his hands. The world moved on its hinges at his command.

In accordance with this belief, he was represented, as in Plate XVII., seated, with two heads, one being that of a youth, to indicate 'beginning,' the other that of an old man, to indicate the 'end,' whence he was styled **Bifrons** (two-headed). In his left hand is a key, to show that he opens at the beginning, and shuts at the end; the sceptre in his right is a sign that he controls the progress of every undertaking.

The first day of January, a month named after him, being
the first day of a new year, was the occasion of a celebration
in his honour.   At the beginning of every month the priests
offered sacrifice to him at twelve altars. He was invoked every
morning as the beginner of a new day. Even at the sacrifices
to other gods he was remembered, and received offerings of
wine and cakes, incense, and other things. The husbandman
prayed to him at the beginning of seed-time. When war was
declared he was invoked.

The public worship of Janus as a god was introduced into
Rome as early as the time of Numa Pompilius, a foundation
for its establishment having been previously laid during the
reign of Romulus.   The story runs, that the Sabines having
once made an assault on the newly built town of Rome, a
spring of boiling water suddenly appeared, and was the means
of destroying these enemies.   On this spot a temple was
erected in honour of Janus, the gates of which stood open so
long as Rome was at war, and were closed with great ceremony and rejoicing only in times of general peace.   Rome
was, however, so continually engaged in war that, in the course
of the first seven hundred years after the foundation of the
city the gates of the temple were closed only three times—in
the reign of Numa Pompilius, after the first Punic war, and
during the reign of Augustus.   Hence the temple of Janus
with its gates shut came to be a very emphatic symbol of peace.

TERMINUS,

Was the god of boundaries, and had, when represented in art,
the figure of a boundary stone or pillar surmounted by a head,
as in the case of the figures of Hermes by the wayside in

Greece. Such figures of Terminus were occasionally surmounted by the head or bust of another god, as, for example,
of Apollo or Athene, and in such cases were styled **Herma-
pollo, Hermathene**. **Pan** and **Priapos**, both rural deities,
were also frequently represented in such a form.

Numa Pompilius is said to have erected the first altar to this
boundary god, Terminus, and to have instituted his worship
among the Romans. To accustom his subjects to respect the
boundaries of their neighbours, he ordered them to be marked
off with figures of the god, and a festival to be held in his
honour annually in February. It was called the **Terminalia**.
Boundary stones were adorned with flowers on the occasion,
and a general sacrifice offered, accompanied by lively songs.

PRIAPOS,

Called also **Lutinus** by the Romans, was a son of **Dionysos**
and **Aphrodite**. He was a god of the fertility of nature, and,
in this capacity, also guardian of vineyards, gardens, and cultivated fields. The idea of representing the productive power
of nature under the form of a god is traceable back to a very
great antiquity, but in later and depraved times it came to be
misused for the purpose of giving expression to coarse sensual-
ity and lust. This accounts for the diversity of his representations, of which, however, that is the most correct in which
he appears as a man of years holding a pruning-knife in his
hand, and fruit in his lap. The principal centre of his worship was Lampsakos, a town in Asia Minor, on the Hellespont,
whence it spread over Greece. His symbols were, like those
of Dionysos, a drinking-cup, a *thyrsus*, or a spear. At the
festivals in his honour the sacrifices consisted of milk, honey,
and asses.

PAN,

(PLATE XIX.)

Was looked upon by the pastoral inhabitants of Greece, particularly in Arcadia, as the god who watched over the pasture-fields, herdsmen, and herds. Woods and plains, hunting and fishing, were under his immediate care and patronage, and on this account he was differently described as a son now of **Zeus**, now of **Hermes**, his mother being in each case a nymph. As god of green fields he was associated with the worship of **Dionysos** (Bacchus), and as mountain god with that of **Kybĕle**. He was fond of sportive dances and playing on the shepherd's pipe, which afterwards took its name of Pan's pipe from him, the story being that he was the inventor of it. It seems that a coy nymph named Syrinx, whom he loved and followed, was transformed into a reed, that **Pan** cut it and fashioned it into a pipe (Syrinx) with such sweet notes when skilfully played, that he once ventured to challenge **Apollo** to a competition.

The judge selected was **Midas**, who awarded the prize to Pan, and was, in consequence, punished by Apollo, who made his ears grow like those of an ass.

As a god of herdsmen and country people, he journeyed through woods and across plains, changing from place to place like the nomadic or pastoral people of early times, with no fixed dwelling, resting in shady grottoes, by cool streams, and playing on his pipe. Hills, caves, oaks, and tortoises were sacred to him.

The feeling of solitude and lonesomeness which weighs upon travellers in wild mountain scenes, when the weather is stormy, and no sound of human voice is to be heard, was as cribed to the presence of **Pan,** as a spirit of the mountains, a sort of Number Nip. And thus anxiety or alarm, arising from no visible or intelligible cause, came to be called "Panic fear," that is, such fear as is produced by the agitating presence of Pan.

His common companions were Nymphs and Oreads, who danced to the strains of his pipe, and were not unfrequently pursued by him with violence. It is said that he rendered important service to the gods during the war with the Titans, by the invention of a kind of trumpet made from a sea-shell, with which he raised such a din that the Titans took fright, and retreated in the belief that some great monster was approaching against them. Another story is, that **Dionysos** being once seriously attacked by a hostile and very numerous body of men on his way to India, was freed from them by a sudden terrible shout raised by Pan, which instantly caused them to retreat in great alarm. Both stories appear to have been invented to give a foundation for the expression "Panic fear," which has been explained above.

Pan, also called **Hylæos** or forest god, was usually represented as a bearded man with a large hooked nose, with the ears and horns and legs of a goat, his body covered with hair, with a shepherd's pipe (syrinx) of seven reeds, or a shepherd's crook in his hand, as in Plate XIX.

From Greece his worship was transplanted among the Romans, by whom he was styled **Inŭus,** because he taught them to breed cattle, and **Lupercus,** because he taught them to employ dogs for the purpose of protecting the herds against wolves. The other forest deities, who were represented like Pan with goat's legs, were called **Ægipanes,** and sometimes **Paniski.**

FAUNUS, or FATUUS,

Was a purely Roman deity, originally resembling the Greek **Pan,** as is implied in the name, which is only another form of the same word. In process of time, however, his character passed through many changes, and became different in many respects from that of the Greek god. It was not till late times, when the religion and myths of the Greeks emigrated into Italy, that the comparison of him with the Arcadian Pan was revived, and the identity of both asserted. The Roman poets frequently call the Greek Pan by the Roman name of Faunus. But the latter had certain myths peculiar to himself, and is represented by them as a son of **Picus,** and grandson of **Saturnus,** or, according to another version, a son of **Mars,** and originally an ancient king of Latium, who, for the good he did his people, by introducing agriculture and civilization, came to be worshipped after his death as a prophetic deity of forest and field, under the name of Fatuus. His oracles were delivered in groves, and communicated by means of dreams, which those desiring them obtained by sleeping in sacred places on the hides of animals that had been offered as sacrifices. **Fauna** also delivered oracles, but only to women. (See below.)

As god of the husbandman and patron of agriculture and cattle-rearing, an annual festival, the **Lupercalia,** or **Faunalia,** was celebrated in his honour by the Romans on the 5th of December. It was accompanied by sacrifices of goats, offerings of milk and wine, banquets, and dancing in the open air in meadows and at cross-roads. In the middle of February also sacrifice was presented to him. He had two temples in Rome. Artistic representations of him are rare, and not easily distinguished from those of Pan. The plural form of the word, Fauni, is merely a Roman expression for what the Greeks called Paniski or Panes.

PICUS, PICUMNUS, AND PILUMNUS.

Picus was also a pure Roman deity, a son and a successor of **Saturnus**, father of **Faunus**, and husband of **Canens**. He was an ancient prophet and forest god. Another story has it that he loved and married **Pomona**. **Circe**, the witch, was attracted by his beauty, and finding her affection not returned, revenged herself by changing him into a woodpecker—a bird which was held to be a sacred symbol of prophecy by the Augurs or Roman priests, whose office was to foretell coming events by observing the flight of birds and by various other phenomena. In early times his figure consisted of a wooden pillar with a woodpecker on it, which was afterwards exchanged for a figure of a youth with a woodpecker on his head, the Romans generally considering the appearance of that bird to be a sign of some special intention of the gods. **Picus**, besides being worshipped as a prophet and a god, was also looked upon as one of the first kings of Italy, and must not be confounded with **Picumnus**, who, with his brother **Pilumnus**, formed a pair of Roman deities whose office was to watch over married life. It was the custom to spread a couch for them at the birth of a child. **Pilumnus**, it was said, would drive away all illness from the childhood of the newly-born infant with the club (*pilum*) with which he used to pound the grain; while **Picumnus**, who had introduced the manuring of land, would give the child growth. Stories were told of the two brothers, of famous deeds in war and peace, such as were ascribed to the Dioscuri (Castor and Pollux).

FAUNA, or FATŬA,

The wife, or, according to other myths, the daughter of
Faunus, was a Roman goddess, whose origin and signification have been rendered very obscure by the variety of stories
about her.   She was identified with the goddess **Ops**, with
Kybĕlē, with **Sĕmelĕ**, the mother of **Dionysos** (Bacchus),
with **Maia**, the mother of Hermes, with **Gaea, Hekăte**, and
other goddesses.   In the earliest times she was called simply
the "kind goddess," her proper name as well as her origin
being given out as a mystery.   Her festival took place on the
first night of May, and was celebrated with wine, music, merry
games, and mysterious ceremonies, at which only women and
girls were permitted to be present.   **Fauna** obtained the
name of the "kind goddess" because, as some thought, her
benevolence extended over the whole creation, in which case
it was not strange that she should be identified with other
deities.   As **Fatŭa** she was represented with the appearance
sometimes of Juno, sometimes of Kybĕlē, but commonly as an
aged woman, with pointed ears, holding a serpent in her hand.

The offspring of Fatua and Fatuus were the Fatui, who were
considered to be prophetic deities of the fields, and sometimes
evil genii, who were the cause of nightmares and such like.
The name and obscure significations of this goddess seem to
have given rise to the fantastic creations of modern times, which
we call Fays—that is, beings with the power of witchcraft and
prophecy, and possessed now with good, now with bad qualities,—now useful and helping to men, now mischievous.

XIX.

Satyr.

Pan.

THE SATYRS,

(PLATE XIX.,)

Like the Roman **Silvanus,** belong to the order of forest deities, and are often confounded with the Panes and Fauni, though quite distinct from them. They represented the genial, luxuriant life in Nature, which, under the protection and with the aid of Dionysos (Bacchus), spreads over fields, woods and meadows, and were, without doubt, the finest figures in all his company. As such at least they appear in the art of the best times, being never figured, like the Panes or Paniski, as half man, half animal, but at most exhibit only such signs of an animal form as small goat's horns, and a small goat's tail, to show that their nature was only a little inferior in nobility to that within the divine or pure human form.

The Satyrs constitute a large family, and may be distinguished into several classes, the highest of which were those who nearly resembled their god (**Dionysos**) in appearance, and whose occupation was either to play on the flute for his amusement, or to pour out his wine. To another class belonged those older figures, distinguished by the name of **Silēni;** and to a third, the very juvenile so-called **Satyriski.** The figure given in Plate XIX. is that of a satyr of the highest order. He is represented as a slender youth leaning carelessly on the trunk of a tree, resting from playing on a flute. His hair is shaggy; on his brow are very small goat's horns. His countenance has a touch of animal expression in it. He wears nothing but a *nebris* or panther's skin thrown over his shoulder.

The life of the Satyrs was spent in woods and on hills,

in a constant round of amusements of all kinds : hunting, dancing, music, drinking, gathering and pressing the grapes, or in the company of the god, whirling in wild dances with the Mænads. Their musical instruments were the syrinx, flute, and cymbals.

We may remark in passing, that the term "satire," commonly applied to poems of abuse, has nothing whatever to do with the **Satyrs**, and for this reason should not be written " satyre," though derived from *satura*. The latter is an old Latin word, which signified originally a poetic dialogue or gossip, which from its nature was admirably adapted for conveying criticism and indirect abuse, or satire in our sense of the word.

KOMOS,

Was worshipped as guardian of festal banquets, of mirthful enjoyments, of lively humour, fun, and social pleasure, with attributes expressing joy in many ways. On the other hand, he was represented frequently as an illustration of the consequences of nightly orgies, with torch reversed, in drunken sleep, or leaning against something.

SILVANUS,

Like **Faunus**, was purely a Roman god, whose function also was to watch over the interests of herdsmen, living in woods and fields, and taking care to preserve boundary lines and banks of rivers. It was said that he erected the first boundary stones to mark off the fields of different possessors from each other, and thus became the founder of a regular system of landowning. He was distinguished according to the three departments of his activity, house, field, and wood. In works of art Silvanus appears altogether as a purely human figure—a cheerful aged man holding a shepherd's pipe, (for he, like the other deities of wood and field, was given to music,) and carrying a branch of a tree to mark him specially as god of the forest. This branch, which sometimes is that of a cypress, is explained as referring to his love for the beautiful **Cyparissus,** whom he is said to have changed into a cypress. There was a figure of Silvanus in Rome beside the temple of Saturn, and two sanctuaries dedicated to him. Women were excluded from his worship. The myths are not clear about his origin. Some of them describe him as a son of Saturn.

PALES,

Was worshipped originally in Sicily, and afterwards by the Romans, as a deity of cattle-rearing, being, according to some, male, according to others, female. A merry festival, called **Palilia,** was held in honour of this deity every year on the 21st of April, the day on which the foundation of the city of Rome was said to have been laid. Offerings of milk and must were presented to her, while pipes were played and cymbals beat round a blazing fire of hay and straw. An ox was driven through this blazing fire, the herdsmen rushing after it, a ceremony intended for a symbol of expiation. This festival, because of its falling on the anniversary of the foundation of the city, served also to commemorate that event.

This ancient deity was represented as an aged woman leaning on a leafless branch of a tree, or holding a shepherd's crook in her hand, and was frequently identified with **Fauna,** sometimes with **Kybĕle,** and even with **Vesta.**

SILENOS, AND THE SILENI.

In some of the myths **Silenos** is represented as a son of **Hermes** (Mercury,) in others, of **Pan** and a nymph, the latter statement accounting for his being figured with the tail and ears of a goat, while the rest of his form was purely human. He was usually described as the oldest of the Satyrs, —of whom, indeed, all those well advanced in years were styled Sileni. Owing to his age, he came to be looked upon as a sort of paternal guardian of the light-headed troops of Satyrs, though, with regard to mythological signification, he was quite different from them. One myth traces his origin, along with the worship of Dionysos (Bacchus), to Asia Minor, and particularly to the districts of Lydia and Phrygia, the original centre of the worship of Kybĕlē (Rhea.) In that quarter he was looked on as a sprite or dæmon of fertilizing fountains, streams, marshy land, and luxuriant gardens, as well as the inventor of such music as was produced by the syrinx (Pan's pipe) and the double flute which was used in the worship of Rhea and Dionysos.

According to other stories, he was born in and was the first king of Nysa, but which of the many places of that name remains untold. It was most probably Nysa in Thrace; for Silenos, with the help of local nymphs, nursed and tended the infancy of Dionysos, as works of art show, and this, according to the myths, was spent in Thrace.

To the Greek mind he appeared specially as a companion of Dionysos, one who knew how to press the grapes for wine, and so much loved that liquid as readily to indulge in it to excess, in which case the Satyrs kept him steady on his ass, or else he would have fallen. To express this feature of his character, he was figured with a wreath of vine tendrils on his head, with a drinking-cup or wine-skin in his hand, or intoxicated and supported by two Satyrs. He was a short, round-bellied, hairy old man, with a bald head.

The ass or mule he used to ride was described as a most intelligent beast, and said to have distinguished itself at the time of the war with the Giants, in which its master, as companion and body-servant, a sort of Sancho Panza, to Dionysos, took part, by braying so loudly as to alarm the Giants, and help to put them to flight.

OKEANOS, TETHYS, PROTEUS.

Okeanos, a son of **Uranos** and **Gaea**, was god of the sea, and, like **Nereus**, was looked upon as the father of a large family of marine deities who went by the general name of Okeanides (see below). He was figured like Nereus, but with the addition of a bull's horn, or two short horns, a sceptre in his hand to indicate his power, riding on a monster of the deep, or sitting with his wife, **Tethys**, by his side in a car drawn by creatures of the sea. He is said to have been the most upright of his brother Titans, and to have had no share in the conspiracy against Uranos. For this reason he retained his office, while the other Titans were consigned to Tartaros. It was under the care of Okeanos and his wife that Hera grew up, and to them she turned for safety during the war with the Titans. So quickly had his offspring spread among the rivers, streams, and fountains of the earth, that the sons alone were reckoned as three thousand in number. He was also identified with the great stream, Okeanos, which was supposed to flow in

10

a circle round the earth, and to be the source of all rivers and running waters. His daughters, the Okeanides, were, like all marine deities, represented with crowns of sea-weeds, strings of corals, holding shells, and riding on dolphins. Painters rendered them as half human and half fish in shape ; but poets described them as beings of purely human form, giving their number very differently.

Prōteus was a son of **Okeanos** and **Tethys,** whose proper dwelling-place was the depths of the sea, which he only left for the purpose of taking the sea-calves of **Poseidon** to graze on the coasts and islands of the Mediterranean. Being an aged man, he was looked on as possessed of prophetic power and the secrets of witchcraft, though he would not be persuaded to exercise the former except by deceit or under threat of violence. Even then he made every effort to evade his questioners, changing himself into a great variety of shapes, such as those of a lion, panther, swine or serpent, and, as a last resource, into the form of fire or water. This faculty of transformation, which both **Prōteus** and **Thetis** possessed, corresponds with the great changeability in the appearance of the sea.

NEREUS and THE NEREÏDES,

Or **Dorides,** as they were sometimes called, are frequently confounded in mythology with **Okeanos** and his daughters, the **Okeanids,** all of them being marine deities of a lower order.

Nereus was looked on as an ancient sea-god, a son of **Pontos** and **Gaea,** who, when the dominion of the sea fell to Poseidon, obtained a position under him, and along with it the power of prophecy. With **Doris,** his wife, he had as offspring fifty, or, according to other accounts, a hundred daughters, called Nereïdes or Dorides, of whom **Amphitrite** and **Thetis**, and next to them **Panope** and **Galatea**, were the most famous, the first mentioned having become the wife of Poseidon, while even Zeus desired to marry the second. But the Fates having announced that from this marriage would issue a son who would surpass his father in might, Zeus relinquished his wish, and gave Thetis in marriage to **Peleus,** to whom she bore **Achilles,** and thereafter returned to live among her sisters of the sea.

Nereus is represented in works of art as an old man with a look of dignity, his daughters as sweet, beautiful maidens. Poets described them as modest nymphs dwelling in a splendid cave at the bottom of the sea, now riding on dolphins or other creatures of the deep, now swimming, sporting, splashing about in troops on the sea, sometimes accompanying the sea-born **Aphrodite,** or playing in the warm sunshine on the shores of bays and at rivers' mouths, drying their wet tresses. In such places they were duly worshipped. To the pious feeling of the Greeks the whole of nature appeared in some way divine, and was accordingly viewed with reverence and sanctity. In this spirit the phenomena of the sea were viewed under the form of divine personifications called Nereïdes, the peaceful shimmering light upon its gently moving bosom being represented by **Galēnē** and **Glaukē,** the play of fantastic waves by **Thoe** and **Halie,** the impetuous rush of billows on island shores by **Nesaie** and **Aktææ,** the fascination of the gaily rising tide by **Pasithea, Erato,** and **Euneike,** the swell and impulse of mighty waves by **Pherusa** and **Dynamene,** who all followed in the train of **Amphitrite.**

It may be that these myths gave rise to the modern legends of mermaids.

TRITON AND THE TRITONS.

(PLATE XX.)

Triton, sometimes said to be a son of **Poseidon** and **Amphitrite,** sometimes of **Okeanos** and **Tethys**, was a marine deity of a lower order, and the herald of **Neptune**, in which capacity he was represented using a long twisted shell as a horn to blow a loud blast from when the sea was to be agitated with storms, and a gentle note when a storm was to be hushed into rest. When Neptune travelled on the waves, it was Triton who announced his approach, and summoned the other marine deities. The Tritons were like him in figure, and had similar duties to perform. Occasionally we find him described in stories as a monster who, by his wantonness and voracity, rendered the sea-shore dangerous, and was in consequence attacked by **Dionysos** and **Herakles.**

In the war with the Giants he rendered considerable service to Zeus, by raising such a frightful din with his shrill trumpet, that the Giants, fearing the approach of some powerful monster, or some fresh danger, retired.

Triton and the Tritons were represented in works of art as beings of human form down to the hips, covered with small scales, holding a sea-shell in their hands, the lower part of them formed by the body and tail of a dolphin. Triton was also described as driving on the sea in a chariot drawn by horses.

Plate XX. represents a family group of **Tritons** with a dolphin in the background.

In the early myths concerning Triton, he appears as the personification of the roaring sea, and, like Neptune and Amphitrite, lived in a golden palace in the depths of the ocean.

XX.

Siren.

Tritons.

LEUKOTHEA

Was regarded by sailors and those who travelled on the sea as their special and friendly goddess, a character which she displayed in her timely assistance of **Odysseus** in his dangerous voyage. She is said to have been a daughter of **Kadmos,** the great-grandson of Poseidon. Originally the wife of **Athamas,** in which capacity she bore the name of **Ino,** she had incurred the wrath of Hera, because she had suckled the infant Bakchos, a son of her sister Sĕmēlē and of Zeus, and for this was pursued by her raving husband, and thrown, along with her youngest son, **Melikertes,** into the sea, from which both mother and child were saved by a dolphin or by Nereïdes. From that time she took her place as a marine deity, and, under the name of **Leukothea,** was known as the protector of all travellers by sea, while her son came to be worshipped as god of harbours, under the name of **Palæmon.** Her worship, especially at Corinth, the oldest maritime town of importance in Greece, and in the islands of Rhodes, Tenedos, and Crete, as well as in the coast towns generally, was traced back to a high antiquity.

THE SIRENS,

(PLATE XX.)

According to one version of the myth, were daughters of the river-god **Achelöos** (hence their other name, **Acheloïdes**) and a **Muse.** According to another version, they were daughters of **Phorkys.** In either case they had been nymphs and playmates of Persephone, and for not protecting her when she was carried off by Pluto were transformed by Demeter into beings half woman and half bird at first, and latterly with the lower part of the body in the shape of a fish, so that they had some resemblance to marine deities such as the Tritons.

Plate XX. represents a **Siren,** half bird and half woman in form, playing on a double flute.

In the Homeric poems their number is not specified. In later times the names of three of them are commonly given: **Parthĕnopē, Ligeia,** and **Leukosia.** It is said that once, during the time when the greater part of their body was that of a bird, they challenged the Muses to a competition in singing, but failed, and were punished by having the principal feathers of their wings plucked by the Muses, who decked themselves with them.

The common belief was that the Sirens inhabited the cliffs of the islands lying between Sicily and Italy, and that the sweetness of their voices bewitched passing mariners, compelling them to land only to meet their death. Skeletons lay thickly strewn around their dwelling; for they had obtained the right to exercise this cruel power of theirs on men so long as no crew succeeded in defying their charms. This the Argonauts, of whom more will be said hereafter, were the first to accomplish, by keeping their attention fixed on the unsurpassably sweet music of their companion, **Orpheus.** The next who passed safely was **Odysseus.** He had taken the precaution, on approaching, to stop the ears of his crew, so that they might be deaf to the bewitching music, and to have himself firmly bound to the mast, so that, while hearing the music, he would not be able to follow its allurements. In this way the power of the Sirens came to an end, and in despair they cast themselves into the sea, and were changed into cliffs.

This transformation helps to explain the signification of the myth of the Sirens, who were probably personifications of hidden banks and shallows, where the sea is smooth and inviting to the sailor, but proves in the end the destruction of his ship. The alluring music ascribed to them may either refer to the soft melodious murmur of waves, or be simply a figurative expression for allurement.

THE RIVER-GODS

Were as a rule looked upon as sons of **Okeanos,** exercising a dominion over individual rivers. They were represented as bearded men, crowned with sedge, and often with horns on their heads, reclining and resting one hand on a rudder, the other on a vase, out of which water flows, to indicate the constant flow of a river.

The names of many of them have been handed down in ancient myths, the most important being **Alpheios, Acheloös, Peneis, Asopos, Kephissos.** Of **Alpheios**, it is said that he loved **Arethusa**, one of the myths in the train of **Artemis**, and so persistently followed her, though his affections were not returned, that **Artemis** interfered, and changed the nymph, to avoid his pursuit, into a fountain, the waters of which, notwithstanding, were said to join those of **Alpheios.**

NYMPHS.

(PLATE XXI.)

The restless and fertile imagination of the ancients peopled with beings of a higher order than themselves every mountain, valley, plain, and forest, every thicket, bush, and tree, every fountain, stream, and lake. These beings, in whose existence both Greeks and Romans firmly believed, were called **Nymphs**, and resembled in many respects the mermaids and fairies of modern superstition.

Generally speaking, the **Nymphs** were a kind of middle beings between the gods and men, communicating with both, loved and respected by both; gifted with the power of making themselves visible or invisible at pleasure; able to do many things only permitted to be done by the gods; living like the gods, on ambrosia; leading a cheerful happy life of long duration, and retaining strength and youthfulness to the last, but not destined to immortality, like the gods. In extraordinary cases they were summoned, it was believed, to the councils of the Olympian gods, but usually remained in their particular spheres, in secluded grottoes and peaceful valleys, occupied in spinning, weaving, bathing, singing sweet songs, dancing, sporting, or accompanying deities who passed through their territories, hunting with **Artemis** (Diana), rushing about with **Dionysos** (Bacchus) making merry with **Apollo** or **Hermes** (Mercury), but always in a hostile attitude towards the wanton and excited **Satyrs**.

Even the earliest of the ancient myths abound with accounts of the various things done by nymphs, while poetic fancy in later times delighted to play with such creations. The Greeks, the great mass of them at any rate, believed firmly in the existence of a vast number of nymphs, and attested their belief by erecting frequently very costly altars in places where the presence and influence of these beings were felt,—as by fountains, or in moist meadows, in woods, and on hills. Grottoes and caves where water dripped or flowed, and where the bees hummed, were sacred to them. Sanctuaries, called **Nym-**

phæa, were also erected for their special honour in well watered valleys, caves, and even in towns. Those in towns being particularly splendid in appearance, and commonly employed for the ceremonies of marriage. The sacrifices presented to them consisted of goats, lambs, milk, and oil, wine being forbidden.

As to the origin of the **Nymphs**, the stories are so many and so different that they cannot be all given here. Very many of these beings, it would seem, were the offspring of **Zeus** and **Thetis**. Separating them in the most convenient manner, according to their local habitations or reputed origin, we have the following classes:—

1. **Dryads**, or **Hamadryads**, also called **Alseïds**, nymphs of woods and trees, inhabiting groves, ravines, and wooded valleys, fond of making merry with **Apollo, Hermes** (Mercury), and **Pan**, and very attractive to the **Satyrs**. Sometimes they appeared as rustic huntresses or shepherdesses.

2. **Oreads**, or mountain-nymphs, sometimes also named after the particular mountains which they haunted, as Peliads (from Pelion), Idæan (from Ida), Kithæronian (from Kithæron), etc.

3. **Limoniads**, or **Leimoniads**, nymphs of meadows and flowers.

4. **Napææ**, or **Auloniads**, nymphs of the mountain vales in which herds grazed. The last three families of nymphs were usually found in the company of **Pan**, rushing gaily and merrily over hills and valleys, through woods and meadows. A favourite and lovely nymph of the vales was **Eurydike**, who, being bitten by a snake, and dying in consequence, was mourned by all her sisters, and sung by **Orpheus** in most touching melancholy strains.

5. **Okeanids,** daughters of **Okeanos,** nymphs of fountains and streams, and named according to the characteristics of streams,—as **Prymno,** "like a cascade which falls over an abrupt height"; **Hippo,** "like a swift current"; **Plexaure,** "like a dashing brook"; **Galaxaure,** "like the refreshing coolness of a shady stream"; **Kalypso,** "like the hidden tide"; **Rhodeia,** "flowing among rose-trees"; **Kallirrhoë,** "like a beautiful stream"; **Melolosis,** "like a river that waters the meadows"; **Telesto,** "nymph of the cool springs," which the Greeks piously used for cleansing and purification.

6. **Nereïds,** daughters of **Nereus,** sometimes also called **Dorids,** after their mother (see Nereus).

7. **Naiads,**—generally speaking, nymphs of the liquid element, daughters of **Zeus.** They were styled "fostering" nymphs, and for this reason were commonly found in the company of **Zeus, Poseidon,** and **Dionysos,** as well as of **Demeter, Persephone,** and **Aphrodite,** and besides were looked on as deities of marriage and sacred rites.

8. **Potamids,** nymphs of the rivers.

9. **Limnads,** nymphs of lakes, marshes, and swamps, most dangerous beings, who allured and misled travellers by their songs or mimic screams for help.

10. **Pleiads,** seven daughters of **Atlas** and **Pleione,** sisters of the **Hȳads.**

11. **Atlantids,** offspring of **Atlas,** and belonging to the same order as the last mentioned.

12. **Hyads,** according to the myth, daughters of **Atlas** and Æthra; sisters, or, according to other versions, daughters of **Hyas.** Languishing of grief at the death of **Hyas,** which was caused by a wild animal, they were changed into stars, being the seven stars which form the head in the constellation

XXI

Pegasos and the Nymphs. S.

Chloris, or Flora.   Tyche, or Fortuna.

of the Bull (Taurus). Their ascension takes place from the 17th to the 21st of May, and usually indicates rain, for which reason they were often called the rainy stars. They were also called **Dodonids**, and described as the nurses of **Zeus** of Dodona. One of them was called **Thyēnē.**

All the most prominent of the nymphs had names of their own.

They were represented as damsels of wonderful beauty, with attributes suitable to their respective avocations.

Plate XXI. represents three of them tending **Pegasos** at a fountain. All three have their hair bound with sedge; two of them have vases.

ECHO : NARKISSOS.

Echo was a mountain-nymph, and at the same time a servant of **Hera,** according to one account, but had to be kept at a distance on account of her talkativeness. In other accounts she is described as a beautiful nymph whom the forest-god **Pan** loved. Happening to meet the beautiful **Narkissos,** a son of the river-god **Kephissos,** she conceived a very tender passion for him, which he unfortunately did not return. **Echo** grieved in consequence, and pined away day by day till at length her voice was all that was left of her. She then took to the mountains and woods which Pan frequented, and occupied herself in mimicking every vocal sound she heard.

Narkissos was a personification of the consequences of self-conceit in the matter of personal appearance, his vanity being such that he used to idle by the brinks of clear fountains, and gaze upon the reflection of his own face, till at last he languished in his unreturned love for it. Other stories affirm that he was punished for this conduct by the gods, by being changed into the flower which still bears his name.

THE HESPERIDES

Were daughters of **Atlas,** an enormous giant, who, as the ancients believed, stood upon the western confines of the earth, and supported the heavens on his shoulders. Their mother was **Hesperis,** a personification of the "region of the West," where the sun continued to shine after he had set on Greece, and where, as travellers told, was an abundance of choice delicious fruits, which could only have been produced by a special divine influence. The **Gardens of the Hesperides** with the golden apples were believed to exist in some island in the ocean, or, as it was sometimes thought, in the islands on the north or west coast of Africa. They were far-famed in antiquity; for it was there that springs of nectar flowed by the couch of Zeus, and there that the earth displayed the rarest blessings of the gods: it was another Eden. As knowledge increased with regard to western lands, it became necessary to move this paradise farther and farther out into the Western Ocean.

As to the origin of these precious golden apples, there is a myth which says that among the deities who attended the marriage ceremony of Zeus and Hera, bringing various presents with them, was **Titæa,** a goddess of the earth, whose gift consisted in her causing a tree to spring up with golden apples on it. The care of this tree, which highly pleased the newly-wedded pair, was entrusted to the Hesperides. But, as they could not resist the temptation to pluck and eat its fruit, it became necessary to place the serpent **Ladon** to watch it. **Herakles,** among his other adventures, slew this serpent and carried off some of the apples, which, however, were afterwards returned to the Hesperides, through the kindness of **Athene.**

The common account speaks of only three Hesperides,— **Ægle, Erytheis** and **Hespere. Arethusa** was afterwards added, and in time three more, so that they were seven in all.

THE MUSES,

Or **Pierides,** as they were also styled, were regarded as nymphs of the springs that bickered down the sides of Mount Helikon and Mount Parnassos, called **Kastalia, Aganippe,** and **Pimpla** or Pimplea, the waters of which were thought to have the property of inspiration. Their origin was traced to **Zeus** and the Titanic nymph **Mnemosyne,** the name of Pierides being applied to them from Pieria, on Mount Olympos, the reputed place of their birth, a locality which appears to have been originally the principal centre of their worship, whence it spread first and most conspicuously to Mount Helikon, in Bœotia, and farther to Athens, Sparta, Trœzene, and elsewhere. It was usual to ascribe this extension of the worship of the Muses to a Thracian named Pieros, of whom it was also said that, having nine daughters, he named them each after one of the Muses, and challenged the latter to a competition in music, the upshot of which was that his daughters lost the award, and were, as a punishment for their daring, transformed into singing-birds. The worship of the Muses on Mount Helikon was celebrated in a grove, in which were the sacred fountains of **Aganippe** and **Hippokrene,** with many monuments of art dedicated to the Muses, contests called **Museia** being associated with the ceremonies.

The nine Muses whom we are accustomed to read of in the Greek and Roman mythology, were looked upon as the patron goddesses of music and song, of poetry, and of the fine arts generally, that tended to promote the civilization of mankind. Their local habitation was on the summits of Mounts Helikon, Parnassos, and Pindos. They would, however, frequently visit Olympos, to gladden the blessed existence of the gods there by the exercise of their arts, especially by music and the recital of songs, the burden of which was probably, as on most other occasions, the glory and omnipotence of Zeus. Sometimes they would lend their presence also to enliven happy incidents in the lives of favourite mortals—such, for example, as the marriage of Kadmos and Harmonia, or that of Peleus and Thetis; and sometimes even at moments of great sorrow, as at the death of Achilles, they would descend to mourn in strains which drew forth tears from gods and men. Their leader was Apollo, who in that capacity bore the title of **Musagetes**. But though generally associated with Apollo, and probably therefore imbued with the form of inspiration peculiar to the god of oracles, they are also found to have been connected with the worship of Dionysos, whose inspiration is known to have been of a wild and excited nature. As nymphs of the sacred streams on the mountains where they lived, their music and song must, for the sake of harmony, have repeated the rushing movement of water, and it may be to this that their association with Dionysos is due.

In addition to the usual nine we hear of three other Muses, **Melētē**, **Mnēmē**, and **Aœdte**, who are described as daughters of **Uranos**, and supposed to have existed from the earliest times. As, however, both Homer and Hesiod appear to know only the number nine, we may assume that the belief in the

XXII

Klio.

Melpomene.   Thalia.

existence of the other three must have originated in the speculations of comparatively later times.

In works of art of the earlier period the Muses were always represented together in company, all wearing the same kind of dress, and all provided with attributes in the forms of musical instruments—such as the lyre, harp, and flute, or with rolls of manuscript. The custom of collecting in such rolls literary works produced under the auspices of the Muses was the first foundation of libraries and **museums,** such as they exist in modern times, and thus the word "museum" carries us back to the early worship of the Muses, and to the early civilization so far as it was due to their inspiration.

The nine Muses were represented according to their various avocations in the following manner:—

1. **Klio** (Plate XXII.), the muse of History, seated wearing a wreath of laurel, and holding out a half-open inscribed parchment roll; beside her a cylindrical box, containing more of these manuscripts. In other cases she appears standing, holding a roll of manuscript in one hand, an instrument for writing with in the other.

2. **Melpomene,** (Plate XXII.), the muse of Tragedy, a serious, dignified figure, standing with her left foot raised on a rock, holding in her right hand a mask, such as was worn by tragedians, and in her left apparently a small roll of a part in a play; her long robe or tunic is girt under her breast, and falls in wide folds; from her shoulder a mantle or *peplos* falls carelessly. In other cases she wears a diadem or a wreath of cypress, and holds a short sword or a club in her hand.

3. **Thalia** (Plate XXII.), the muse of Comedy and Burlesque, standing, clad in a robe or tunic, over which is a mantle, with a fringe, thrown over the left shoulder, and

wrapped round the legs, leaving the right arm free; in her right hand a shepherd's crook, in the other a mask, such as was worn by actors in the Satyric plays.

4. **Kalliope** (Plate XXIII.), the muse of Heroic Poems, and looked on as the chief of the Muses, on which account she sometimes appears as their representative; seated, holding a writing tablet and a *stylus*. In other cases she is standing, crowned with a wreath, and holding a manuscript roll in her hand, or a pipe (*tuba*) round which a branch of laurel is twined.

5. **Urania** (Plate XXIV.), the muse of Astronomy, seated beside a globe, holding a pair of compasses in one hand, while with the other she points upwards towards the heavens. In other cases she wears a crown of stars, and holds a lyre, her eyes turned towards the stars, and pointing out at the same time something on a globe beside her.

6. **Euterpe** (Plate XXIV.), the muse of the art of Music, the "giver of pleasure," as her name implies, standing, playing on a double flute. In other cases she plays on other instruments.

7. **Polyhymnia**, or **Polymnia** (Plate XXIV.), the muse of Song and of Oratory, her name signifying "rich in song," was also described as the inventor of myths, on which account she was represented in the attitude of contemplation, with one finger raised to her lips; on her head a laurel wreath. In other cases she appears in a quiet, attentive, observant mood, leaning forward on a pillar, her arms concealed under her drapery, and wearing at times a veil, to indicate the hidden truths within the myths, while her posture was intended to indicate the process of revolving the meaning of them. For this reason she was also viewed as the goddess of serious and sacred poems and hymns.

Urania.

Euterpe.   Polyhymnia.

Mother of the Muses.

Kalliope.

XXV

Erato.   Terpsichore.

Horæ.

8. **Erato** (Plate XXV.), the muse of Love and Marriage Songs, wearing a wreath, and playing on a large lyre with many strings. In other cases she appears holding a lyre by her side in one hand, and in the other an arrow or a wreath of myrtle and roses.

9. **Terpsichore** (Plate XXV.), the muse of Dancing, wearing a wreath, and playing on a lyre. At other times she holds cymbals, has her robe girt up, and appears in the attitude of dancing.

The mother of the **Muses** was called, as has already been stated, **Mnemosyne,** that is, " Memory," and especially the memory or recollection of great events, such as the war with the Titans, that was said to have occurred at the commencement of the world's history, and must continue to occur until the universe is brought into perfect harmony. In later times she came to be viewed merely as goddess of memory, and worshipped along with the Muses.

Plate XXIII. represents her standing in a quiet, thoughtful attitude, both arms under her drapery, to indicate the silent mysterious action of memory.

It was the custom of the muses to play, under the leadership of Apollo, at the banquets and marriage ceremonies among the gods, while the Horæ, Charites (Graces), Aphrodite, and other deities given to mirth and gaiety, danced. In this fashion the ancients represented under the form of persons the union of joy, music, poetry, dance, and merriment.

11

IRIS,

(PLATE XXVI.,)

Goddess of the rainbow, was a daughter of **Thaumas** and **Elektra**, a grand-daughter of **Okeanos** and **Gaea**, and a sister of the **Harpies**. As messenger of Hera and Zeus, she lived among the other deities of Olympos, which she only left for the purpose of conveying the divine commands to mankind, by whom she was looked on as a guide and adviser. She travelled with the speed of wind always, from one end of the world to the other, could penetrate to the bottom of the sea, or to the Styx, and in this respect formed a female counterpart of **Hermes** (Mercury) in his capacity of messenger of the gods, she holding much the same position towards Hera as he did towards Zeus.

It was Iris, the ancients believed, who charged the clouds with water from lakes and rivers, in order that they might let it fall again upon the earth in gentle fertilizing showers; and, accordingly, when her bow appeared in the clouds the farmer welcomed it as a sign of rain to quicken his fields, and gladly paid honours to the goddess whose presence he recognized in the rainbow with its splendid colours.

She was represented as a beautiful virgin with wings of varied hue, in robes of bright colours, and riding on a rainbow; at other times with a *nimbus* on her head, in which the colours of the rainbow were reflected.

Plate XXVI. gives a figure of her standing, clad in a long robe, holding in one hand a herald's staff, such as Hermes also carries (*caduceus*), and in the other a helmet.

XXVI

Iris.

Hymen.

Hebe.

ÆOLOS

Was the son of a king named Hippotes, and lived on one of the abrupt rocky Lipara islands close to Sicily, along with his offspring, six sons and six daughters, who were married in pairs, and made life merry with their music. In the caves of the island were imprisoned the winds, Æolos letting them out in gales, or in a soft favouring breeze, at the will of the higher gods.

The idea of the winds beings thus kept in a cavern under the restraint of a divine person, appears to have suggested itself to the ancients from the strong draught that is felt on entering a cave or subterraneous passage; but whether the belief in the existence of such a personage reached back to primitive times, when mankind lived to a great extent in places of that kind, is not certain. The influence of Æolos was felt both genially and the reverse on land and on sea, but principally on sea, which he could more readily command from the island where he lived.

As an instance of his kindliness to travellers by sea, we may here mention his hospitable reception of **Odysseus** (Ulysses) on that errant homeward voyage of his. On departing, Æolos gave him a great bag containing all the contrary winds, putting it on board the ship, so that he might reach Ithaca with a fair wind. Odysseus himself remained steadily and anxiously at the helm for several days, but his native land coming at length in sight, he sank overpowered with sleep. His followers observing this proceeded to indulge their curiosity to see the costly presents which they fancied the bag contained, opened it, and out burst the imprisoned wind with a roar and a force that drove the ship again far out of her course.

But besides this conception of the winds as mere elements in the hands of Æolos, there was another which represented them as each personified by a separate divine being, living apart, and being directly under the control of Zeus and Poseidon.

THE WIND GODS,

Of whom the principal were **Boreas**, the north wind, **Euros**, the east wind, **Notos**, the south wind, and **Zephyros**, the west wind, were, as we have previously said, the offspring of **Eos** and **Astræos**, the parentage of fierce destructive winds being assigned to **Typhon**. According to another report, neither the origin nor the number of the deities of the winds was known, the prevalence in particular districts of winds blowing from this or that point between the four chief quarters, naturally giving rise to a set of personifications such as north-west wind, south-west wind, and others.

The character and appearance ascribed to each of these deities was, as usual in Greek mythology, such as was suggested by the phenomena of each wind—as, for example, the strength and fury of the north wind, or the genial warmth of the south-west. Some were thought to be male, some female, and all winged. **Euros**, who brought warmth and rain from the east, was represented holding a vase inverted, as if pouring rain from it. **Lips**, who from the south-east wafted home the ships as they neared the harbour of Peiræus at Athens, held the ornament from a ship's stern in her hands. **Zephyros**, coming from the warm, mild west, was lightly clad, and carried a quantity of flowers in his scarf. **Apeliotes**, the south-east wind, carried fruits of many kinds, wore boots, and was not so lightly clad as the last mentioned. So they were represented on the "Tower of the Winds" at Athens.

Though the winds were looked on as each under the control of a separate divine being, whose favour it was necessary to retain by sacrifice, no particular story or myth is told of any one of these persons excepting Boreas and Zephyros, the rival lovers of **Chloris** (Flora), Zephyros being the successful suitor. **Boreas** carried off, it was said, Oreithyia, the beautiful daughter of Kekrops, king of Attica; and remembering this, the Athenians in their distress, when the Persians advanced the first time against Greece, called upon him for aid, which he rendered by sending a terrible north wind, which overtook the Persian fleet near the promontory of Athos, scattering and largely destroying it. From that time the Athenians had an altar to him, and offered sacrifice at it for their preservation.

The scene of Boreas carrying off Oreithyia is represented on a beautiful bronze relief found at Calymna, and now in the British Museum. The wind-god is powerful in form, bearded, but still young, and wearing thick high boots, and a mantle thrown across his body.

EOS, or AURORA: LUCIFER.

Eos was a daughter of the Titan pair, **Theia** and **Hyperion**; the latter, to judge from the meaning of his name, having been at one time god of the sun, "who travels high above earth." Helios and Selene, the deities of sun and moon, were her brother and sister, while she herself was a personification of the dawn of morning. A fresh wind was felt at her approach, the morning star still lingered in the sky, and ruddy beams "shot the orient through with gold"; and because these beams appeared like outspread fingers, she was called "rosy-fingered Morn." The star and the winds of the morning, **Zephyros, Boreas, Notos,** and **Euros,** were her offspring by **Astræos,** the god of starlight. The moon and the other stars vanished gradually as she advanced but Helios followed her closely. To poets she seemed to lift the veil of night with rose-tinted fingers, and to rise in the east out of the ocean in a car with four white steeds, shedding light upon the earth. Others imagined her coming riding on the winged horse, Pegasos, which Zeus had given her after **Bellerophon's** failure to ride on it up to Olympos.

She loved all fresh young life, and showed special favour to those persons whose active spirit led them abroad in the morning to hunt or to make war. When struck with the beauty of a youth she would carry him off, and obtain immortal life for him, as she did with **Kleitos, Orion, Kephalos,** and **Tithonos.** So it appeared to the Greeks, who recognised in the brief duration of the freshness and glow of morning a comparison with the early death of promising and beautiful youth, and from the comparison proceeded to construct a myth which should trace both to the same divine cause.

Tithonos became her husband, and she lived with him pleasantly beside the Okeanos so long as his youth and beauty lasted. Unfortunately, in obtaining immortality for him from Zeus, she had omitted to add to her request, "and eternal youth." When white hairs showed themselves on his head she was not the same to him as before, though still supplying him with ambrosia and fine raiment. But he became quite helpless at last, and, to avoid the sight of his decrepitude, she shut him up in a chamber, where only his voice was heard like the chirp of a grasshopper, into which creature, it was said,

XXVII.

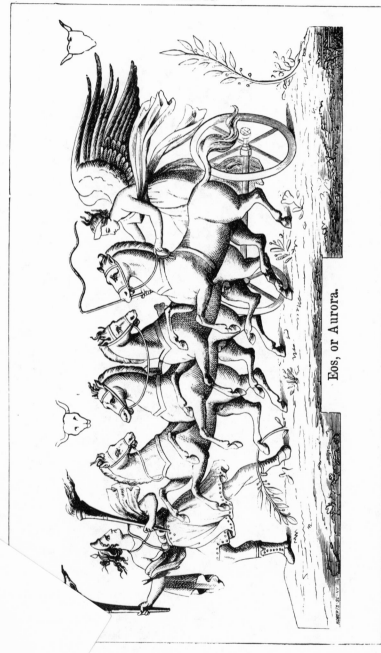

Eos, or Aurora.

he became transformed. By the story of Tithonos we would understand day, in its eternally returning course, fresh and beautiful at dawn, wearied and worn at the close.

Of **Kephalos** it is said that from love to his wife, **Prokris**, he resolutely withstood the advances of **Aura,** the goddess of the morning wind, and that the latter in revenge stirred up discord between him and his wife. Another version of the story is, that Aura caused him to kill his wife by mistake when out on the chase. Prokris, it would seem, jealous of her husband's meetings with the goddess, had secreted herself in a thicket to watch them; but happening to stir, Kephalos caught the noise, and suspecting it to be caused by some lurking animal, hurled his spear, and slew his wife.

Eos and Tithonos had two sons, Memnon and Emathion, the former widely celebrated for his beauty, and mourned for his early death at the hands of Achilles. His dead body was carried by his weeping mother to Ethiopia; and at Thebes, in Egypt, she erected in his memory, so story goes, that wonderful monument which, when the first rays of the morning sun touched it, gave forth a sound like the snapping of a harp-string.

In art she was represented as a spirited maiden, with large wings, clad in robes of dazzling white and purple, a star or cap on her head, a torch in her hand, and driving in a chariot with four horses, or riding on Pegasos; at other times she appeared floating in the air, and pouring morning dew from a vessel down to the earth.

In Plate XXVII. she is figured driving a *quadriga* with great speed, as is indicated by the flow of her drapery. The bulls' heads signify that the moon and stars are still in the sky. Lucifer precedes her with a torch. Flowers and plants quick-

ened by her dew, wake and raise their heads.   In the British
Museum is a beautiful example of early gem engraving, representing a head of her.

In other representations we find Hermes advancing before
her, a duty which **Lucifer,** the morning star, and a favourite
of Aphrodite and Hera also, most usually performs.

EROS, or AMOR: PSYCHE.

Amor, or **Cupīdo,** as he was also called, was not, it should
be noticed, a native Roman deity, but had been introduced
from the mythology of the Greeks by poets, his name being
a direct translation of the Greek Eros.   It should further be
observed that this translation presents an instance of the
difference in character of these two ancient races; the word
for "love" among the Greeks being feminine, while its
Roman equivalent was masculine.

We must at the outset distinguish the double character of
Eros; first, as we find him described taking part at the creation of the world out of Chaos, and secondly, as a mere god
of love, a son of **Aphrodite** and **Zeus,** or **Ares,** as some
said, or even of **Uranos.**   In the former phase of his character he is represented as sorting the shapeless mass of the world,
with its conflicting elements, into order and harmony, dis-
pelling confusion, uniting hitherto jarring forces, and making
productive what was barren before.   In the latter phase he is
the deity who sways the passions of the heart both of gods and
men.   In the one case he was conceived as having existed
before the other gods, as being the god of that love which
operates in nature; and in the other case as the youngest born
of them all, the god of that love which holds the hearts

XXVIII

Cupid.

Cupid and Psyche.

Ganymedes.

Mars and Venus.

of men in tyranny. It seems to have been as a combination of both characters that Pheidias* represented him at the birth of Aphrodite, receiving her as she rose out of the sea, in presence of the assembled deities of Olympos.

The chief and oldest centre of his worship was Thespiæ, in Bœotia, where a festival called **Erotidia** was celebrated in his honour, and continued to be a source of attraction down to Roman times. Thence his worship spread to Sparta, Athens, Samos, and Crete, the Spartans and Cretans having a custom of sacrificing to him previous to the commencement of a battle, in the belief that he was also the god of that patriotism or love of country which best unites an army. In Athens there was an altar to him and his counterpart, **Anteros.**

In early times his worshippers at Thespiæ were content with a rude stone as an image. But in later times, and in contrast with this, we find him the most attractive figure among the works of the second Attic school of sculptors, the school of Scopas and Praxiteles,† both of whom directed their splendid talents to adding fresh grace and beauty to his form. While artists rivalled each other to this end, poets were no less zealous in singing his praises. In daily life his influence became more generally acknowledged. In the gymnasia where the youth practised athletics his statue was set up between Hermes and Herakles ; for he was then represented as lithe of limb and graceful of form—a model of ripening youth. As time went on, however, his figure became more and more that of the chubby boy who plays all manner of tricks with the hearts of men, with which we are most familiar. He was supposed

---

* On the base of the statue of Zeus at Olympia.

† The famous statue of him by Praxiteles was afterwards carried off to Rome, and is known to us through copies of it made by other sculptors.

to exercise his influence over the hearts of deities as well; and to show him in this light, he was represented at times now with the symbol of one god, now of another.

To the later age of Hellenistic and Roman poetry and art belongs the touching story of **Psyche**—a personification, as she appears to have been, of a soul filled with the passion of love, and as such conceived under the form of a small winged maiden, or, at other times, as a butterfly which bore the same name. Psyche, the story runs, was a king's daughter, and most beautiful. The fame of her beauty awoke the jealousy of Aphrodite, who to get rid of the rival, charged her son Cupid to visit the princess, and inspire her with love for some common man. Cupid obeyed so far as to pay the visit, but being himself struck with the maiden's beauty, carried her off to a fairy palace in a vale of paradise, where they spent happy hours together, with only this drawback, that she was not permitted to look upon her lover with her mortal eyes. Even this she would not have considered a drawback, had not her envious sisters stirred up her curiosity in the matter. Yielding to their temptation, she took one night a lamp, and stole into the chamber where the god lay asleep. Alarmed at the discovery she had made, she let a drop of hot oil fall upon his shoulder. He awoke, and charging her with disobedience to his express command, left her alone to her despair. She searched for him everywhere in vain, finding her way at last to the palace of Aphrodite, who after subjecting her to menial service of various kinds, finally ordered her to go down to the lower world, and fetch a box of beauty's ointment from Persephone. This most painful task she accomplished; but, on opening the box, sank overpowered by its odour. Cupid could resist no longer, ran to her help, and brought her back to life. The anger of Aphrodite was appeased, and the marriage of Cupid and Psyche was forthwith celebrated with great rejoicings, in presence of the higher gods, Psyche obtaining immortality.

The purpose of the story is obviously to illustrate the three stages in the existence of a soul,—its pre-existence in a blessed state, its existence on earth with its trials and anguish, and its future state of happy immortality.

Plate XXVIII. represents the two embracing tenderly. Eros has laid aside his bow and quiver, with its dangerous arrows ; roses are strewn on the ground before them, and a shoot of a rose-tree grows behind to symbolize the sweetness and beauty of young love. Psyche has the wings of a butterfly, and links by which she may be chained on her ankles and arms. Behind her is a mirror. In the other figure Eros appears riding on a lion, and playing on a lyre, the soft music of which soothes the savage beast, as love was supposed to soothe the fiercest temper.

In works of art he is frequently to be seen in company of his mother Aphrodite, or playing with the Muses and Graces, or struggling with his opposite **Anteros**, or accompanied by **Pothos**, whose name, like the Roman **Cupīdo**, signifies a "desire of love," that is, a "desire of union in love," and **Himeros**, a "soft yearning for love." In later times artists often surrounded Aphrodite, and occasionally also Dionysos, with troops of little winged figures of children, which we call **Erotes** or **Amorettes**.

The word *Psyche*, signifying originally the "soul," came afterwards to mean also a "butterfly,"—a likeness being observed between the manner in which a soul and a butterfly, freed from the body or chrysalis in which they have been confined on earth, rise on wing, and waft themselves in the light.

The flame of love which often scorched the soul was compared with the torch which attracts the butterfly to its doom. When this happened, Eros turned away his face and wept. Such is the meaning of the allegory represented in Plate XXIX. Behind Eros stands **Nemesis**, holding a twig from an apple-tree, her customary attribute, and before him **Elpis**, or Hope, holding a lily.

HYMEN or HYMENÆUS,

(PLATE XXVI.,)

Was worshipped as the god of marriage both by the Greeks and the Romans. His origin is variously stated to have been now from Apollo and Kalliope, now from Dionysos and Aphrodite, while at other times he is said to have been by birth a mortal, and afterwards deified. Properly speaking, he is a personification of the marriage song. There are various accounts of his life and deification, and among them the following:

Young, and of a soft delicate beauty, so that he might be mistaken for a girl, Hymen loved a young Athenian maiden, whom, however, because of his poverty, he could not hope to obtain for his wife. To be near her, he once joined a troop of maidens, among whom she was engaged in celebrating a festival to Demeter at Eleusis. Suddenly a band of robbers appeared from a hiding-place, carried the maidens off to their ship, and set out with the intention of selling them as slaves in some distant country. But landing on the way on a dreary island, the robbers indulged so copiously in wine that they all fell into deep slumber. Hymen, seizing the opportunity, incited his fellow-captives to take the weapons from the robbers and slay them all, which they did. Thereupon he set off to Athens in the ship, and finding the people there in great distress, presented himself to the parents of the maiden he loved, and undertook to bring her back unharmed on condition of their giving her to him as his wife. This was readily promised. Finding a crew, he at once set sail for the island, and speedily returned with all the maidens on board. For this he obtained the title of **Thalassios,** as well as the wife that had been promised him. So happy was his wedded life that at marriage ceremonies generally his name was on the lips of all the company, and he himself in course of time came to be looked on as a god, and the founder and protector of marriage rights. At bridal festivities a sacrifice was offered to him, festal songs were sung, and flowers and wreaths strewn.

As a deity he was placed among the playmates of Eros, and in the company of Aphrodite. His home, it was believed, was among the Muses on Mount Helikon in Bœotia. There is a story which says that he lost his voice and his life in singing the marriage song of Dionysos and Ariadne or Althæa. He is always a picture of youthful beauty, and of the charms of love and song.

Hymen was represented as a beautiful youth with a mantle of a golden colour—sometimes nude—and carrying a torch, as in Plate XXV., or a veil.

THE CHARITES, or GRACES,

Were looked upon by the Greeks as the goddesses of the gracefulness and the charms of beauty, and of cheerful amusement, which were observed both in nature and in the intercourse with men. As such, their worship dated from a very early time in Orchomenos in Bœotia, in Sparta, Athens, and Crete; the games held in their honour in the last-mentioned place being said to have existed even in the time of the pre-historic king Minos. Their oldest sanctuary was said to be that at Orchomenos. It contained images of them in the form of rude stones which were supposed to have fallen from heaven.

The manifold beauty which the works of nature, especially in spring-time, display, would seem to have given rise in very early times to a belief in the existence of certain goddesses at first simply as guardians of the vernal sweetness and beauty of nature, and afterwards as the friends and protectors of everything graceful and beautiful—an idea which the poets further developed. Pindar, in one of his most delightful songs of victory, singing of the Graces, associates with them the source of decorum, of purity and happiness in life, of good will, beneficence and gratitude among men.

They were represented as beautiful young modest maidens, winning and charming, always dancing, singing, and running, or bathing in fountains, or decking themselves with early flow‑ ers, especially with roses; for the rose was sacred to them, as well as to Aphrodite (Venus), in whose company, and doing her many a service, according to the myth, they were usually to be found. Their home was among the Muses in the neighbourhood of Olympos, where they often appeared as companions of Aphrodite, and danced before the other deities.

Their origin is variously stated,—now Zeus and Eurynome, an Okeanid, being assigned as their parents, now Dionysos and Aphrodite. There is a difference also in the statements of their names and number. From Orchomenos, it would seem, come **Aglæa, Euphrosyne,** and **Thalia.** In Sparta and in Athens there were only two, the pair worshipped in the former town being called **Kleta** (clang) and **Phaënna** (glimmer), in the latter town, **Auxo** and **Hegemone**. In the Iliad a whole race of them is mentioned, old and young—the youngest being **Pasithea**. According to another account, the youngest was Aglæa, the wife of Hephæstos; the object in assigning him such a wife being probably to indicate the perfect beauty of the works of art produced by that god. Beauty and sweetness, the best charm of poetry, came from the Graces. Athene (Minerva) called in their aid in the serious business of life over which she presided, because without gracefulness all labour was in vain, the Greeks believed. They assisted Hermes (Mercury) in his capacity of god of oratory. From these instances of their activity it will be seen how highly the Greeks prized this quality of gracefulness.

In Greece there was a number of temples and beautiful groups of statuary in their honour, sometimes devoted to them alone, sometimes to them in common with other deities; as, for example, Aphrodite, Apollo, and the Muses. Annual festivals, called **Charitesia**, accompanied with games, music, and dance, were held in their honour. It was the custom also to call upon them in taking an oath, and at banquets the first cup of wine was offered to them.

In early times they were represented in art as draped figures, but in later times as quite nude, or but sparingly clothed, and occupied in a dance. Their attributes were the rose, the myrtle, and dice, as a symbol of cheerful amusement. At other times they hold apples or perfume-vases, or ears of corn, or heads of poppies, or musical instruments—such as the lyre, flute, and syrinx.

PEITHO, or SUADA,

Or **Suadēla**, was the goddess of persuasion, and like the Graces, formed part of the escort of Aphrodite, whose daughter she was said to be.

Her worship, along with Aphrodite, was introduced into Athens by Theseus, at the time when he succeeded in persuading the various isolated tribes inhabiting Attica to unite into one people, with Athens as their chief town. But she had temples in other places also, and was looked on as a deity to whose influence much was due.

HEBE,

(PLATE XXVI.,)

Or **Ganymeda**, or **Dia**, as she was called in the vine-growing district of Phlius, where she was worshipped as the principal deity, was daughter of Zeus and Hera, and was the goddess of youth, herself remaining always young, and warding off age, like the other deities, by means of nectar and ambrosia. Her name among the Romans was **Juventas**. In Olympos she held the office of cup-bearer to the gods, for which it is supposed that she was peculiarly adapted, first, because of her association with the vine-growers of Phlius, and, secondly, because she was the youngest daughter of the regal pair of Olympos, and as such, on the analogy of human arrangements, would be expected to wait upon the divine guests, as Briseis did on Achilles, or Hippodameia on Oenomaos or as, in real life, Melissa, the daughter of Prokles, king of Epidauros, poured out wine for her father's men with a grace which captivated Periander. The difficulty of explaining how Hebe and Ganymedes would both hold the same office was met in various ways, of which one was to assume her to have been cup-bearer in general and him cup-bearer to Zeus in particular, while another ingeniously supposed that Hebe only held the office while Ganymedes was absent from Olympos during the Trojan war, so as to avoid witnessing the misfortunes of his native country. Among her other duties she had to assist Hera to yoke her car. When Apollo and the Muses played she danced with other deities. At times she accompanied Aphrodite. But the character in which she was best known and most admired was that of the bride and wife of **Herakles**, when he was raised to Olympos in reward for his extraordinary labours on earth. This union of Hebe, the favourite daughter of Hera, with Herakles, whom she had constantly persecuted while on earth, is unknown to the Iliad. The character of the myth, however, appears to point to a very early origin. The singular climax of events, which made Herakles the guest of the gods of Olympos and the husband of the most attractive of the goddesses, was a subject which was made the most of by the comic poets. Representations of the marriage procession, and of Herakles receiving a cup of wine from Hebe, occur in ancient sculpture. In other cases she appears in the company of her mother Hera, or alone, or in the character of Ganymeda, fondling the eagle of Zeus, or giving it drink from a cup, as occurs not unfrequently on engraved gems.

At the town of Phlius, in the district of Argolis, there was, in a fine grove, a celebrated temple in her honour, which served as a place of refuge or asylum, in which slaves who had been set free hung up their chains among the cypresses sacred to the goddess.

12

In Rome **Juventas** had two sanctuaries, one on the Capitol, the other beside the great race-course. It was the custom—dating, it was said, as far back as the time of Servius Tullius—to pay into the temple of Juventas a piece of money for every boy who lived to enter the stage of youth. When the young Roman assumed the *toga virilis*, he went up to the Capitol and prayed to Jupiter and Juventas. At the beginning of every year sacrifice was offered to both deities in behalf of the youth of the city.

GANYMEDES,

(PLATE XXVIII.,)

Was a son of the Trojan king **Tros** and **Kallirhoe,** and was therefore great-grandson of **Dardanos,** the founder of Troy. Zeus finding him on Mount Ida, and admiring his beauty, carried him off to Olympos, where he appears to have succeeded Hebe in the office of cup-bearer to the gods.

He was represented as possessed of eternal youth and extraordinary beauty, wearing a Phrygian cap to indicate his birth-place. The cup in his hand indicates his office of cup-bearer, while the eagle of Zeus by his side shows that that office was performed among the gods of Olympos.

ASKLEPIOS, OR ÆSCULAPIUS,

(PLATE XXXI.,)

Was, according to the most common version of the myth, a son of Apollo and Koronis, a daughter of a Thessalian prince, —whence his title Koronides. At his birth his mother died, struck by the arrows of Artemis; but the father saved the child, and taking it to Mount Pelion, gave it in keeping to the famous physician, **Chiron,** who carefully instructed the boy from early youth onwards in the mysteries of the healing art, training him at the same time to expertness in the chase. In the former the pupil soon excelled the master, curing the most malignant diseases, and working real miracles with his art. There was but one whom his success could injure, and that was **Pluto,** the monarch of the lower world, who urged his complaint before Zeus. The latter, astonished at the boldness of a mortal in thus defying the decrees of fate, felled the great doctor with a thunderbolt, to the indignation of Apollo, who was only silenced by banishment from Olympos for some time. After his death Asklepios was looked upon as a god in Greece ; festivals called **Asklepia** were held in his honour, and temples were erected to him, of which the most celebrated was that of Epidauros, in the Peloponnesos. Thither even the Romans sent ten deputies once, to inquire the will of the oracle with regard to a pestilence that was raging in Rome. The deputies had hardly entered the temple, when from behind the gold-and-ivory statue of the god a serpent appeared, the symbol of Asklepios, and followed them through the streets of the town, on to the harbour, and into their ship. They received it joyfully as a happy portent, and set out homewards. On reaching Italy the serpent left the ship, and proceeded to a temple of Æsculapius, in the town of Antium, but afterwards returned to the ship, and did not leave it again until, on going up the Tiber, it stopped at an island. Thereupon the pestilence ceased, and the temple was erected on the island to Æsculapius, to commemorate the event. Thither patients were conveyed and cured—a short statement of the symptoms of each case, and the remedy employed, being inscribed on tablets, whic' were i. ing up in the temple, and were found to be a great boon to posterity.

Besides the serpent, he frequently has as an attribute a cock, —that animal being also sacred to him. The serpent, by its periodic change of skin, indicates rejuvenescence; the staff marks him as wandering from place to place, to give help; while the dish, which he sometimes holds, is a symbol of his healing potions. It was the custom of invalids to sacrifice a cock to him, as Socrates did after drinking the cup of poison, as a token that he did not fear death, but rather looked upon it as a cure and a convalescence.

Among the children of Æsculapius, **Hygiea** is specially mentioned. The name of his wife was **Epigone**—"the soothing." Like many other deities of the lower order, in common with heroes, he was in after times placed as a star in the sky.

In Plate XXXI. the god of medicine is represented as a man of years, bearded, gentle, and earnest, draped, and resting on a staff, round which a serpent, as emblem of rejuvenescence, is coiled. His type of face resembles that of Zeus so much, that in the case of the fine marble head in the British Museum absolute agreement has not yet been arrived at as to which of the two gods it was intended to represent. The head in question was found in the island of Melos, on the site of what is supposed to have been a temple to Asklepios, from the discovery in the same place of a native tablet, dedicated to the god and to his daughter Hygiea. A person who had recovered from a local illness would dedicate a sculptured representation of the part that had been affected. Of such sculptures there are a number of examples in the British Museum.

HYGIEA,

(PLATE XXXI.,)

Or **Hygieia**, or **Hygea**, was, as we have just said, the daughter of Asklepios, and the goddess of health. Others said she was the wife of Asklepios.

She was represented as a young, active, smiling goddess, in whom Apollo took a special interest. In Plate XXXI. she appears draped, and holding a serpent—which, as in the case of Asklepios, is the symbol of health. She feeds it from a plate or *patera*.

At other times she is figured wearing a wreath of laurel, or of plants known for their medicinal properties—a *patera* in her hand, a serpent coiled round her arm or body.

MEDITRINA

Passed in Rome for a sister of Hygea and a goddess of health, a festival called **Meditrinalia** being annually held in her honour at the beginning of October, the ceremony consisting in drinking some old and some new wine together, and exclaiming, " I drink the new and the old wine—with new and old wine I heal infirmities."

The distinction between the two goddesses of health lay in this—that while Hygea preserved good health, Meditrina restored it. The Greek goddess **Jaso** appears to have been identical with Meditrina.

TELESPHOROS

Was looked upon as a *genius* or deity of that secret and mysterious vitality which sustains the convalescent. He was re-

presented (Plate XXXI.) by the side of Æsculapius, or standing between him and Hygea, as a small barefooted boy,
wrapped closely in a mantle, with a hood on his head. This
careful wrapping-up seems to indicate the secret shrouded
nature of the vital force which he personifies, and may also
have been meant to express the care in wrapping-up so essential to convalescence.

The principal centre of his worship was on the coast of
Asia Minor.

TYCHE, or FORTUNA.

(PLATE XXI.)

The idea that a great part of the incidents and circumstances
of life was due to chance, had taken hold of the mind in very
early times, and had come to be personified in the form of a
goddess of luck, whom the Greeks called Tyche and the
Romans Fortuna. She was the daughter of Zeus. The Parcæ,
or Fates, were her sisters. It was believed that she guided
the career of men, whether prosperously or the reverse; and
to show her in this capacity, she was figured holding a double
rudder in her hands—the one to steer the barque of the lucky,
the other that of the unlucky. In later times she was represented with wings, or with her eyes bound, standing on a ball
or a wheel, to indicate that luck rolls like a ball, without choice,
undoing all the efforts of this one, and overwhelming that one
with wealth and prosperity. Sometimes she was represented
with a ball on her head, or with a cornucopia in her hands.

In Plate XXI. she appears draped, her arms bare, a horn of
plenty in one hand and a rudder in the other,—the ball beside the rudder indicating the rapid turns of fortune.

XXX

Nike, or Victoria.

Herakles (Hercules).

Tyche was worshipped in many places in Greece, but especially at Athens, where she was popularly believed to reside constantly as a favouring deity. In Italy the worship of Fortuna was wide-spread, and a general festival held in her honour annually on the 24th of June. Her principal worshippers, however, were newly-married women. She had an oracle of considerable fame in the towns of Præneste and Antium.

NIKE, or VICTORIA,

(PLATE XXX.,)

The goddess of victory, was a daughter of the giant **Pallas** and the Okeanid nymph **Styx**, and was regarded by the Greeks as inseparable from Zeus and Athene. Except in works of art of an early period, she was represented with wings. Her attributes were a palm-branch, a wreath, and a trophy of armour. Sometimes she carried a staff (*caduceus*) like that of Hermes, as a sign of her power, and floated in the air with outspread wings, or appeared coming down to earth—now pointing the way to a victor, now reaching a wreath down to his brow, or driving his horses. As goddess of victories by sea, suitable emblems were assigned to her.

In Plate XXX. she appears standing on a globe, draped, winged, holding a wreath and a palm-branch. On coins apparently struck to commemorate victories, or, as it sometimes happened, success in the national games,—on engraved gems, sculptures,—figures of Nike are of frequent occurrence. She is also draped, and of a youthful appearance : a favourite subject, to judge from the repetition of it on gems, seems to have been that in which she was represented in the act of sacrificing an ox.

EIRENE or PAX,

The goddess of peace, was also represented holding a palm-branch. At other times she stood with armour under her feet, or was engaged in closing the temple of Janus. In Greece she was reckoned one of the Horæ—the most cheerful, indeed, of the three sisters. In Rome she had a temple, and enjoyed the honour of an annual festival on the 30th of January.

FATE,

The Greek name being **Ananke**, the Roman **Fatum**, was a personification of the unalterable necessity that appeared to control the career of mankind and the events of the world. Gods, as well as men, were subject to its unchanging decrees. This deity was the offspring of Night and Erebos. Her sentences were carried out by the Parcæ, who, however, were also looked upon as independent deities of fate. She was represented standing on a globe, and holding an urn.

MŒRA and the MŒRÆ, or PARCÆ.

In very early times the management of the world in regard to social matters involving right and reason, was supposed to be directly under the control of a goddess called Mœra, who, in her own province, acknowledged the superiority of no other deity, not even of Zeus, the ruler of the world, who, as supreme god, could not be thought to insist on anything unreasonable or wrong. In later times we find, instead of this single deity,

XXXI

One of the Horæ.

Perseus.

Hygiea.   Æsculapius.

three Mœræ (or Parcæ) answering respectively to the three stages of human life—birth, years, and death. In this form, however, they no longer retained the high position of superiority to Zeus, but, like the other deities, became subject to him, thus showing that he possessed in its highest form the consciousness of right and reason, and was entitled to be called **Mœragetes**, or leader of the Mœræ.

They were described as daughters of Night—to indicate the darkness and obscurity of human fate—or of Zeus and Themis, that is, "daughters of the just heavens." Another story has it, that it was they who united Themis and Zeus in marriage, the same ceremony, according to another version of the myth, having been performed by them to Zeus and Hera. It was natural to suppose the goddesses of fate present and taking part at marriages and births.

The names of the three sisters were **Klotho, Lachesis,** and **Atropos.** To express the influence which they were believed to exercise on human life from birth to death, they were conceived as occupied in spinning a thread of gold, silver, or wool; now tightening, now slackening, and at last cutting it off. This occupation was so arranged among the three, that Klotho, the youngest, put the wool round the spindle, Lachesis spun it, and Atropos, the eldest, cut it off, when a man had to die. Tyche, or Fortuna, has been taken as a fourth sister, on account of the similarity of her functions. It is not, however, so.

They were represented in art as serious maidens, always side by side, and in most cases occupied as we have mentioned; there being instances, however, in which Atropos, the 'unalterable,' is represented alone.

They were worshipped very seriously both in Greece and Italy: sacrifices of honey and flowers, sometimes of ewes, were offered to them, while in Sparta and in Rome they had temples and altars.

NEMESIS,

Called also **Adrasteia** and **Rhamnusia**, from Rhamnus in Attica, the principal centre of her worship, was a personification of the vengeance which appeared to overtake every act of wrong. She was the goddess of punishment, and as such a figure of her was placed beside the bench of the judges. A mysterious power, watching over the propriety of life, she was conceived as shaping the demeanour of men in their times of prosperity, punishing crime, taking luck away from the unworthy, tracking every wrong to its doer, and keeping society in equipoise. She was represented as a thoughtful, beautiful figure of queenly aspect, with a diadem or crown on her head, winged, except in the case of early sculptures, or driving in a car drawn by gryphons. Among her several attributes were a wheel, to indicate the speed of her punishments, a balance, a bridle, a yoke, a rudder, a lash, a sword, and an apple-branch. Special festivals, called **Nemesia**, accompanied by public sacrifices to assure her good will, were held annually in Athens and in Smyrna.

Now Erebos, now Okeanos, is mentioned as her father, while Zeus is said to have been her lover, and Helena their daughter.

To execute her commands she had three attendants, **Dike, Pœna**, and **Erinys** (respectively justice, punishment, and vengeance). She was a terror to evil-doers. At the same time her endeavours to preserve an equal balance in the attitude of man to man were recognized as springing from a deep-seated love, and therefore she was placed beside the Graces. In Smyrna several winged beings of her type were worshipped.

ERIS,

Called by the Romans **Discordia,** the goddess of strife, was employed by the other gods to stir up fierce disputes and mortal quarrels among men. It was she who caused the dispute between Hera, Athene, and Aphrodite for the possession of the golden apple, the prize of beauty, which she threw among the company assembled at the marriage of Peleus.

Terrible in form and aspect, with attributes like those of the **Eumenides**, with whom her home was in the realms below, she was looked on as the sister and companion, sometimes as the wife, of Ares, the god of massacre. Her daughter was

ENYO,

Whom the Romans called **Bellona,** now believing her to be the wife and now the sister of Mars. Similarly among the Greeks, Enyo, the murderous goddess of war, delighting in devastation, was associated with Ares, who also bore the title of **Enyalios,** either driving his chariot or rushing in front of it to battle. The peculiar fierceness and fury with which she spread terror and alarm in a battle distinguished her from Pallas-Athene. She was represented as of frightful aspect, with flowing hair, rushing wildly hither and thither, with a lash in her hand, and armed with shield and spear. Her most celebrated temple was that at Komana, in Asia Minor.

At the close of the war against the Samnites a temple was erected to her in Rome by Appius Claudius. There the Senate used to meet when they had to deliberate with an embassy from a hostile power, or when they had to decide whether the honour of a triumphal entry into the city should

be bestowed upon a general. At the entrance to the temple
stood a pillar, which, on the occasion of declaring war, was
viewed as márking the boundary between Roman and hostile
territory. The ceremony of declaring war was to throw a
spear over this pillar—that is, into the territory of the enemy.
There festivals of din and wild excitement were held in her
honour. Her priests were styled **Bellonarii.**

PHEME, or FAMA,

The goddess of fame or report, whether good or bad, was said
to be a daughter of Gaea, and born at the time of her great
indignation at the overthrow of the Giants. Sleepless, always
prying, swift of foot, Pheme announced whatever she saw or
heard of, at first in a whisper addressed only to a few persons,
then by degrees louder and to a larger circle, until finally she
had traversed heaven and earth communicating it. She was
represented as a tender, gentle figure, winged, and holding a
trumpet.

ATE

Was the goddess of infatuation, mischief, and guilt, misleading
men to actions that involved them in ruin. For this her
father, Zeus, cast her in anger from Olympos, and from that time
she wandered about the earth in search of victims to her
malignant influence. She was spoken of as powerful in person
and swift of foot, running before men to mislead them. Her
sisters were the

LITÆ,

Sweet-natured goddesses, whose special duty was to recom-
pense the persons whom Ate had reduced to distress and ruin.

XXIX

One of the Erinys.

Eros Grieving for Psyche.

Their name signifies "prayers of the penitent," and the allegory in this case is not far to seek. Prayers atone and make amends for what a man does to the harm of others in thoughtlessness or from infatuation, without wicked thought or design. In the Homeric poems they are described as lame, wrinkled, and squinting—those deformities being caused by the trouble they had in making good the harm done by Ate. Penitent prayers were at best but sorry aid in making good the evil done from infatuation or carelessness.

The Litæ were supposed to be daughters of Zeus, and to place before him the prayers of those who invoked his assistance.

THE ERINYS, or FURIÆ,

(PLATE XXIX.,)

Called also **Diræ, Eumenides,** or **Semnæ**—that is, the "revered" goddesses, were daughters of Night, or, according to another myth, of the Earth and Darkness, while a third account calls them offspring of Kronos and Eurynome. They were attendants of Hades and Persephone, and lived at the entrance to the lower world. Their first duty was to see to the punishment of those of the departed who, having been guilty of some crime on earth, had come down to the shades without obtaining atonement from the gods. At the command of the higher gods, sometimes of Nemesis, they appeared on earth pursuing criminals. Nothing escaped their sharp eyes as they followed the evil-doer with speed and fury, permitting him no rest.

A sad instance of this is the story of **Orestes,** the son of **Agamemnon,** who slew his mother, **Klytæmnestra,** to avenge his father's death. The atrocity of the crime committed

by Klytæmnestra was held by Zeus and Apollo to be no excuse
for the act of Orestes, and accordingly he was subjected to the
long and cruel pursuit of the Furies, from which he was at
length freed by bringing, on the advice of an oracle of Apollo,
an image of Artemis from Tauros to Argos.

In Plate XXIX. is represented one of the Erinys pursuing
Orestes ; the face reflected on the mirror which she holds is
perhaps that of Klytæmnestra.

The number of the Erinys, varying in early times, was afterwards fixed to three : **Tisiphone** (the avenger of murder),
Alekto (the unwearied persecutor), and **Megæra** (the grim).
They were represented as female figures of odious aspect, clad
in black, sometimes winged, with hair formed of vipers, and
carrying a serpent, a knife, or a torch in their hands. In time
this grim conception of them fell away, and they came to be
represented as beautiful serious maidens, clad something like
Artemis. As divine beings, whose office it was to punish
neglect of duty, breach of faith, and crimes committed against
parents, they came to be looked upon as aiding the preservation of a high morality, and were called Eumenides, or the
"well-minded goddesses." When sacrifices were offered to
them, the place chosen for the occasion was of a wild character, the time night, and the animals sacrificed, black. In
Greece there were several temples and solemn groves dedicated to them—as, for example, at Colonos, close by Athens.

THE HARPYS,

Also were creatures employed, according to the belief of the
Greeks and Romans, by the higher gods to carry out the
punishment of crime. They were three in number : **Aëllo,**

Okypete, and Kelæno, or Podarge; and were said to be daughters of the giant Thaumas and the Okeanid nymph Elektra. Their body was that of a bird, their head that of a woman; and it would seem that they were originally goddesses of the storm,which carries everything along with it.

Their manner of punishing those whom they were sent to punish was to carry off all the food set before their victim, and devour it, or failing that, to render it uneatable. Among others who were punished in this way was Phineus, a king of Thrace, his crime having been cruelty towards his own son and contempt of the gods. For showing the Argonauts the way to Kolchis he was, however, freed from their persecution by Kalais and Zetes, the winged sons of Boreas, who, in gratitude, killed them. At other times, as the case of the daughters of Pandareos, they are described as carrying off their victims bodily from the earth; while, on the so-called Harpy tomb in the British Museum, they appear to be represented as dæmons of death carrying away the souls of deceased persons.

THE GORGONS,

By name Stheino, Euryale, and Medusa, were daughters of Phorkys and Keto. Two of them were believed to be immortal, while the third, Medusa, the youngest and most beautiful of them, was mortal. She loved Poseidon, and having met him once in the temple of Athene, to the desecration of that building, was punished by having her beautiful hair turned into snakes, thus making her appearance more ghastly than that of her sisters. Her face was terrible to behold, turning the spectator into stone. At last Perseus, finding her asleep, cut off her head with his curved sword, and presented it to Athene, who had assisted him in the enterprise, to be worn on her *ægis* or shield as a terror to her enemies.

The ancient poets describe the Gorgons generally as horrid, aged women, and frequently place them by the side of the Furies. In early times there was only one Gorgon—Medusa—instead of the three of later times. The winged horse, **Pegasos**, was the offspring of her and Poseidon.

In Plate XXXI. Perseus is represented standing with sword in one hand and the head of Medusa in the other, turning his face away to avoid seeing it. The subject of Perseus cutting off the head of Medusa occurs in one of the earliest examples of Greek sculpture—one of the *metopes* of the oldest temple at Selinus, in Sicily; and from the conventional manner in which her face is represented, compared with the other parts of the sculpture, it is agreed that the type must have been familiar for some time to Greek art. To possess a representation of a Gorgon's face was to be provided with a charm against ills, and accordingly it was frequently employed as a personal ornament. Many hundreds of such faces worked in thin gold, and intended to be stitched down on garments, were found in the tomb of a priestess of Demeter in Kertch, and are now in the hermitage of St. Petersburg. A representation of Perseus escaping after cutting off the Gorgon's head, and being pursued by her sisters, occurs on a small vase in the British Museum, where also is to be seen, on a fragment of a terra-cotta relief, Athene holding up the shield, the polished surface of which reflected her face, and thus guided Perseus to the spot without his encountering its deadly stare.

THE GRAEÆ,

Daughters of **Phorkys** and **Keto**, were three in number; **Deino, Pephredo,** and **Enyo**; their names meaning respectively "alarm," "dread," and "horror." Sisters and at the same time guardians of the Gorgons, they were conceived as misshapen hideous creatures, hoary and withered from their birth, with only one eye and one tooth for the common use of the three, and were supposed to inhabit a dark cavern near the entrance to Tartaros. The belief in their existence seems to have been originally suggested by the grey fog or mist which lies upon the sea and is a frequent source of danger to the mariner. It is said that Perseus obtained from them the necessary information as to the dwelling of the Gorgons by seizing their solitary eye and tooth, and refusing to return them until they showed him the way.

NYX, or NOX,

Was, it will be remembered, a daughter of **Chaos.** She became the wife of **Erebos** (darkness), and bore to him two children, **Æther** (the pure air) and **Hemera** (day). In the earliest form of the myth she was one of the seven elements that constituted the world—fire, water, earth, sky, sun, moon, and night.

In time the lively imagination of the ancients associated with this mysterious goddess of night a control over illness. sufferings, dreams, misfortunes, quarrels, war, murder, sleep, and death; everything inexplicable and frightful that befell men being personified and described as her offspring.

She was supposed to inhabit a palace in the lower world jointly with Day. When the latter entered the palace, Night
13

rode out in a chariot drawn by two black steeds, and accompanied by many stars, traversed the heavens till daybreak,
when she returned to the palace.

She was represented as a serious figure clad in long heavy
drapery, on her head a black star-spangled veil; with black
wings, and carrying two children in her arms (one of them
being white to personify Sleep, the other black, to personify
Death), or riding in a black chariot, holding an extinguished
torch inverted.

HYPNOS, or SOMNUS,

Was, as we have just said, a son of Night, twin-brother of
Thanatos (death), with whom he lived in deep subterranean
darkness at the entrance to Tartaros.   His influence extended
to gods as well as men, and by the latter he was viewed as a
special benefactor, giving the weary refreshing rest, and suf-
ferers alleviation of their pain.

He was represented in different forms and attitudes, with
different attributes,—now nude, or lightly or heavily clad, now
standing, or striding hastily, or reposing heavily; or as a
powerful youth holding a poppy or a horn, from which sleep
trickled down on those reposing; or as a child, and sometimes
as a bearded aged man.   On his head were the wings of a
hawk or a night bird, and beside him frequently a lizard. He
was looked on as a favourite of the Muses, apparently because
of the dreams he was supposed to communicate to men.

In the British Museum is a very beautiful bronze head of
Hypnos, with the wings of a hawk growing out from the temples.   In the Iliad, Hera commands him to take the form of
the bird which men call a hawk.   How the idea originated
of attaching wings to the temples, is uncertain.

ONEIROS and MORPHEUS

Are two different forms of the god of dreams. According to the meaning of their names, the office of the latter would be to fashion dreams, as the gods desired them to be sent to men. In this task he was assisted by **Ikelos,** who fashioned those dreams that had all the appearance of reality, by **Phobetor,** the author of alarming dreams, and **Phantasos**, who tricked sleepers with innumerable and strange phenomena. But we find Morpheus also represented in the capacity of a sort of watchman and guardian of dreams, as Æolos was of the winds.

Oneiros was properly a personification of dreams, whether idle or deceptive or really prophetic. Dreams of the former class were supposed to issue from the ivory gates, those of the latter class from the horn gate, of the palace where they were kept, beside the Western Okeanos. They were called children of Night, sometimes children of Sleep, and were directly under the control of the superior order of gods, who, as they pleased, despatched deceptive or prophetic dreams to men.

MOMUS

Was a deity whose delight and occupation was to jeer bitterly at the actions both of gods and men, sparing no one with his insinuations except Aphrodite, in whom he could find nothing to blame, and vexed himself to death in consequence. As an example of his behaviour, it is said that he complained of the man that **Prometheus** had made, because there was not a. window in his breast through which his thoughts might be seen.

THANATOS, or MORS,

The god of death, was, as we have said, a son of Night and twin-brother of Sleep. He was, however, also described as a son of Earth and Tartaros, to whom it was his office to introduce, some time or other, the whole of mankind. The relentless severity with which he discharged the task caused him to be frequently regarded with pain, and to be represented as of a powerful figure, with shaggy beard and fierce countenance, with great wings to his shoulders, and resembling, on the whole, the figure of Boreas, the god of the wild north wind of winter. This form, in the case of both deities, was expressive of the violent nature of their functions.

Thanatos was, however, more frequently regarded with submission, or as coming opportunely, and in such cases was represented in the form of a quiet pensive youth, winged, standing with his legs crossed, often beside an urn with a wreath on it, and holding an extinguished torch reversed. Or, as a personification of endless repose, he appeared in the form of a beautiful youth leaning against the trunk of a tree, with one arm thrown up over his head—an attitude by which ancient artists usually expressed repose. It was probably owing to the spread of the belief that death was a transition from life to Elysium, that in later times this more attractive representation of the god of death took the place of the former repulsive representations whether, as a powerful and violent god, or as a black child in the arms of his mother, Night. Among the figures sculptured on the chest of Kypselos, a description of which we have still in Pausanias, was that of Night carrying twin children in her arms—the one white, representing Sleep, and the other black, representing Death. On Roman sarcophagi, Mors, or the genius of death, was represented in the form of a winged boy, resembling Cupid, resting and holding a torch.   In the Alcestis of Euripides he is described as armed with a sword.

DÆMONS, OR GENII,

Were an order of invisible beings, one of whom was assigned by Zeus to every man, to attend, protect, and guide him. They were nameless, and, like the multitude of mankind, innumerable.   Some of them acted as personal attendants to deities of a higher order, and in that case were represented under particular forms, and enjoyed distinctive names, while others were believed to watch over particular districts, towns, or nations. While the Greeks regarded these Dæmons as deities of an inferior order, the Romans believed them to be a sort of intermediate beings linking mankind to the gods.   The Dæmons assigned to women were supposed to be feminine.

To every man was assigned a Dæmon at his birth.   Identifying itself with him, it endeavoured, throughout his life, to guide him in a wise course, and at his death died with him. To be of a cheerful mood, and to be careful of prolonging life, was to live in obedience to a man's Dæmon or Genius. To be sad and vexed, or to shorten life by recklessness, was to wrong the attendant spirit.   On birthdays it was usual to offer a sacrifice of wine, milk, flowers, or incense to the Genius, while at most meals some unmixed wine was poured out to the "Good Dæmon" (Agathodæmon).

The usual representation of a being of this class was in the form of a youth holding a horn of plenty and a dish in one hand, and some heads of poppies and ears of grain in the other.   The presence of a Dæmon was also symbolized by the figure of a serpent.

Besides the general family of Genii, the Romans had one great Genius whom they reckoned among the gods of the second rank, and esteemed highly, believing that he had some control over the others.

LARES AND PENATES

Were beings peculiar to the religion of the Romans.   Every household was supposed to be under the protection of one Lar and several Penates, whose presence was symbolized by images in the form of a youth wearing a short tunic, girt at the waist, and holding a horn of plenty in one hand, and a *patera*, or flat circular dish, in the other.   Such images of the Lares and Penates were kept in a particular part of the house called the *Lararium*, received constant offerings of incense and libations, and were decked with garlands of violets and rosemary. When a slave obtained his freedom, it was the custom of his former master to hang a chain upon the figures of his Lares. When a youth left the paternal roof he prayed: "Ye Penates of my fathers, and you, Lar, father of our family, I commend to you my parents, that you may protect them.   Other Penates and another Lar I must now seek."

Besides these private household deities there were also public Lares, who were recognized as the protecting spirits of whole states and towns.   Of these there were originally two in Rome, and later three,—the spirit of Julius Cæsar having been added as the third; for the Lares were considered to be the spirits of deceased persons who continued to watch over and influence the living.   The other two were, however, regarded sometimes as sons of Mercury and a nymph called Lara. Statues and temples were erected in their honour. Sacrifice and prayers for the safety of the state were offered up at their altars, which in spring and in summer were frequently decked with flowers. They were protectors of highways and travellers, and in this capacity had the honour of a festival called **Compitalia,** which was annually celebrated at cross-roads, a few days after the **Saturnalia,** and consisted of a banquet and sacrifice of cakes, the ceremony being conducted by slaves. To the Lares who protected the fields, sacrifices of lambs, calves, and pigs were offered.

It was believed that the Genii of good people became after their death kindly Lares, while the Genii of evil-doers became **Lemures** or **Larvæ**—that is, evil spirits who wandered about the earth afflicting mankind with illnesses for which there was no remedy but expiatory sacrifices to the gods. Persons who died without expiation for every wrong they had done were pursued by these Larvæ in the lower world.

THE MANES,

Generally speaking, were the souls of the departed inhabiting the realm of shadows. Survivors, however, who believe that departed souls sustained a higher and nobler existence, regarded them as divine beings, calling them Dii Manes, offered sacrifice to them at tombs, and thought it possible to call them up from the lower world.

III. DEMIGODS, OR HEROES.

DEMIGODS, or heroes, were a class of beings peculiar, it would seem, to the mythology of the Greeks. They were regarded partly as of divine origin, were represented as men possessed of godlike form, strength, and courage ; were believed to have lived on earth in the remote dim ages of the nation's history; to have been occupied in their lifetime with thrilling adventures and extraordinary services in the cause of human civilization, and to have been after death in some cases translated to a life among the gods, and éntitled to sacrifice and worship. They were described as having been the first sovereigns and legislators of the nation, and as the founders of all the kingly and noble families. Monsters that devastated particular localities were destroyed, the oppressed were set free, and everywhere order and peaceful institutions were established by them. They were, in short, the adventurous knights the history of whose deeds formed for the mass of the people the first chapter of the national history, and that in a manner worthy both of the civilization to which the nation had attained, and of the gods to whose influence the progress was due. The legends of their adventures furnished to poets and artists an inexhaustible treasure of striking figures, wonderful deeds, and strange events, while they formed at the same time a most powerful element in the national education.

It has been suggested that the belief in these beings may have originated in later times, in an impulse to people the blank early pre-historic age with ideal figures of a sublime order of men, to whom the nation might look back with pride; or that it may have originated in a desire to dwell on the memory of distinguished persons who had actually existed, and in time, by so doing, to exaggerate their actions to a degree quite beyond human powers. But it is far more probable that, like the gods, the heroes had originally been divine personifications of certain elements of nature, and the legends of adventures ascribed to them merely a mythical form of describing the phenomena of these elements. The idea, for example, of a long struggle and ultimate victory over grim enemies, which is so characteristic of these adventures, is the same idea that we find pervading the early myths, in which the powers of light are represented as struggling with, and finally overcoming the powers of darkness. But while the gods always maintained their relationship to the elements of nature, of which they were divine personifications—marine deities for instance, dwelling in the depths of the sea, and celestial deities in the pure ether—the heroes or demigods, on the other hand, had ceased to be identified with any particular element, and though retaining the form, strength, and courage of gods, came in time to be regarded as men of high order that had once inhabited Greece, but had passed away. The legends, which, as we have said, had been intended to be the mythical descriptions of certain natural phenomena, were expanded so as to embrace the new variety of adventures which imagination with its wide scope now assigned to the heroes.

There appears to have been a time when the gods generally were in danger of being reduced in this manner to the condition of demigods or heroes,—such events, for instance, as the war of Zeus with the Titans and Giants, the contests of Apollo with Tityos and Python, or of Dionysos with his enemies, being calculated, from their adventurous nature, to present their authors more in the light of heroes than of gods, and to form readily subjects for the epic poets, as indeed the contests of Dionysos did. This tendency was, however, arrested by the necessity of defining, for the purposes of worship, the provinces of the various deities. From that time the position of the gods was determined, while the heroes became less and less distinguishable from men, the legends concerning them assuming gradually more of a historical than of an ideal character. Traditions of early battles and victories that still lingered among the people, were made to circle round these imaginary heroes, who in time became the centres of all the earliest national recollections, the accredited founders of most of the elementary institutions of social life, and the guides of colonists.

It does not, however, follow that the particular elements of nature over which the heroes or demigods had originally presided, were left after this separation unrepresented by divine beings. For in addition to the vast number of gods in the Greek national religion, whom we have already described as identified with this or that department of the universe, there must have been in the early ages a large number of local deities, who, when the tribes to which they were peculiar, coalesced in after times into one Greek nation, must have appeared in many cases quite identical in character, though probably very often different in regard to the details of the deeds or adventures ascribed to them. Thus many who may have been dispensed with as gods would be retained, on account of their local adventures, as heroes or demigods.

Turning to the oldest examples of the Greek epic poetry which we possess—the Iliad and Odyssey—we find the heroes represented as hardly distinguishable from men. More powerful, more beautiful, and more courageous they certainly were than the ordinary men of their day, and on this account were looked on as descendants of the gods; still their ways of life were distinctly the ways of men, not of gods.

By the time of Hesiod we find this opinion of the heroes changed. The heroic age is lamented as a thing of the past. The people of his time, aware of their weakness and wants, looked back with reverent feelings to the happy age in which the great heroes stood between the gods and feeble mankind. Zeus, it was taught by Hesiod, had translated the heroes to the islands of the blest, far removed from men, where they lived in a perpetual golden age under the sovereignty of Kronos. The people, however, thought otherwise, believing that the ancient tumuli in Greece and in Asia Minor were the graves of the heroes. The imposing tumuli at the entrance to the Hellespont, for instance, were viewed as the tombs of Achilles, Patroklos, and Ajax. Sanctuaries and temples were erected to heroes, their bones were searched for, and when found regarded as a great source of strength to the town that possessed them; all relics of their stay on earth were hallowed, and a form of worship was specially adapted to them.

In later times the heroes came to be identified more or less with the Dæmons. The consequence of this was that all individuals who on account of extraordinary strength, courage, beauty, talent, or self-sacrifice, were supposed to be possessed of special Dæmons, were reckoned as heroes. And this was not confined to persons remarkable for their good qualities; successful daring entitling a robber to this rank as much as did the bravery of the men who fell at Marathon and Platææ.

In still later times, as the belief gained ground that every soul had something of the nature of a Dæmon in it, and was destined to a higher and nobler life, heroic honours were paid to almost all the dead; so that when a man of particular distinction died, the only course left open of paying him signal honours was to regard him as having been, after the manner of Herakles, translated to a life among the gods, and to worship him as a god.

It is, however, only with the heroes or demigods that occur in the mythology and the epic poetry that we have to do. They may be divided into three classes: First, the demigods, associated with the creation of mankind and the earliest incidents of human history and civilization,—the most striking figure among them being that of Prometheus. Secondly, the earlier heroes properly so called—such as Herakles, Theseus, Minos, Pelos, Perseus, or Bellerophon, who were distinguished for their extraordinary adventures, labours, and expeditions, such, for example, as that of the Argonauts to Kolchis. Thirdly, the more recent heroes, the tales of whose deeds and expeditions—for instance, those against Troy and Thebes—read more like historical traditions magnified by the imagination of the poets, than allegorical narratives such as those of the two preceding classes.

THE CREATION OF MAN.

PROMETHEUS AND THE FIRST DEMIGODS.

AMONG the various opinions in ancient times concerning the origin of mankind, the most generally accepted one appears to have been that in which it was asserted that man and all other forms of life had, like the gods, originally sprung from the common mother earth. It was not supposed that the whole human race could trace its lineage back to one primeval pair; on the contrary, it was believed that a primeval pair had been created in all the chief districts in which mankind was afterwards found settled. As the natural features of these districts varied, so varied the opinions with regard to the exact substance from which the first beings had sprung. In wooded and mountainous districts, for instance, they were held to have sprung from rocks and trees; in valleys, from the moist element of nature. As to the time at which this creation took place, and whether it took place simultaneously throughout the various inhabited regions, we have no means of knowing the current belief.

From the primitive condition of savages living like animals in the forests and caves, they advanced slowly in the direction of civilization,—sometimes visited with terrible punishments, and sometimes assisted by the gods; the different classes or tribes becoming in time united into two great races,—the Pelasgic and the Hellenic. The former traced its origin to the Argive **Phoroneus,** and appears to have been resident mainly in the Peloponnesos, while the latter looked back to **Deukalion** as its founder, and was resident in Thessaly and round Parnassos. According to the story, a great flood had swept away the whole human race except one pair, Deukalion and Pyrrha, who, as the flood abated, landed on Mount Parnassos, and thence descending, picked up stones, and cast them round about, as Zeus had commanded. From these stones sprang a new race—men from those cast by Deukalion, and women from those cast by his wife. From Hellen, the son of Deukalion, the Hellenic race derived its name, while its four great branches, the Æolians, Dorians, Achæans, and Ionians, traced their descent and names from four of his sons.

In such a primitive condition of life, perhaps nothing was regarded as of greater importance, or more mysterious in its nature, than fire. Its beam dispelled the dread of darkness, and its warmth removed the chill of winter. The fire of the hearth was the centre of domestic life. At the forge, tools and weapons were fashioned. It was an emblem of the life of man, with its flash and sudden extinction on the one hand and the illumination of its prolonged blaze on the other. In storms it was seen descending from the sky, and in volcanic eruptions it was seen issuing from the earth. The source of it all was readily believed to be in the close keeping of the gods; and how mankind came to obtain the use of it was explained in the story of **Prometheus.**

Zeus, foreseeing the arrogance that would arise from the possession of so great a blessing, had from the first refused to transmit any portion of his sacred fire to men. Their deplorable condition, however, owing to the want of it, found a champion in the person of Prometheus (a son of the

Titan Japetos), who had previously identified himself with the cause of humanity in a dispute that arose at Mekone (Sikyon) as to the rightful share of the gods in all sacrifices offered to them. On that occasion an ox had been slaughtered as a sacrifice, and Prometheus, having wrapped up all the eatable parts in the skin of the animal as one portion, and having cleverly covered the bones and worthless parts with fat as the other portion, asked Zeus to select what he thought the better portion for the gods. Zeus, though perfectly aware of the deceit, chose the worthless parts, and more firmly than ever determined to withhold his fire from men. Prometheus, however, resolved to obtain it for them, and succeeded in snatching some of it from the hearth of Zeus, or, as another version of the story has it, from the forge of Hephæstos in Lemnos. As a punishment, he was condemned to be chained alive to a rock in the remote Caucasus mountains, and to submit while every day a vulture came to gnaw away his liver, which daily grew afresh. For a long time he bore this suffering, and indeed would never have been released but for the secret which he possessed concerning the ultimate fate of the dominion of Zeus, who, for the purpose of learning the secret, permitted Herakles to shoot the vulture, to free Prometheus, and bring him back to Olympos.

Meanwhile the human race enjoyed the many benefits of fire, and continued to advance in civilization rapidly. But that their cup of happiness might be mixed with sorrow, Zeus ordered Hephæstos to fashion a woman of clay, of divine beauty, but possessed of all the weaknesses as well as charms of human nature. Athene instructed her in the industrial occupations of women, Aphrodite gave her grace of manners, and taught her the arts of a beauty, while Hermes qualified her for the part of flattering and soothing. With the help of the Graces and Horæ, Athene robed her with costly, beautiful robes, and decked her with flowers, so that, when all was done, **Pandora,** as they called her, might be irresistibly attractive to gods and men. Hermes conducted her to **Epimetheus,** who, though warned by his brother Prometheus to accept no gift from Zeus, yielded to the besetting weakness from which he obtained his name—that of being wise when it was too late. He received Pandora into his house, and made her his wife. She brought with her a vase, the lid of which was to remain closed. The curiosity of her husband, however, tempted him to open it, and suddenly there escaped from it troubles, weariness, and illnesses, from which mankind was never afterwards free. All that remained was Hope.

We have thus, in contrast with the general belief described above as the spontaneous origin of man from the earth, an instance of a human being directly fashioned by the gods from clay. From this mean substance it was also asserted the first men were made by Prometheus, Athene assisting him by breathing life into his figures. But this was probably only a learned speculation, indulged in to account for the zeal displayed by Prometheus in the cause of human civilization. It is better to account for that zeal by assuming Prometheus to have been originally a god of fire, who, asserting his right to employ that element for the benefit of mankind, provoked the hostility of the other gods, and from that time forward identified himself with the cause of men. There is good ground for assuming this in the fact that Prometheus was intimately associated with Hephæstos in the very ancient worship of that god in Lemnos and in Attica.

While the progress of civilization, as far as it had depended

on, or could be symbolized by, fire, was connected with Prometheus, the progress of agriculture in primitive times was
reflected in the story of the two giants Otos and **Ephialtes,**
sons of Alöeus (the planter) and Iphimedeia. Small and puny
at their birth, they grew quickly, living on grain, and soon
became the wonder of men for their great size and beauty.
Finding that war and agriculture could not go together, they
seized Ares, the god of war, bound and confined him in a
large brazen vase for thirteen months. He would have perished in it had not Hermes at length heard of his imprisonment, and set him free. Becoming more and more arrogant
in the pride of their strength, the two brothers next determined
to assail the immortal gods in Olympos itself, and for this
purpose they had placed Mount Ossa on the top of Mount
Olympos, and upon Ossa had heaped Mount Pelion, when
the shafts of Apollo felled them. They perished in youth,
ere their beards had grown.

THE EARLIER RACE OF HEROES.

IT will be convenient to separate, for the present, the
legends of the adventures of Herakles, together with those
that relate to combined expeditions of heroes from different
districts,—such as the expedition of the Argonauts,—from the
other legends of this earlier race of heroes, and to arrange the
latter class according to the localities assigned as the principal scenes of their actions, beginning with

14

(*a.*) ARGOS.

At the head óf the Argive line of heroes stands **Inachos,**
the river-god, a son of Okeanos, like all the other river-gods.
With the nymph Melia for his wife, he became the father of
Phoroneus and Io, of whom the former, according to Argive
legends, was the first man upon the earth.   Such services as
Prometheus was elsewhere believed to have rendered to early
civilization, were there ascribed to Phoroneus.   He was
reputed to have founded the town of Argos, and to have established there the worship of Hera.   With regard to Io, we
have already related (in connection with Hermes) how she
was loved by Zeus, and, to escape the jealousy of Hera, was
transformed by him into a cow—how Hera, discovering the
transformation, set a watch over Io, in the person of Argos,
a giant with a hundred eyes, and how Hermes slew the watchman and released Io.   Another version of the story says that
it was Hera who transformed Io into a cow, for the purpose
of thwarting the love of Zeus for her.   Argos had tethered
her to an olive-tree in a grove sacred to Hera, between the
towns of Mykenæ and Argos, and was there keeping guard
when Hermes arrived and slew him.   Though set free, Io did
not yet regain her human form, but was compelled to wander
through distant lands in the form of a white horned cow,
goaded by a vexatious insect sent by Hera.   At last, on
reaching Egypt, she obtained rest, was restored to her human
form, and became the mother of **Epaphos.**

Io, the white horned cow, appears to have been a personification of the moon, like the Phœnician goddess **Astarte,** who
was also represented in this form.   Her wanderings were like
the wanderings of the moon.   Hera, who punished her, was

the supreme goddess of the heavens. Argos, with his many eyes, reminds us of the stars. The slaying of Argos by Hermes was a favourite subject with ancient artists.

Epaphos became king of Egypt, and had a daughter called Libya (after the district of that name on the shore of the Mediterranean), who bore to Poseidon, the sea-god, two sons—**Agenor** and **Belos.** While the former became the head of a race that spread over Phœnicia, Cilicia, and on to Thebes in Greece, Belos remained in Egypt, succeeded to the throne, and marrying **Anchirrhoe,** a daughter of the Nile, had two sons, **Ægyptos** and **Danaos.** The latter was appointed to rule over Arabia, the former over Libya. Ægyptos had fifty sons, and Danaos the same number of daughters. A dispute arose between the two families, and Danaos yielding took ship with his daughters and sailed to Argos, pursued all the way by the sons of Ægyptos. At Argos, the home of his race, he was kindly received by the reigning king, and protected against the pursuers.

At that time the district of Argos was suffering from a drought which Poseidon had angrily caused. Danaos sent out his daughters to search for a spring, and while they were so engaged it happened that one of them, **Amymone,** throwing her spear at a stag missed it, and hit a Satyr who was asleep in the brake. Pursued by the Satyr, she called on the name of Poseidon for help, and the god instantly appeared, drove off the Satyr, and for love of the beautiful Danaid caused a perennial spring to flow at Lerna, where he met her. Amymone bore to Poseidon **Nauplios,** the wrecker of Nauplia, who by false lights misled many ships to their destruction among rocks, and enriched himself from their cargoes. By a singular fatality he perished in this way himself at last. He had three sons:

Palamedes, celebrated for his inventive faculty, **Oiax**, the steersman, and **Nausimedon**, the ship captain.

Meantime the sons of Ægyptos, it is said, having besieged Argos for some time, at length proposed to forget their difference with Danaos, and to marry his daughters. Without relenting in the least, he agreed to give his daughters to them in marriage, but to each daughter he presented a knife, and commanded them all to slay each her own husband on the marriage night. All obeyed his order except **Hypermnestra**, who preferring to be regarded as of weak resolution than as a murderess, spared her husband, **Lynkeus**, and became the mother of the Argive line of kings. While Zeus approved the murderous deed of her forty-nine sisters, and sent Athene and Hermes to give them expiation, Hypermnestra was cast into a dungeon by her indignant father, her husband, Lynkeus, saving himself by flight. On being brought to trial she was however publicly acquitted; her husband returning to Argos, succeeded Danaos on the throne, and in after times was widely respected, among other things for having founded the great festival in honour of the Argive Hera. The prize of victory in the games that accompanied that festival was a shield, not a wreath, as was elsewhere usual; the tradition being that on the first occasion of these games Lynkeus presented his son Abas with the shield which had belonged to Danaos.

Whether it was to obtain husbands for his daughters who had accomplished their own widowhood, or whether it was to decide among a multitude of suitors for their hands, Danaos held a kind of tournament, the victors in which were to be accepted as husbands. On the morning of the contest he ranged his daughters together on the course, and by noon each had been carried off by a victorious athlete, a scion of some noble house.

It was said that after death the Danaïdes, with the exception of Hypermnestra, were punished in Tartaros by having continually to carry water, and pour it in the vain endeavour of filling a broken cistern. It may be that this form of punishment was selected for them as the most suitable for women, who generally in Greece were the drawers of water. At the same time it was very suggestive of the dry parched soil of Argos, the streams of which were always dried up in summer.

From **Abas**, the son of Hypermnestra and Lynkeus, sprang the brothers **Akrisios** and **Prœtos**, famous for their hatred of each other from infancy onwards. When they had grown up, Prœtos, finding himself constantly defeated in the fraternal encounters, fled to Lycia, and was there hospitably received by the king, **Iobates**, and the queen, **Amphianax**, whose daughter, **Sthenebœa**, he married. With the assistance of a Lycian army he was reinstated in his rights of sovereignty over Argos and Corinth, fortifying himself in the citadel of Tiryns, while his brother Akrisios held out in that of Larisa. Of both citadels, the massive structures, now in ruins, still bear witness to the fierce assaults which must have been made upon them.

Prœtos had three daughters, whose exceeding beauty made them prizes which the noblest youth of the country sought to win. But they were haughty, despised the common usages of the times, scorned to take part in the worship of Dionysos, and made ridicule of the sanctity of Hera's ancient image and shrine. For this they were punished by a form of insanity which drove them ever to wander restlessly among the woods and hills of Argos and Arcadia. It is further said that, being under the hallucination that they were cows, they lowed like kine as they wandered about. The father summoned **Melampos**, the prophet and priest, to work a cure upon his daughters, but on the prophet's stipulating a third of the kingdom as his reward, dismissed him again. The evil grew worse, for the other women of the country began to yield to the infatuation of abandoning their husbands and slaying their children. Melampos was recalled, and this time demanded an additional third of the kingdom for his brother, **Bias**. Prœtos agreed, and Melampos, collecting a body of active youths, pursued the three princesses over the mountains, and on to Sikyon, where the eldest of the three died, and the other two, after being purified, were given in marriage to Melampos and Bias respectively.

This legend also would seem to have originated in connection with the very ancient worship of Hera, as queen of the heavens, at Argos; the wanderings of the three daughters of Prœtos, under the imaginary form of cows, having reference, like the similar wanderings of Io, to the moon.

Returning to Akrisios, we find him troubled at the prospect of having no heir to his throne. To this question the oracle at Delphi replied that a daughter would be born to him, and that she would bear a son who would slay his grandfather, and rule in his stead. The daughter, **Danäe** by name, was born, and to prevent the latter part of the oracle from being fulfilled, she was imprisoned in a subterranean chamber. But a shower of gold, sent by Zeus, penetrated to her, and she became the mother of an infant destined to fulfil the oracle and to become conspicuous among the ancient heroes. He was named Perseus, probably with reference to his being a son of Zeus, the great god of light, and to his having been born in dark-

ness, in which respect, as in several others, he may be compared with Apollo, whose mother was **Leto** (darkness), while
his father was Zeus. The shower of gold would thus signify
a beam of golden light.

Akrisios, hearing the voice of the child, summoned his
daughter to the altar of Zeus to give a solemn explanation of
the circumstance. Disbelieving her story, he placed mother
and child in a closed box, and committed them to the waves.
After rocking about on the bosom of the sea, the box was at
last carried towards the island of Seriphos, and was there
caught in a net belonging to a fisherman named **Diktys,** who
took the waifs to his house, and acted kindly by them. It was
a very barren island, affording little but shelter to the families
of fishermen that inhabited it. The chief or king of it was
Polydektes, a brother of Diktys, just mentioned, and as
notorious for the gaiety of his habits as was his brother for
his simplicity. Struck with the beauty of Danae, and finding
that her son Perseus stood in the way of the fulfilment of his
desires, Polydektes became anxious to get rid of him, and
gladly availed himself of the opportunity that presented itself
when Perseus, not to be outdone in professions of loyalty,
vowed that he would even fetch the head of the Gorgon
Medusa for the king, should he wish it.

Perseus set forth sadly on his mission, but took courage
when Hermes and Athene, who often lent their aid in heroic
adventures, appeared to him, and led him to where the Graeæ
lived,—three aged women, with only one eye and one tooth
in common. Perseus, seizing the indispensable eye and tooth,
refused to give them back until they told him where to find
the nymphs who had in keeping the helmet of Hades, the
winged shoes, and the pouch necessary for his future move-

ments. On arriving at where the nymphs lived, he obtained from them the objects in question, to which Hermes added the knife (*harpe*) with which he had cut off the head of Argos. Buckling on the winged shoes, he proceeded towards the Gorgons with the speed of a bird, the helmet of Hades making him invisible, but concealing nothing from his sight. It is further said that Athene instructed him how to approach Medusa without being petrified, as was usual, by her stare. To this end she gave him a shield of polished brass, on which, as in a mirror, he could see the reflection of the Gorgon, while he himself, unseen, advanced and cut off her head. The instant he had done this there sprang from the trunk of Medusa Pegasos, the winged horse, and Chrysaor, the father of Geryoneus. Perseus, placing the head quickly into the pouch which the nymphs had given him, hastened from the scene, pursued by the two sisters of Medusa for some distance.

Among his adventures on the way back to Seriphos were the turning of Atlas into stone because the giant refused to receive him hospitably, and the release of **Andromeda**, whom he found, on passing over Æthiopia, bound to a rock on the sea-shore as a victim to a great sea-monster. She was a daughter of **Kepheus** and **Kassiepeia**, the king and queen of Æthiopia. The latter having vaunted herself equal in beauty to the Nereids, gave offence to them and to Poseidon also, who thereupon visited the country with a flood, and sent a dreadful monster from the sea to destroy both men and cattle. On appealing to the oracle of Ammon in Libya, Kepheus was told that the evil would not abate until he exposed his beautiful daughter, Andromeda, to the monster. Compelled by his subjects to yield, the luckless father took her to the shore, and chained her to a rock, in the position in which Perseus found her. Struck with her beauty, Perseus undertook to save her on condition that she should become his wife. Kepheus agreed to this, and Perseus, after slaying the monster, unchained the maiden. She had, however, been engaged beforehand to **Phineus,** her father's brother, who, arriving with a strong body of soldiers, burst in upon the marriage feast. But the sight of the Gorgon's head turned them all to stone, and Perseus triumphantly carried off his bride.

Arriving at Seriphos, he found that his mother and Diktys were being persecuted by Polydektes, and obliged to seek protection at the altars of the gods. His course was to announce his arrival to the king, who at once assembled his nobles to witness how the young hero had kept his word. Perseus appeared in the assembly, and producing the Gorgon's head, turned the king and all his nobles instantly to stone. Not content with punishing in this manner the principal persecutors of his mother, Perseus is said to have turned the island itself into a great barren rock, and to have spared only the excellent Diktys and the fishing population attached to him. Even the frogs of the island became dumb, said an ancient proverb.

Having thus fulfilled his promise, and rescued his mother, Perseus handed over the winged shoes, the pouch, and the helmet that made him invisible, to Hermes, to be restored to the nymphs. The head of Medusa he gave to Athene, who ever after wore it on her shield. Accompanied by Danäe and Andromeda, he set out for Argos to find his grandfather, Akrisios, who, however, in the meantime having left Argos in consequence of an increasing dread lest the oracle should be fulfilled regarding his death, had established himself at Larisa in Thessaly. Thither Perseus proceeded, and found, on his arrival, the king, Teutamias, occupied with public games in honour of his deceased father. Perseus took part in the games, and by a fatality which justified the oracle, the disc which he threw fell upon the foot of Akrisios, and caused his death. After burying his grandfather honourably at Larisa, Perseus returned to Argos to his mother and wife, but instead of establishing himself there, exchanged Argos for Tiryns, which was then held by **Megapenthes**, a son of **Prœtos**, and soon after founded the ancient Mykenæ, with its massive walls.

Perseus and Andromeda had two sons—**Elektryon** and **Alkæos**. **Alkmene**, the mother of Herakles, was a daughter of the former, and her husband, **Amphitryon**, a son of the latter. It was also said that before leaving the court of her father, Kepheus, Andromeda had born a son, whom they called Perses, and left behind with his grandfather. From this Perses the Persian kings traced their lineage. The kings of Pontos and Cappadocia, claiming the same descent, introduced a figure of Perseus on their coins. In Tarsos and in Egypt also were traditions of ancient benefits derived from the Greek hero.

While the wanderings of Io remind us of the wanderings of the moon, and lead us to connect the origin of the legends concerning her with the worship of Hera at Argos, the adventures of Perseus similarly suggest the apparent movement of the sun, and the effect of his light, particularly in slaying the dread monsters with which the imagination peoples darkness. It would seem, therefore, that the origin of the belief in these adventures must have had some connection with the Argive worship of Zeus and Athene.

His adventures, either as an entire story or in parts, formed a most attractive subject to ancient poets, and were frequently represented in works of art, many of which we still possess. One of the earliest examples of Greek sculpture to which an approximate date can be assigned, is a group on a temple at Selinus in Sicily, which represents him cutting off the Gorgon's head, and belongs to the seventh century B. C.

In Plate XXXI. he is figured holding the head of Medusa in one hand and the curved sword in the other. In Plate XXXII. is the rescue of Andromeda.

(b.) CORINTH.

Owing to its convenient situation on the isthmus between two seas, Corinth was from very early times an important seat of commerce; and as such being chiefly dependent for its prosperity on the benignity of the sea-god Poseidon, had at an early period established his worship, and exalted him as its principal god. In the legends concerning the Corinthian heroes we would therefore expect to find decided traces of this worship, just as in those of Argos we found traces of the early worship of Hera.

With regard to **Sisyphos,** the first of these heroes, the legend was that he had chanced to see Zeus carrying off Ægina, the daughter of the river-god **Asopos,** and having marked the direction of their flight as towards the island of Ægina, determined to make capital of his knowledge, by informing Asopos of what he had seen, on condition that the river-god would create a spring of water on the parched citadel of Corinth—Acrocorinth, as it was called. The terms were agreed

to, and Sisyphos at once secured the afterwards famous fountain of Peirene.   But Zeus could not permit the act of treachery to pass unpunished.   He sent the god or dæmon of death
to claim him.   Instead of yielding, Sisyphos bound the dæmon
with strong chains, and retained him, no one dying in the
meantime, till Ares arrived and broke the chains.   Sisyphos
was then handed over to the dæmon, but before departing
charged his wife, Merope, not to offer the customary sacrifices
for the dead, and thus to disappoint Pluto and Persephone.
Arrived in Hades, he began to denounce this neglect on the
part of his wife, and repeated his complaint so often that he
was at last allowed to return to the upper world.   Another
version of the story has it that Herakles carried him off by
force from Hades.   In either case he returned to Corinth, lived
to an advanced age, and after death was punished, as we have
already related, by having to roll a huge stone up a height,
which when it had gained the summit immediately rolled back.

It may be that the idea of such a punishment was suggested
by the backward and forward rolling of stones by the treacherous waves on the shore.   At any rate we find a connection of
Sisyphos with the worship of Poseidon in the statement that
he, at the command of the Nereïdes, received the dead body
of Melikertes from his mother, and instituted in his honour
the Isthmian games, which afterwards were held in honour of
Poseidon.

More directly connected with the worship of the sea-god is
the legend of **Glaukos**, the son of Sisyphos.   The reference
in his name to the colour of the sea is strengthened by the
title of **Pontios** which he bore, and yet it is not with the sea
directly, but with horses the accredited symbols of the waves,
that he is associated.   For some reason—from having been fed

XXXII

Bellerophon.

Perseus and Andromeda.

on human flesh, according to one report—his horses became furious, and tore their master to pieces. In after times his name was a terror to equestrians in the hippodromes, the current belief being that Glaukos survived as an evil spirit wandering about and frightening horses.

A figure of far greater importance than Glaukos in the legendary history of Corinth, was his son **Bellerophon.** Not that Corinth had been to any extent the scene of his exploits; for, except the incident of the bridling of Pegasos, his memorable adventures were all conducted elsewhere—in Argos at first, and afterwards in Lycia. His story was, moreover, strangely blended with that of the Argive Perseus. It may be that the proximity of the two towns, and the political dependence of Corinth on Argos, wrought in time an assimilation in the legends of two heroes originally quite distinct. Or, on the other hand, it may be that the difference in the pursuits and religious inclinations of the two towns acted on the imagination in such a way as to alter a legend originally common to both, so much that each might in time fairly claim a separate hero of its own. Whichever way it may have been, the Corinthians were proud of Bellerophon, and in early times had a figure of his horse, Pegasos, on their coins.

With regard to that wonderful winged horse, we have already related how it sprang from the neck of the Gorgon Medusa, when Perseus cut her head off. The legend proceeds to tell how it flew through the air, and did not set foot on earth until it reached the citadel of Corinth, where it halted to quench its thirst at the famous fountain of Peirene. Bellerophon, after trying in vain to catch it, applied to the seer Polyidos for advice, and was told to lay himself down to sleep at night beside the altar of Athene. This he did, and in the course of his sleep dreamed that the goddess came and gave him a golden bridle, bidding him show it to his father, Poseidon, and at the same time sacrifice a white ox to him. Waking, he found the bridle, sacrificed the ox, and, on the advice of the seer, dedicated an altar to Athene. The horse at once took the bit, and from that time proved of the most service to its master.

According to the ancient derivation, the name of Bellerophon signifies the "slayer of Belleros," the story being that he had accidentally caused the death of a person of that name, either his own brother, or a Corinthian noble. To obtain the necessary purification, he repaired to Argos, and was there kindly received by Prœtos, the reigning king. Unfortunately, however, the wife of Prœtos, **Stheneboea** (or, as Homer calls her, Anteia), resembled Potiphar's wife in the bent of her passions, and finding the young hero firm against her temptations, resolved to accomplish his ruin, to this end charging him before the king with an attempt to violate her. Prœtos, on hearing the charge, decided to send the youth to Lycia, to the court of Iobates, the father of Stheneboea, with a letter written in strange characters, in which the Lycian king was instructed to compass the death of the bearer. The parting scene, where Bellerophon receives the letter, and Stheneboea still gazes affectionately on him, is represented on several ancient painted vases.

Arriving at the Lycian court, Bellerophon was entertained hospitably for nine days. On the tenth day the king inquired the business of his guest, and received the letter of Prœtos. Acting on the instructions of the letter, Iobates despatched him with orders to slay the **Chimæra*** (a monster composed

---

* It was represented in art as a lion with a goat's head springing from

of a lion in front, a goat in the middle, and a serpent behind), which infested the mountains, and slaughtered all who attacked it. But Pegasos carried his master up in the air beyond the reach of the monster, and yet not too far for his spear to have deadly effect. (Plate XXXII.) Bellerophon returned triumphant. Though his scheme had not succeeded, the king had at any rate got rid of a terrible enemy to his subjects, and determined a second time to profit by the prowess of the young hero, if he should fail in causing his death. Accordingly he sent him to fight against the Solymi, a hostile neighbouring tribe, from which he again returned victorious. With like success he fought against the Amazons, those warlike women of Asia Minor, whom the ancient poets and artists delighted to represent as fighting stoutly against the best heroes of Greece, but always being vanquished. With this result they opposed, for example, Herakles and Theseus, and afterwards, in the Trojan war, took part against the Greeks. (See Plate XXXIII.) It would seem from their connection with the Ephesian Artemis, among other reasons, that the legends concerning them originated in the worship of the moon goddess.

In a last effort to secure the death of Bellerophon, the Lycian king planned an ambush for him of his bravest knights, all of whom, when the time came, perished at the hands of the hero, who, it then became clear, could be no other than the son of a god. Instead of being put to further encounters, he received the hand of the king's daughter in marriage, and with her the half of the kingdom. The grateful Lycians bestowed on him a large estate, well wooded and fitted for

---

its back. The statement of its spitting fire may have reference to the volcanic features of Lycia.

agriculture.   His wife bore him three blooming children:
Isandros, Hippolochos, and **Laodameia.**   In short, he
had reached the pinnacle of happiness.   But the gods prepared a catastrophe for him.   He became insane, and wandered about sad and alone, avoiding the company of men.
His son Isandros was slain by Ares, his daughter Laodameia,
by Artemis.   According to another report, repeated success
in hazardous adventures had inflamed him with the desire to
mount to Olympos on the back of his wonderful horse.   In
the attempt he fell to earth, smitten by the thunderbolt of
Zeus, and died.

(*c.*) THEBES.

It is a relief to turn from the bloodshed and perilous adventures of the Corinthian and Argive heroes, to the comparatively
tranquil tone of the Theban legends, with all their variety of
character and incident.   We would not be understood to say
that the tales of Thebes are free from horrors, but only that
the general impression left, especially by the earliest of them,
concerns the daring and achievements of mind rather than the
exploits of physical courage.

First among the heroes of Thebes is **Kadmos,** the founder
of the ancient city—the Kadmeia, as it was called—who, while
rendering important services to the population gathered round
him there in the management of their public affairs, is said to
have conferred on Greece generally an inestimable blessing in
the form of an alphabet, or means of communicating thoughts
in writing, previously unknown in that land.   It is this
alphabet, more or less modified, that we still employ.   That
he found the letters of it in use among the Phœnician traders
who visited Greece in remote early times, establishing factories

in many places,—among others, in the neighbourhood of Thebes,—is probable; but to believe, as the Greeks did, that Kadmos was a Phœnician by birth, and that the system of civilization which he introduced was, like the alphabet, Phœ· nician, was only another instance of the readiness with which the Greeks listened to stories that traced the beginnings of their civilization back to the influence of the more ancient nations of the East.

The genealogy of Kadmos, according to the legend, com· menced with the sea-god Poseidon and Libya, who had two sons—Belos (Baal) and Agenor; the former becoming king of Egypt, the latter of Phœnicia. By his wife, Telephassa, Agenor had one daughter—**Europa**—and three sons,—**Kadmos**, **Phœnix**, and **Kilix.** The sister having disappeared — carried off, it was said, on the back of a white bull, into which Zeus had transformed himself for love of her—the brothers were sent to search for her in different directions. Phœnix and Kilix, wearied of searching in vain, settled down in the countries named after them, while Kadmos, accompanied by his mother, proceeded through the Greek islands northwards to the coast of Thrace. There his mother died and was buried. He proceeded to Delphi, to ask the oracle concerning his sister. The advice was to search no longer, but to follow a cow which should come in his way, and where it lay down to rest there to found a city. Leaving Delphi, he saw a cow, and followed it through Bœotia, till it reached the place where Thebes was afterwards built, and there lay down. Intending to sacrifice the cow in honour of Athene, his protecting goddess, Kadmos sent his attendants to a fountain not far off to fetch water. It happened, however, that the fountain was watched by a terrible dragon, which killed his men. With

15

the aid of Athene, Kadmos slew the monster, and, at the command of the goddess, sowed its teeth in the ground, from which there instantly sprang a number of wild armed giants, called Spartæ. By throwing a stone among them, Kadmos so roused their passions that they fell upon each other with such fury and effect that only five of them survived. From these five the noblest families of Thebes afterwards traced their lineage.

To appease Ares, whose dragon he had slain, Kadmos was compelled to devote himself to the service of that god for eight years, or a "long year" as it was called, the usual period prescribed for penance in such cases. His term of service having expired, he was raised by Athene to the throne of Thebes; and to complete his happiness Zeus gave him **Harmonia**, the beautiful daughter of Ares and Aphrodite, for his wife. The gods of Olympos went to the marriage feast, and made presents to the pair. The Muses sang a marriage song. The gift of Kadmos to his wife consisted of a splendid dress (*peplos*), which Athene had worked for him, and the famous necklace made by Hephæstos. From the marriage sprang four daughters,—**Semele, Ino, Autonoë, Agaue,**—and one son,—**Polydoros.**

Autonoë married **Aristæos,** to whom she bore Aktæon, the young huntsman who, for the misfortune of having once seen Artemis bathing, was transformed into a stag, and devoured by his own hounds. Ino married **Athamas,** of whom it is said that, being seized of a frenzy, he pursued his wife to do her violence, and that she eluded him by leaping into the sea, after which she was regarded as a marine goddess under the name of **Leukothea.** Semele became the mother of the wine-god Dionysos, and at the birth of her child was, as has been already related, struck dead by the thunderbolt of Zeus. Agaue, marrying **Echion**, one of the five surviving Spartæ, became the mother of **Pentheus**, who, after the death of Polydoros, succeeded to the sovereignty of Thebes.

Semele being dead, her statement that Zeus himself was the father of her child was disbelieved by her sisters, especially by Agaue. But after her son Dionysos had grown up, and returned to Thebes from his triumphant journey eastward to India, Agaue and the other women of Thebes changed their minds, and embraced his worship with its extravagant rites. Pentheus, then king of Thebes, opposed the introduction of the new religion, but in the course of his opposition was slain by his mother and her excited companions. **Labdakos**, the son of Polydoros, succeeded to the throne. Meantime Agaue, recovering her senses under the affliction, fled to Illyrium.

Grief at the calamities that fell so thickly on their children at last drove Kadmos and Harmonia from Thebes. They wandered to Illyrium, and there found peace in the grave. Their bodies, it was believed, had been transformed into two snakes that lay beside their tomb, while their spirits had been placed in Elysion by Zeus.

After Kadmos, the next figures of importance are the twin-brothers **Amphion** and **Zethos**, who resemble in many respects the "great twin-brethren" Castor and Pollux, being like them represented riding on white horses, and appearing with aid in times of distress. Between the two brothers there was a great difference of character, Amphion being devoted to music, and excelling in the skill with which he played the lyre given him by Hermes, while Zethos applied himself wholly to rough life, such as hunting and herding. What Zethos did by physical force, Amphion accomplished by the persuasion of his strains, as was shown in the case of their building the walls of Thebes, the population of which had so far outgrown the limits of the old town founded by Kadmos as to require new barriers against invasion. While Zethos toiled in bringing huge stones for this purpose, Amphion, like Orpheus, had only to strike his lyre, and still larger stones followed whither he led the way. Such was the story, the intention of which seems to have originally been to point to the combination of actual strength with harmony in placing the blocks required in good masonry. The same idea recurs in the legend of the building of the Trojan walls by Apollo and Poseidon, the former god corresponding to Amphion and the latter to Zethos. The seven gates of Thebes answered to the seven strings of the lyre.

The mother of the two Theban brothers was **Antiope**, who, according to an early report, was a daughter of the river-god Asopos. In the usual genealogy, however, she was described as a daughter of **Thebe** and **Nykteus** (the "dark and stormy"), who held the office of regent in Thebes during the minority of Labdakos. Zeus having approached Antiope in the form of a Satyr, she was driven from her father's house, and forced to seek refuge, which she found with **Epopeus**, the king of Sikyon. Under his protection she remained some time, the father meanwhile demanding in vain that she should be given up to him. Ultimately she was given up to **Lykos** ("light") the brother of Nykteus, but, as his name implies, of quite an opposite character. Returning with him, she gave birth to twin boys on the way, in the neighbourhood of Eleutheræ. The infants were entrusted to a herdsman to be brought up. The mother was carried off to Thebes, where, as a contrast to the gentle treatment she had experienced from Lykos, she was subjected by his wife, **Dirke**, to relentless cruelty. After enduring continued persecution for some years, Antiope fled from Thebes, and taking the direction of Mount Kithæron, where her children had been left, at last reached the house of the herdsman who had taken care of them. She did not, however, recognize him, nor was she aware that the two youths, who took kindly to her, were her sons. It happened just then that Dirke, who had come to Mount Kithæron to take part in some Bacchic ceremony, detected her escaped victim, and ordered the two young herdsmen to fetch a wild bull from their herd, and to bind her to its horns, that she might be dragged to death. They would have obeyed her command, had not the old herdsman at the moment recognized Antiope, and revealed her as their mother. On hearing the story of her former troubles, Amphion and Zethos, in their indignation, seized Dirke, bound her to the bull which they had brought, and looked on while she perished miserably. The legend adds that Dirke was transformed into a fountain, which bore her name.

On the return of Antiope with her sons to Thebes, Lykos abdicated in their favour, and then commenced the building of the walls, of which we have already spoken. Amphion married **Niobe**, the daughter of the Lydian king Tantalos, and had a family of sons and daughters, whose beauty, in their mother's eyes, might measure with that of Apollo and Artemis. How she was punished for her pride has already been related. After the death of Amphion and Zethos, caused, it was said, by the arrows of Apollo, the sovereignty of Thebes finally passed to Labdakos, of whose reign little is said, his fame consisting chiefly in his being the father of **Laios** and grandfather of **Œdipos.**

This Laios married **Jokaste,** a daughter of Menoikeus, and

had by her a son, Œdipos.   An oracle had said that the child,
on growing to manhood, would cause the death of his father.
To avert this danger, Laios exposed the newly-born infant on
Mount Kithæron, expecting it to perish.   It was, however,
found by some herdsmen, conveyed by them to Corinth, and
there given over to the king, **Polybos,** whose wife was childless, and took readily to the castaway.   Arriving at years of
manhood, Œdipos inquired at an oracle concerning his parentage, and was told in reply to avoid the lands of his ancestors,
for otherwise he would cause his father's death, and thereafter
marry his own mother.   Puzzled by an answer so mysterious,
and being uncertain whether Polybos might not have been his
father, he left the court at Corinth, and wandered about the
country.   In the course of his wanderings he met Laios tra-
velling with a retinue.   A quarrel arose between Œdipos and
some of the royal attendants.   Laios took the part of his men,
and was slain in the fight by his son, who, unaware of the
blackness of the crime he had committed, proceeded on his
way to Thebes.   There he found great distress prevailing, in
consequence of the loss of life caused by a **Sphinx**—a monster with the body of a lion, and the head, breast, and arms
of a woman.   This creature had a riddle which she propounded
to all who approached her, and on their failing to resolve it,
as always happened, threw them from the high rock where she
lived.   Not so Œdipos, who read the riddle rightly; upon
which the Sphinx cast herself from the rock, and perished.
The prize offered to the man who should succeed in getting
rid of the Sphinx was the hand of Jokaste, the widow of Laios,
along with the throne of Thebes.   Œdipos married her, and
fulfilled the oracle.

They had two sons, **Eteokles** and **Polyneikes,** and two

daughters, **Antigone** and **Ismene**, neither being aware of the criminality of their marriage, until, on inquiring at the oracle the cause of certain misfortunes that had befallen the country, they received an answer which revealed the facts in all their horror.   Jokaste slew herself, while Œdipos, after putting out his eyes, forsook Thebes, and wandered about accompanied by his faithful daughter, Antigone.   His two sons succeeded him in the government, quarrelled with each other, however, and ultimately fell, both of them, in a personal encounter, as we shall relate afterwards.

The various acts of this terrible tragedy were reproduced on the Athenian stage with all the poetic power of Æschylus and Sophocles.

(*d.*) THESSALY.

In harmony with the wild, rocky features of the country, the early legends of Thessaly tell of furious wars, in which the combatants fought with trunks of trees, or hurled rocks and even hills at each other.   It was there that the war of the gods against the Giants and Titans took place.   There the brothers Otos and Ephialtes heaped hill on mountain in their ambition to scale the heavens.   There Poseidon cleft the mountain-range asunder with his trident, and formed the pleasant vale of Tempe.   Mount Olympos, with its clouded summit, where the gods were once supposed to dwell, was there, and there also was Iolkos, the seat of the ancient race of the Minyæ. Gryton was the hold of the **Lapithæ**, and the scene of those combats between them and the **Centaurs** which formed in after times so attractive a subject to Greek sculptors.

Among the Lapithæ the two principal figures are **Ixion** and his son **Peirithöos**.   Ixion's wife was **Dia**, a daughter of **Deioneus.** Previous to the marriage he had promised her father, according to ancient usage, many valuable presents, which he afterwards refused to give. Deioneus endeavoured to indemnify himself, but in the course of the attempt perished in a great hole, full of fire, which had been cunningly prepared for him by Ixion. For this—the first murder of a relation, it was believed, that had taken place in the world—Ixion was punished with frenzy, and wandered about, unable to obtain expiation from gods or men, till at last Zeus received him compassionately, and purified him. But the purification was not so complete as to prevent him from conceiving a passion for the goddess Hera, who, knowing his desires, deceived him with a cloud shaped like herself. From this union sprang the race of Centaurs. Ixion, being blind enough to boast of his supposed success with Hera, was despatched by Zeus to Tartaros, and there bound by Hermes to a winged wheel, which constantly revolved, as an eternal example of the punishment due to such crime.

The same passion for a goddess descended to his son Peirithöos, who tried to carry off Persephone from Hades, for which he was placed in chains in Tartaros. But the event on which his fame chiefly turns was his marriage with **Deidamia.** By his invitation, the Centaurs of the neighbouring mountains went to the banquet, and, being unused to the influence of wine, could not suppress excitement. The wild **Eurytion** laid hold of the bride, his fellows rushed towards her maidens, and a scene of grand confusion took place; Peirithöos and the Lapithæ, with the help of his friend **Theseus,** from Attica, at last succeeding in driving the Centaurs away.

Of Kaineus, another of the Lapithæ, it is related that, having been originally a beautiful virgin, she was changed into a man by Poseidon, and made invulnerable, as was proved in a fight with the Centaurs; for, in spite of the rocks and trunks of trees which they struck him with, and heaped above him, he remained unwounded, and sank into the earth alive,—a scene represented in several ancient works of sculpture and vase-painting still in existence.

With regard to the Centaurs, the usual form in which they were represented was that of the body and legs of a horse, with the head, arms, and body of a man down to the waist. In early works of art, however, they have the legs of a man in place of the forelegs of the horse.

Cheiron seems to have had nothing in common with them but his form; for he was wise and just, well-meaning and kindly, a friend of gods and heroes, and skilled in medicine, music, and various arts. The young Achilles was brought up under his care and tuition, in the cave where he lived, on Mount Pelion. So also were Jason and Asklepios. He was the friend of Peleus and of Herakles, and his death was an example of the self-sacrifice which had characterized his life. In trying to make peace between Herakles and the Centaurs, he had been accidentally hit by a poisoned arrow from the bow of Herakles. The wound baffling all his skill, and causing acute pain, he offered himself to die in the room of Prometheus, and was accepted by the gods.

(e.) THRACE.

The burden of all the early Thracian legends is the strange divine influence of music and song. Whether the passion for music, which may be supposed to have given rise to the legends, originated among the ungenial northern hills and valleys of Thrace, or whether, as is supposed, it was transplanted thither by immigrants from the district of Pieria, with its ancient fountain of the Muses, it would be hard to decide. All that is certain is, that the belief concerning **Orpheus,** the principal figure in these legends, was common to both regions.

Orpheus was regarded as a son of the muse Kalliope and the god Apollo. From his mother he inherited the fascinating power with which he played the lyre and sang, so that the birds of the air, the fish in the streams, wild beasts, even trees, rocks, and hills, gathered round him to listen. The subject of his song was always the beautiful **Eurydike,** whom he had loved and lost. She had died through the poisoned bite of a snake that lurked in the grass over which she had to run to escape from **Aristæos,** who also loved her. Her sister nymphs, accompanied by Orpheus, wandered over the hills and valleys, filling the air with plaintive strains to call her back again. Orpheus carried his search for her even down to the gloomy shades of the lower world, the sweetness of his music soothing the monsters and wicked spirits that dwell there, and otherwise would have resisted his progress. Even the hardened hearts of Persephone and the merciless Erinys were touched by his passionate grief. It was agreed that Eurydike should be permitted to return with him to the upper world,—the only condition attached to the agreement being that he should not turn to look upon her face all the way back. His patience, however, gave way. The bargain became null, and Eurydike must instantly retrace her steps, and be lost to him for ever. For seven months he sat in doleful mood by the banks of the river Strymon, under the open sky, refusing food or drink. Then he withdrew to the higher wintry regions of the mountains

Rhodope and Hæmos, to nurse his sorrow in greater solitude, but was discovered by a band of Mænads out upon some wild Bacchic mission, and torn by them limb from limb. The Muses, it was said, gathering the limbs, conveyed them to Pieria, on Mount Olympos, and buried them there. His head and lyre floated down the Hebros, and were carried by the sea, the lyre sounding sweetly with the swell and fall of the waves, to the island of Lesbos, celebrated in after times for its poets and musicians. There the head was buried, and nightingales sang sweeter beside it than elsewhere in Greece. But in Thrace also a tomb was pointed out as being that of Orpheus, while a sanctuary was established in his honour.

In later times a religious system with mysterious rites and ceremonies, said to have been instituted by Orpheus, and bearing his name, was widely propagated in Greece. It may be that his connection with the worship of Dionysos, referred to in the legends both of Pieria and Thrace, was regarded as sufficient warrant for associating with his name religious institutions having much in common with the Dionysiac mysteries.

It is said that Orpheus accompanied the expedition of the Argonauts, but at what period of his life we do not know.

To the same region of Thrace belongs the legend of **Thamyris,** a son of the king **Philammon** and the nymph **Argiope,** distinguished for his personal beauty as well as his minstrelsy. He was, however, inordinately vain, and on the occasion of a visit to the court of **Eurytos,** at Œchalia, boasted himself not inferior to the Muses themselves, the daughters of Zeus. But on his way homeward he was met by them ; they put his eyes out, and took away his power of song and music.

(ƒ.) ATTICA.

The people of Attica, generally speaking, believed that their first ancestors had sprung from the earth, and by some process been transformed from trees or rocks, or perhaps from animals, into men and women. The change was not supposed to have been direct and instantaneous, as we may infer from the form ascribed to **Kekrops,** the first of the race, which was that of a man with extremities in the shape of snakes in place of human legs. In later times of learned speculation this Kekrops was thought to have been an immigrant from Egypt. Proofs of an early immigration into Attica are certainly not wanting, but they do not point to Egypt as the source of it. They point to Crete, which in the time of **Minos** held Attica, as it probably held other places, as a dependency.

Kekrops according to the legend, ruled as king over the primitive race of Attica, established himself on the Acropolis of Athens, and gathered a township round him, which he called Kekropia. He gave his people laws, and taught them to worship Zeus and Athene-Polias. It was during his reign that the celebrated contest took place between Poseidon and Athene for the control of Attica. Kekrops was chosen to decide, and, arguing that the sea was common to all, while the olive was peculiarly adapted to the soil of his country, gave his decision in favour of the goddess. He had three daughters,—**Hersē, Aglauros,** and **Pandrosos,**—all three names apparently referring to the fertilizing fall of dew. The last mentioned was the first priestess of Athene. Of the other two, Hersē became the mother of **Keryx,** from whom the priestly family of heralds in Attica derived their lineage. His father was Hermes, the divine herald. Aglauros bore a daughter to the god Ares. Her name was **Alkippe,** and her story, that she loved **Halirrhotios,** a son of Poseidon, and was slain by Ares. For that crime a court called the **Areopagus** was appointed to try the god, and continued thereafter to sit on cases of murder.

The successor of Kekrops was **Erichthonios,** who was described as being altogether of the form of a snake. He was the offspring of Hephæstos and Gaea, was the fondling of Athene, and when he obtained the throne of Attica, taught his people to worship the ancient wooden image of the goddess, and instituted in her honour the famous Panathenaic games. The story of his infancy was that Athene handed him in a closed box to the three daughters of Kekrops, with orders not to open it. Two of the sisters, Herse and Aglauros, yielded to curiosity, opened the box, and on seeing a snake within, were seized with frantic terror and threw themselves from the rocks of the Acropolis. Erichthonios was brought up within the sanctuary of the goddess.

Erichthonios was succeeded by his son **Pandion,** and he again by his son **Erechtheus,** with whom the dynasty of the line of Kekrops came to an end, passing over to Ion, a reputed son of Apollo, and the ancestor of the Ionian race. Erechtheus and all his family perished in a battle against **Eumolpos,** the prince of Eleusis. The result of their death, however, was that the old strife between Attica and Eleusis was put an end to, and the two kingdoms united in one.

Besides his son Erechtheus, Pandion had two daughters, **Prokne** and **Philomela,** of whom a touching story is told. It would seem that in the course of a war with Labdakos of Thebes, Pandion had obtained important assistance from **Tereus,** a king of Thrace, and for this offered him the hand

of his daughter Prokne.   Afterwards the Thracian desired her
sister also, and, pretending that Prokne was dead, obtained
Philomela as his wife.   To prevent the former from revealing
the truth, he tore out her tongue, and placed her in a cage in a
wood.   But his end was not thus gained; for Prokne con-
trived to send her sister a piece of drapery on which she had
embroidered a representation of the facts, which her sister
readily understood.   The two sisters then combined to execute a terrible revenge on Tereus, placing the flesh of his son
Itys, whom they killed, before him as a dish.   Tereus drew
his sword, and pursued the sisters till all three were changed
into birds—he into a lapwing, Prokne into a swallow, and
Philomela into a nightingale.   The Latin poets reversed the
story of the two sisters, saying that it was Philomela whose
tongue was cut out, their object being, since her name is the
same as that of the nightingale, to account for the silence of
that bird except in the springtime.

The Attic legend of **Boreas**, the wind-god, who carried off
Oreithyia, has already been given, as has also that of Kephalos and Prokris.   We shall therefore pass on to **Ion**, who,
when the male line of Kekrops had become extinct, succeeded
to the throne of Attica.

Ion was a son of Apollo and **Kreusa**, a daughter of Erechtheus, and at his birth was taken away from his mother, who
afterwards married **Xuthos**, and remained childless.   Going
to Delphi to consult the oracle about their prospects of posterity, Xuthos and Kreusa were told by the god to adopt as
their son the first youth they should meet.   This happened to
be Ion, who had been brought up in the temple of Delphi,
and who, agreeably to the command of the god, was adopted
by the childless pair.

According to another legend, Pandion was driven from Attica by the sons of **Metion**, and took refuge with **Pylos**, the king of Megara, where he found and adopted Ægeus, who, after Pandion's death, advanced upon Attica, and, with the assistance of his brothers, Pallas, Nisos, and Lykos, recovered the kingdom of his adopted father, reigned in Athens, and became the father of the renowned hero, Theseus, whose exploits we shall relate hereafter.

(*g.*) CRETE.

The position of the island of Crete, its extent and fertility, appear to have attracted the early Phœnician traders to its shores. They founded the towns of Knosos and Gortys, and so developed the resources of the island as to give it a powerful ascendency over the other islands of the Archipelago, and extending to various districts of the mainland of Greece, including Attica, as has just been said. They introduced the worship of Astarte and Moloch; and when, generations afterwards, the island had become completely Hellenized, through the successive immigrations of Achæans and Dorians, there were still found current among the people legends that could only be explained in connection with the religion of the Phœnicians. Of this kind were the legends of **Talos, Itanos,** and the river **Jardanos.** The Greek immigrants settled in the towns that had been planted by the Phœnicians, adapting themselves to existing arrangements, it appears, and accepting the ancient traditions of the island as a basis for legends of a purely Greek construction.

These legends commence with **Europa,** whom Zeus saw and loved while she was gathering spring buds near Sidon, where her father, Agenor (or Phœnix, as some said), was king. The god, transforming himself into a white bull, carried her off on his back over the sea towards the south coast of Crete, and landed with her in the district of Gortys and Phæstos, where **Asterion** was then the reigning king. Europa gave birth there to three sons,—**Minos, Rhadamanthys,** and **Sarpedon,**—who grew up under the care of Asterion, to whom Zeus had commended their mother. How familiar the people of the island must have been with the various phases of this legend, may be seen from the ancient coins of Gortys and Phæstos, with their representations, now of a bull alone, now of Europa riding on him, and at other times of Europa seated among the branches of a plane-tree.

The oldest traditions describe Minos as ruling the island with exemplary justice, extending its maritime power and its supremacy over the neighbouring islands and countries. He established among his people a wise system of laws, which formed, it was believed, in after times, the basis of the legislation of Lykurgos. These laws, he said, were communicated to him by his father, Zeus, with whom he went every ninth year to hold communion in a sacred cave in the island. So high was his reputation for justice, that when he died, so people thought, he was appointed a judge in the lower world.

The wife of Minos was **Pasiphäe,** a daughter of the sungod **Helios** and **Perseis.** It is necessary to bear her parentage in mind for the sake of obtaining a right clue to the explanation of the legend concerning her. For, as a daughter of Helios and Perseis, she may well have been originally a goddess of the moon, and as such represented under the form of a white cow. Her name, Pasiphäe, would be appropriate for such an office. She bore to Minos two daughters—**Ariadne** and **Phædra**—of whom more will be told hereafter.

Minos, it was said, on being chosen king of the island, proceeded to the sea-shore to offer, in presence of his people, a sacrifice to his father, Zeus, calling on the sea-god Poseidon to send up a victim for that purpose from the sea. Poseidon heard, and sent a shimmering white bull. In this act of compliance on the part of the sea-god, Minos perceived that his supremacy at sea was secured. Instead, however, of sacrificing the white bull, he placed it among his own herd which browsed near Gortys—a herd which is elsewhere said to have belonged to the sun-god. Poseidon, taking offence at the deceit, caused the bull to become wild, and at the same time inflamed the queen, Pasiphäe, with an unnatural desire towards it. The bull broke from his stall, and was pursued by Pasiphäe over hills and through woods, till finally the great artist **Dædalos** succeeded in holding him to the meadow, and in satisfying the desires of the queen, who afterwards gave birth to **Minotauros,** a creature with the body and limbs of a man, and the head of a bull. Dædalos had now to employ his skill in making a vast **labyrinth,** with intricate winding passages, from which no one who entered could find his way out. Within it Minotauros was placed, and received as victims the persons sent to Minos periodically by tributary states. Such tribute, consisting of seven boys and seven girls of noble families, Minos had levied on Athens as a satisfaction for the murder of his son **Androgeos** by Ægeus, the king of Attica. Every eight years the grievous levy was despatched to Crete, till **Theseus,** the son of Ægeus, put an end to it in a manner which we shall afterwards have occasion to relate.

Minos met his death at Agrigentum, in Sicily, whither he
16

had pursued Dædalos, who had escaped from the labyrinth, into which he and his son **Ikaros** had been thrown for making a figure of a cow for Pasiphäe, so lifelike as to be mistaken by the herd. He had escaped by means of wings which he had made for himself and his son. The latter fell into the sea, and was drowned, while his father, reaching Sicily in safety, was received under the protection of King Kokalos, whose daughter killed Minos by pouring boiling water on his head while he was in a bath. Minos was buried there, and had a tomb erected in his memory.

On the coins of the town of Phæstos is the figure of a youth, winged and nude, rushing with great strides, and holding what appears to be a stone in each hand. This figure has been identified with the legends of **Talos,** who is described as having been made of bronze, a remnant of the bronze age, or, as others said, a living work of art produced by Hephæstos. Hè had been placed in Crete by Zeus, to watch over Europa, his duty being to run round the island three times a day, and see who landed on the coast. When the Argonauts arrived, he opposed their landing, but unsuccessfully ; for it happened that they were aware of the fact that, though apparently altogether made of bronze, he still had a vein reaching from neck to heel, and containing his life-blood. This vein Pœas, the father of Philoktetes, managed to hit with an arrow from the famous bow of Herakles. Talos fell, and died. Others said that Medea, who accompanied the Argonauts, overcame him by witchcraft. It had been the practice of Talos, when he caught any one landing on the coast, to seize his victim in his arms, to leap with him into a fire, and press him to his burning bosom, the while laughing at the pain. This was the origin of the phrase "Sardonic laughter."

Though the appointment of **Rhadamanthys** as a judge in the lower world was said to have been due to the sense of justice which he had displayed on earth, the region or country that benefited by his decisions is not given. It may be right to assume that he acted with his brother Minos in Crete. **Sarpedon,** the third of the brothers, passed over to Lycia, and there became the founder of an illustrious line of heroes.

(*h.*) ELIS AND ARGOS.

With **Pelops** commences a lineage of heroes famous in Elis and Argos for their deeds of violence, and for the retribution that awaited them. How Niobe, the sister of Pelops, was punished for her pride, we have already seen. What his father, Tantalos, had to endure in Tartaros has also been described. Tantalos had ruled his kingdom of Phrygia, in Asia Minor, well, and on that account gained the esteem of the gods, who invited him to a banquet. But he betrayed their secrets, and, to crown all, invited them to a feast, at which, to test their power of knowing all things that happened, he set before them the flesh of his own son Pelops. The gods, perceiving the outrageous attempt, restored the child to life, giving him in place of the shoulder that had been eaten, whether by Demeter or Thetis, a shoulder of ivory. His father was despatched to Tartaros.

When Pelops had grown to manhood under the care of the gods—especially of Poseidon, from whom he learned his skill in managing horses—he resolved to win **Hippodameia,** the daughter of the king of Elis, **Œnomaos,** a son of Ares, and the owner of horses swift as the wind. The story was that Œnomaos had been informed by an oracle that his death would be caused by the husband of his daughter. Trusting to the extraordinary speed of his horses, he freely offered his daughter's hand to any suitor who should outstrip him in a chariot race. Those who failed, it was stipulated in the challenge, should perish at his hands. This fate had befallen many an ardent suitor previous to the arrival of Pelops, who, with a golden chariot and winged horses, given him by Poseidon, won the race. It is said, however, that his success was rather due to Hippodameia, who had conceived a great love for the youth, and gave practical effect to her passion by bribing her father's charioteer, **Myrtilos,** to take a spoke out of his master's wheel.

With the hand of Hippodameia, Pelops obtained the throne of Elis, and had, among other children, two sons, named **Atreus** and **Thyestes.** He established, or at least greatly promoted, the Olympian games. His grave, the house of Œnomaos, and other monuments of his excellent rule, were afterwards gratefully pointed to at Olympia.

Atreus and Thyestes, having slain the beautiful young Chrysippos, a son of Pelops and a nymph, were compelled to leave Elis. They found refuge in Mykenæ, establishing themselves in the old fort of Midea, until the death of Eurystheus, when Atreus obtained the government of Mykenæ, the ruins of which still attest the power of its ancient kings. Atreus married a daughter of Minos—Ærope—who allowed herself to listen to proposals from Thyestes, and assisted him to carry off the ram with the golden fleece, the possession of which was supposed to secure the government of the country. But Zeus interfered in the cause of Atreus, the elder of the brothers, and, as a sign of his will, caused the sun to rise in the west. Thyestes returned to his brother's house, asking to be forgiven, and was received with an appearance of good-will. Instead of being forgiven, however, he was presented, on sitting down to eat, with the flesh of his own son. Thyestes fled in horror, and thereupon famine stalked over the land. On consulting an oracle with regard to the famine, Atreus was told to find Thyestes, and take him back. He did so, and moreover placed him in confinement in Argos, at the same time trying to persuade Ægisthos, the son of Thyestes, to kill his father. But events took a different course, Thyestes preferring to make a victim of Atreus. On the death of Atreus, Agamemnon succeeded to the throne of Argos, and his brother Menelaos to that of Sparta. Of these two brothers more shall be said in connection with the war against Troy.

HERAKLES.

(PLATE XXX.)

Though regarded sometimes as a god, and honoured in the way appointed for immortals, it was chiefly as the hero of a long series of arduous labours, difficulties apparently insurmountable, and sufferings, that Herakles obtained the numerous honours paid to his memory throughout Greece. In the gymnasia, where the youth of every town were instructed in athletic exercises, the statue of Herakles was pointed to as a model of what a perfect athlete should be; while the tales of his wrestling with this or that giant were repeated as examples of fearlessness and extraordinary strength. Soldiers going to battle thought of his fatigues and ultimate triumphs. Labourers oppressed by toil relieved their sorrows by recalling the laborious incidents of his life. Even the Athenians valued the rugged, stubborn endurance of Herakles higher than the litheness and more perfect form of their own Theseus. So far,

Herakles was looked upon merely as an example of extraordinary physical strength and patient toiling to the end; but in
later times he came also to be held up as an ideal of virtue
and duty, in which capacity a story invented by the sophist
Prodikos concerning him, found great applause. That story
was entitled " The Choice of Herakles," and represented him
as being met at a crossway, while yet a youth, by two figures
—Pleasure and Duty—the one promising him all possible enjoyments, the other a life of labour and trouble, if he would
follow her. He chose to follow Duty.

According to the genealogy, Herakles was a son of **Zeus**
and **Alkmene**, the wife of **Amphitryon**, a descendant of
Perseus, and resident in Thebes. On the day on which he
was to have been born, **Hera**, to whose persecution all the
labours and sufferings of Herakles in after life were due, obtained from Zeus, in presence of the assembled gods, a vow
that the boy to be born on that day should have power and
dominion over all that dwelt about him. Hastening to Argos,
she lent a helping hand to the wife of Sthenelos, and enabled
her to give birth to Eurystheus, a weakly seven-months' child.
Meantime she had delayed the birth of Herakles, who, in
consequence, became the subject of Eurystheus. With all
this hostility on the part of Hera, it is curious to compare a
scene which not unfrequently occurs on ancient painted vases,
representing Hera sucking the infant Herakles. The story
was that Hermes, at the command of Zeus, had carried the
newly-born child to Olympos, and put it to Hera's breast,
without her knowing whose child it was. From this divine
milk Herakles drew his godlike strength, the first promise of
which was given soon after his birth, by his strangling the
serpent sent by Hera to kill him.

His youth was spent under the instruction of the most celebrated heroes of the day, the wise Rhadamanthys teaching
him to be wise and virtuous, and Linos the practice of music.
Unluckily, Linos had to punish him for some neglect, and in
doing so enraged the boy so much, that he turned and slew his
master. For this Amphitryon carried his son away to the
hills, and left him under the care of herdsmen, with whom,
like Romulus, or Amphion and Zethos, he enjoyed a wild life
of hunting and exposure to climate, his limbs growing to enormous size, and his eyes sparkling with unusual fire. At the
age of eighteen he slew an enormous lion that infested Mount
Kithæron, destroying the flocks of his father, Amphitryon, and
of Thespios, the king of Thespiæ. Returning to Thebes from
the lion-hunt, and wearing its skin hanging from his shoulders
as a sign of his success, he met the heralds of the king of the
Minyæ, coming from Orchomenos to claim the annual tribute
of a hundred cattle levied on Thebes. Herakles cut off the
ears and noses of the heralds, bound their hands, and sent
them home. A war followed, in which Amphitryon and his
two sons, Herakles and Iphikles, did wonders on the part of
Thebes, and were duly honoured for the same.

But the part taken by Herakles in that war was the last act
of his own free will; for Hera, annoyed at the fast-rising fame
of the young hero, persuaded Eurystheus to exercise the au-
thority given him at his birth by Zeus, and to call on Herakles to enter his service. Herakles inquired at the Delphic
oracle whether it was possible to escape the summons, but was
told in reply that he must carry out successfully twelve tasks
to be imposed on him by Eurystheus, and that, having done
so, he would be reckoned among the number of immortals. With this answer in his mind, he presented himself to

Eurystheus at Mykenæ, and commenced the serious labour
of life.

THE TWELVE LABOURS OF HERAKLES.

It may be, as has been often suggested, that the legend of
the labours of Herakles, like those of Perseus in the service of
Polydektes, or of Bellerophon in that of the Lycian king, or
of Siegfried in that of the king of Burgundy, was intended to
convey an illustration of the course and operations of the sun.
His first labours are performed near home, the distance from
which increases with each new labour that is imposed, till at
last, after carrying off the golden apples of the Hesperides in
the remote west, he descends to the lower world, and brings
back with him the hated dog Cerberus.   In later times the
twelve labours were openly brought into connection with the
twelve signs of the zodiac.   It is, however, more likely that,
originally, this number had no more signification than in the
case of the twelve higher deities of Olympos, that it was
adopted by the poets, such as Pisander and Stesichoros, who
first made these labours their theme, and that through their
influence it became stereotyped both in poetry and art.   In
Homer, though the labours are known, there is no mention
of their number.   In the Iliad (v. 395) Herakles is the hero
whose unerring arrows wounded Hera and Hades.   In the
Odyssey (viii. 224) Herakles and Eurytos are described as
the most celebrated marksmen of bygone times; and in early
works of art, it is his character as a bowman that is principally
represented.   But after the time of Pisander and Stesichoros,
a change is introduced.   The club becomes his favourite weapon; and instead of a linen garment wrapped round his loins,

he now appears either carrying the skin of the Nemean lion over his arm, or wearing it hanging down his back—the skin of its head fitting to his crown like a cap, and the fore-legs knotted under his chin.

1. *The Nemean lion*, the offspring of Typhon and Echidna, had been sent by Hera to devastate the neighbourhood of Nemea, and had succeeded, to the horror of the natives. What made the matter worse, was that the plain of Nemea was sacred to Zeus. The lion was known to be invulnerable,—proof even against the arrows of Herakles. It was therefore necessary to adopt novel means for its destruction. Herakles entered the cave where its lair was, closed the entrance behind him, and at once grappling the monster in his arms strangled it. The skin he tore off with his fingers, and, knowing it to be impenetrable, resolved to wear it henceforth in his own defence. To the legend as it thus stands was added, by the Alexandrian and Roman poets, the story of Molorchos, a native of the district, on whom Herakles called on his way to the cave, and who, when about to kill his only goat to make a feast for his guest, was told by the hero to desist and to wait his return. It was arranged that should he not return within thirty days Molorchos was to sacrifice to him as to a dead person. The thirty days had just elapsed when Herakles returned and found his friend in the act of preparing the sacrifice. It is possible that the thirty days may refer to the period of greatest heat in summer, when the lion and dog are ascendant.

2. *The Lernean hydra*, also the offspring of Typhon and Echidna, and sent by Hera. Herakles killed it with his sword, being assisted in the enterprise by Iolaos and Athene. The legend is given more fully by Apollodorus, whose version, though late, is proved to have been founded on an earlier form

of it by the remains of poetry and art of high antiquity. The *hydra* was a monster with nine heads, of which eight were mortal and the ninth invulnerable. It lived in the marshy ground beside the fountain of Amymone, and even the smell which spread from its poison was fatal to any one who passed near it. Herakles arrived at the spot in a chariot, attended by Iolaos, and succeeded in driving the hydra from its hole by firing his arrows in upon it. The fight began, and Herakles found that for every head of it which he cut two fresh heads started up, and to increase the difficulty a huge crab came and seized him by the heel. It was necessary to try another form of attack. Herakles ordered Iolaos to set the neighbouring wood on fire and to fetch him a brand from it; with the brand so obtained he proceeded, the moment he had cut off a head, to burn it up, and in this way destroying them one by one, he at last came to the invulnerable head, cut it off also, and buried it under a huge rock. He dipped his arrows in the poison of the hydra. When his success was reported to Eurystheus, the latter refused to reckon it as one of the labours, on the ground that Iolaos had rendered assistance. The interpretation of the legend is that the hydra or water-snake is a symbol of the horrors of a marshy district, and that its poison, with its fatal smell, represents the miasma which arises from such districts.

3. *The Erymanthian boar,* like the Keryneian stag and the Stymphalian Birds, carries us to a mountainous and wild rustic scene. Its haunt was on Mount Erymanthos, in the north of Arcadia. But the name of Erymanthos was also applied to a stream which flowed down the mountain side; and it is not improbable that the wild boar was only a legendary illustration of the ravages produced in winter and early spring by the descent of this river with swollen torrents. The orders of

Eurystheus were that the boar should be brought back alive to Mykenæ; but at the sight of Herakles returning with it alive on his shoulders, fear took possession of the king, and he hid himself in a large bronze vessel, into which Herakles, as frequently represented on ancient vases, proceeded to put the boar, as the safest possible place. The consternation of Eurystheus may be imagined. In connection with the capture of the boar is told the story of a visit which Herakles paid on his way to the Centaur, Pholos, who lived in a cave on Mount Pholoe. The hero was hungry, and Pholos gave him to eat. He was also thirsty, and required some wine. Now Pholos had at hand a large vase full of choice wine, but it was the common property of the Centaurs who lived in other parts of the mountain. On the other hand the wine had been a present from Dionysos, and had been accompanied with the command that it should not be opened till his good friend Herakles arrived. Pholos accordingly had no hesitation in tapping the vase, and both drank freely from it. The strong aroma of the wine, however, reached the nostrils of the other Centaurs, who now flocked towards the cave of Pholos in wild confusion, armed with pine branches, rocks, axes, and torches, and fell upon Herakles. A violent fight ensued, in which Herakles, besides with superior numbers, had also to contend with the disadvantages of a flood of water sent by the clouds, who were the mothers of the Centaurs. Ultimately he succeeded in wounding many, and dispersing the others into the woods,—the only melancholy part of the issue being that his friend Pholos lost his life, under circumstances which remind us of the death of that other kindly Centaur, Chiron, who lived on Mount Pelion, and brought up Achilles. Pholos was stooping over a Centaur who had fallen by an arrow from

Herakles, and after drawing out the arrow, was wondering how so small a thing could produce such an effect, when it fell from his hands, and striking severely on his foot, its poison entered his body and he died. The legend appears to have been popular both with poets and vase painters.

4. *The Keryneian stag*, an animal of wonderful fleetness, with antlers of gold and hoofs of brass, was sacred to Artemis, to whom it had been dedicated by Taygete, one of the Pleiads. It took its name from the hill and hunting district of Keryneia, on the borders of Arcadia and Achaia; at other times it was called the Mænalian stag. The task imposed on Herakles was to capture and bring it back alive. The chase lasted for a whole year, Herakles pursuing it over hills and plains, ravines and meadows, on to the Hyperborean region, and thence back to where it had started among the Arcadian hills. It sought shelter in the sanctuary of Artemis, but being dislodged was overtaken by Herakles at the banks of the river Ladon. He would have slain it had not Apollo and Artemis appeared on the scene. The stag running a whole year on to the regions of the Hyperboreans, and thence returning to where it had set out, appears to be a mythical illustration of the course of the moon, and may be compared with the much simpler story of the huntress Arge—the "shimmering being" who pursued a stag, crying out, "I will catch you should your speed equal that of Helios;" for which boast the angry god transformed her into a deer.

5. *The Stamphalian birds.* The vale of Stamphalos, lying among the mountains in such a way as to be constantly exposed to the floods and storms of winter, was described in a mythical form as being subject to the ravages of a numberless flock of birds, which, with their iron talons and feathers sharp

as arrows, delighted in human flesh. From the description of the figures of some of them, which were preserved in the sanctuary of Artemis, it appears that they resembled in form the Harpys, and like them, too, they were, there is every reason to believe, symbols of the cold, destructive storms of winter. To get rid of them, Herakles first raised an alarm by ringing a large bell; and when the birds came out from the thick wood where their nests were, many were shot down by his arrows, and the rest flew away in fright. They flew, as it appears from the story of the Argonauts, to an island, sacred to Ares, in the inhospitable Black Sea, where the Argonauts suffered severely from the heavy falls of their sharp biting feathers, and only obtained relief by again frightening them by raising a great din. As the birds flew over the sea their feathers fell like a thick snow-storm, the flakes of which, it should be remembered, are frequently in the legends of other peoples compared with feathers. Herakles, as a hero representing the influence of the sun, was very properly called in by the myth-makers to destroy beings of this kind, more especially as in the neighbouring district of Pheneos he had long been regarded as a beneficent hero. The statement of his having alarmed the birds by ringing a bell may have been suggested by a common practice of raising birds from their nests. At the same time it may also refer to a custom which is known at any rate in more recent times—that of ringing bells during severe storms, from a belief that such a proceeding availed against all evil spirits of the air.

6. *The Augeian stables.* Augeias, the rich prince of Elis, and his daughter Agamede, the sorceress who knew the potency of all the herbs in the world, were known to the author of the Iliad (**xi.** 701, 739). His seat was at Ephyro, a name which

occurs in connection with the worship of the heavenly powers, while Augeias itself means "a being of streaming light." Light streamed from his eyes, and it was said expressly that he was a son of Helios. His daughter Agamede is obviously identical in character with Dirke, Medea, and Megamede, all of whom represented by their witchcraft the occult powers of the moon. Another feature of the story, which confirms the opinion that Augeias in some way was intended to illustrate the phenomena of the sun's light, is his possession of herds of lambs and cattle, fabulous in numbers as are the fleecy clouds, and including twelve bulls, white as swans, and sacred to Helios— one of them being called Phæthon, and described as glittering like a star. The court of Augeias was by the banks of the river Menios, and the task assigned to Herakles was to clear out his endless line of stalls alone and in one day. To accomplish this, the hero made an opening through the wall at a part where the river approached it. The stream, rushing in at the opening, swept with it, as it flowed along the stables, their accumulated dung. Augeias had promised to reward Herakles with a tenth of his herds; but declined to fulfil his agreement on hearing that the task had been imposed by Eurystheus. This refusal afterwards led to a war between Herakles and Elis.

7. *The Cretan bull* had been presented by Poseidon to Minos, and by him placed among the herd of cattle sacred to the sun. How it became wild, and how Pasiphäe, the wife of Minos, conceiving a passion for it, followed it over the island, has been told in connection with the legends of Crete. The task imposed on Herakles was to bring this bull to Mykenæ. The first difficulty was to capture and subdue it, an act in which he is frequently represented on the painted vases. The

second was to bring it over the sea to Mykenæ, which he did by sitting on its back while it swam, as did Europa with Zeus, in the shape of a bull. As to the fate of the bull, it is said that Eurystheus sacrificed it to Hera, and, again, that it escaped, roved wildly over the Peloponnesus, and was finally captured at Marathon by Theseus.

8. *The horses of Diomedes*, a king of Thrace, and reputed to have been a son of Ares, the god of war and the personification of storm. Like the people whom he ruled, Diomedes was fierce in war. His seat was in the neighbourhood of Abdera, where in later times the remains of his citadel was pointed out. He was the owner of certain horses which fed on human flesh, and by that means became furious and so powerful that they had to be fastened with iron chains. The human flesh on which they fed was generally that of persons who had been wrecked on that inhospitable coast. Herakles was ordered to bring these horses to Mykenæ. To Abdera he went by sea; and on arriving overpowered the guards, and led the horses away to the shore, when he was overtaken by a crowd of the subjects of Diomedes. A terrible fight ensued, in which the king fell at the hands of Herakles, and was himself given as food for his horses. In the course of the combat, Abderos, a beautiful youth, of whom Herakles was very fond, fell: and in his honour the hero raised a mound, and instituted games in his honour, which the people of Abdera afterwards continued annually. After the horses had been conveyed to Mykenæ and presented to Eurystheus, it is said that they escaped among the hills of Arcadia, and were there ultimately devoured by wild beasts—probably by the wolves of Zeus Lykæos. Their allegorical signification is clearly that of storms and billows, and hence the legend was located in

Thrace, a country with which we are familiar in connection with other personifications of storm—such as Ares, Lykurgos, and Boreas.

9. *The girdle of Hippolyte*, the queen of the Amazons, had been a gift from Ares, and was a symbol of the power of a rushing headlong storm. The task imposed on Herakles was to fetch this girdle for Admete, the daughter of Eurystheus, of whom we learn elsewhere that she was a priestess of the Argive Hera. Herakles slew the Amazon, and returned with the girdle. From this adventure appears to have arisen the legend of a war conducted by Herakles against the Amazons.

10. *The cattle of Geryon* or Geryoneus, who was a son of Chrysaor and the Okeanide nymph Kallirrhoë. In one person he had three bodies, three heads, three pairs of legs, and six arms. He was gigantic in size, heavily armed, powerful, and provided with wings. The great point of his character was that he was the lord of immense herds of cattle. Considering that the possession of herds of cattle was also a prominent feature in the character of Apollo and Helios, in whose case the cattle represented the days of the year, and considering further that the local habitation of Geryon, though assigned to various localities, is always assigned to a place in some way connected with the worship of Helios, it may be inferred that Geryon also was an illustration of some of the phenomena of the sky; and of these phenomena none but those of wintry storms correspond with his personal appearance and vehemence. Geryon keeps his cattle at night in a dark cave in the remote west, into which Herakles penetrates, and drives them away eastward towards the region of morning light. The expedition had three stages: first, the journey to Erytheia, where Geryon lived, and which, judged by the meaning of its name, seems

to be connected with the red glow of sunset; secondly, the contest with Geryon; and, thirdly, the return to Mykenæ with the cattle.   Erytheia was an island somewhere in the remote west, beyond the pillars of Herakles; and to reach it the hero employed a vessel, obtained, some said, from Nereus, while others believed that he had compelled Helios to lend him for the occasion the cup or vessel in which he was accustomed to sail every night round the world from west to east.   On the passage Herakles was alarmed, or at any rate disturbed, by a storm, which was only appeased by his drawing his bow on Okeanos.   Reaching the island, he placed himself on Mount Abas, but was observed by the two-headed dog of Geryon, and attacked by it.   He slew the dog, and was next attacked by the herdsman Eurytion, who also fell at his hands.   Then Meno-itios, who was there watching the cattle of Helios, pointed out to him the cattle of Geryon, grazing in a meadow by the river's side.   He was in the act of driving them away, when Geryon himself, in all his strength and fierceness, appeared on the scene. The combat was ended by a fatal shaft from Herakles.   Ship-ping the cattle into the vessel of the sun, and landing them safely, Herakles commenced his homeward journey on foot, through Iberia, Gaul, over the Alps, and down through Italy, with many adventures, in all of which he was successful.   At Rome occurred the incident with the robber Cacous, which the Romans incorporated among their national legends, though the elements of it were obviously of a Greek origin.   At the Phlegræan fields, near Cumæ, he fought the Giants.   On the mountains between Rhegium and Locri, his rest was disturbed by the noise of the grasshoppers, and at his prayer the gods removed these creatures from the district for ever.   From the south of Italy one of his bulls escaped across the sea to Sicily,

17

and as it was necessary to follow it, Herakles, holding on by
the horns of another bull, crossed with his herd to that island,
through the length and breadth of which he appears to have
wandered, encountering giants like Eryx, experiencing kindness from the nymphs of Himera and Egesta, at whose warm
springs he was refreshed, and everywhere leaving reminiscences
of his visit.   Thence he passed up the shores of the Adriatic,
round by Illyria and Epirus to Ambracia, where a gadfly, sent
by Hera, caused his cattle to run away in great numbers to the
mountains.   With the remainder he reached the Hellespont,
and thence proceeded to Mykenæ, where Eurystheus sacrified
them to the goddess Hera.

   11. *The apples of the Hesperides.*   According to later story,
the last labour imposed on Herakles was to procure three of
the golden apples which grew in the garden of the Hesperides;
and hence in works of art which represent him as *invictus*, the
invincible, he appears holding the apples in his hand.   As in
the case of the cattle of Geryon, here also the chief interest of
the legend resides in the adventures on the way.   As regards
the locality where this wonderful garden was to be found, there
was a difference of opinion; some, apparently under the influence of Phœnician traditions, believing it to have been in
the remote west, while Æschylos and others conceived that
Atlas and the Hesperides lived in the northern region of the
Hyperboreans.   From the combination of both beliefs in later
times, a very wide scope was given to the adventures of the
hero on his way there and back.   Herakles himself, not knowing what direction to take, is said to have first passed through
Macedonia and on to the Rhone, where he met certain nymphs
who advised him that Nereus, the sea-god, knew the secret,
and could be made to give it up.   In spite of the many trans-

formations of Nereus, Herakles compelled him to tell him the way.   He then proceeded to Libya, where he found Antæos, a giant of enormous strength, whose habit was to kill all travellers who crossed the waste where he lived.   He was a son of Poseidon and the Earth, deriving from his mother a strength which rendered him invincible to those who could not lift him from the ground, which Herakles did.   The wrestling scene between the two was a favourite subject in ancient art, and commended itself largely to the Greek youths as they practised in the palæstra.   When he had conquered Antæos, Herakles lay down to rest, and in a little while found himself covered with a host of creatures called Pygmies, who sprang up from the waste.   He wrapped them in his lion's skin and killed them. From Libya he went into Egypt, where he was seized by the orders of Busiris and conveyed, as were all strangers, to be sacrificed.   He burst his bonds, and offered up instead Busiris, his son, and retinue.   From Egypt he went to India, and thence returned in a northerly direction towards the Caucasus mountains, where he set free Prometheus, and in return for that kindly act was told the way on through Scythia to the region of the Hyperboreans, where lived Atlas and the Hesperides.   Part of the arrangement was that Atlas should pluck the three apples for him; and to relieve him for that purpose it was necessary that Herakles should take the burden of the world on his shoulders.   Atlas returned with the apples, and naively proposed that he himself should convey them to Eurystheus.   Herakles appeared to appreciate the proposal, and only wished first to find a pad to save his head from the weight. Atlas did not see the joke, and willingly took the world on his shoulders again.   Herakles, of course, did not return.   Another report has it that Herakles himself entered the garden, slew the dragon which watched the tree, and carried off the apples and returned with them to Eurystheus.

12. *Cerberus*, the three-headed dog of Hades, which guarded the entrance to the lower world, was a symbol of the eternal darkness of Hades. The task of bringing it to the upper world was regarded in the earlier epic poetry as the most difficult of the labours of Herakles. It was supposed that he entered from the upper world through a chasm near Tænarum, returning by the same way. The shades of the dead fled in terror when they beheld him. Near the gates he found his friends Theseus and Peirithöos seated on a rock, to which they were attached as if they had grown from it, and in great trouble. He freed Theseus, but the earth shook when he tried to do the same for Peirithöos. To impart life to the shades of his friends whom he freed, he obtained blood from one of the cows of Hades, which he killed after a severe fight with Menoites, the herdsman. At last he reached Pluto, who agreed that he might take Cerberus provided he could do so without the assistance of arms of any kind. This he succeeded in doing, and leading the hated dog to Eurystheus, completed his twelve labours.

The labours of Herakles were a favourite subject with the ancient vase-painters and sculptors, and of the latter especially those of later times who worked for Roman patróns, in whose estimation the Greek hero stood high. The manner in which each of the labours was represented, seldom varied; and from this it may be assumed that the type of each had originally been established by Greek artists of celebrity, from whose models it would have been presumption to depart. As an instance of how these labours were represented collectively, we would cite a marble sarcophagus in the British Museum, dating probably from the third century A. D. Without caring to follow the chronological order usually accepted, the sculptor has chosen to dispose his groups according to his ideas of artistic effect, or perhaps according to his ideas of their importance. On the extreme left of the front we find Herakles dragging Cerberus out of Hades, the mouth of which is represented as the rocky entrance to a cave. Among the rocks is hiding a nude diminutive figure, which may be taken to be one of the shades of the dead, who, as it was said, fled in terror when they beheld the hero. Next to this is a group of Herakles removing the girdle of the Amazon Hippolyte, who lies dead at his feet. Then we have the scene in the garden of the Hesperides, then the taming of the horses of Diomedes, and lastly, the strangling of the Nemean lion. On one end of the sarcophagus he appears slaying the Lernean hydra, and on the other capturing the Keryneian stag. In these last three groups he is figured represented as beardless and of a youthful figure, while in the others his form has become colossal, and his features marked with toil. On the lid are sculptured on a smaller scale, the five remaining labours, of which the first, beginning from the left hand, is the bringing of the Erymanthian boar; next to that we find Herakles hard at work with a pickaxe, making an opening, as it seems, into the wall of the Augeian stables; the third scene represents him shooting the Stymphalian birds; in the fourth he is engaged in subduing the Cretan bull; and in the fifth he fights with the triple-bodied giant, Geryon. These five labours are shut in on the left by the scene where Herakles, as an infant, strangles the snake sent by Hera, and on the right by a group representing him seated after his labours, and receiving a cup of wine from the goddess Victory, while Athene stands by.

Herakles as a National Hero.

In addition to the twelve labours imposed by Eurystheus, and apparently after the expiry of his servitude to that monarch, Herakles performed many other wonderful feats, which caused his name to be surrounded with glory. Of these it has already been mentioned that he wrestled with and vanquished the Giant **Antæos**, who lived in Cyrene, on the north coast of Africa, and slew all who came in his way, and that in Egypt he slew **Busiris**, whose practice had been to sacrifice all strangers that entered his dominions. Next we find him among the Caucasus mountains, where, having shot the bird that gnawed the liver of **Prometheus**, he set the Titan free. He saved **Alkestis**, the wife of **Admetos**, king of Pheræ, under the following circumstances: Admetos, being sick, had caused an inquiry to be made of an oracle as to the issue of his illness, and was told in reply that he would die unless some one could be found to volunteer to lay down his life for him. For this his wife, Alkestis, offered herself, and would have been carried off to the shades, but for Herakles, who seized the god of death in his strong arms, and held him till he promised to allow her to remain with her husband.

He accompanied the expedition of the Argonauts in search of the golden fleece, and took part in the first war against Troy, along with **Telamon**, the father of Ajax, **Peleus**, the father of Achilles, and **Oïkles**, the father of Amphiaraos. The cause of this war was a breach of faith on the part of **Laomedon**, the king of Troy, who, in consideration of Herakles having rescued his daughter **Hesione** from the jaws of a sea-monster, had promised her hand to Herakles.

Laomedon was besieged in his citadel, finally was taken prison-er, and slain along with his sons—all except **Podarkes,** whose life was spared on the entreaty of Hesione. Telamon was rewarded with the hand of Hesione. Podarkes assumed the name of **Priamos,** and, after the withdrawal of Herakles and his expedition, established a new dynasty in Troy. On the way home Herakles and his companions were compelled to take shelter from a storm at Kos, but were refused hospi-tality by the inhabitants. For this they destroyed the town.

In an expedition against Pylos, Herakles succeeded, with the assistance of Athene, in overcoming **Periklymenos, a** strange being, who had the power of assuming any form he pleased. He next proceeded to Lacedæmon, to assist his friend **Tyndareus,** the rightful ruler of that state, against the family of **Hippokoöntides,** by whom he had been expelled, —this undertaking being also crowned with success, though it entailed the loss, among others of his companions, of the sons of Kepheus, king of Tegea. Tyndareus was reinstated.

Whether it was on the conclusion of the labours imposed on him by Eurystheus, or at some other period of his life, Hera-kles is said to have once returned to Thebes, exhausted by toil, and to have fallen into violent illness, followed by raving, in the course of which he committed many unfortunate acts, among others attempting to carry off the sacred tripod from the sanctuary of Apollo at Delphi. Being afterwards informed by the oracle of Apollo that the crimes he had committed through his insanity could be expiated by a period of three years' servitude, he offered his services to **Omphale,** queen of Lydia, and there, as elsewhere, distinguished himself chiefly for the assistance he rendered to the oppressed, and for the valour of his deeds.

THE DEATH AND DEIFICATION OF HERAKLES.

Herakles, it would seem, had wooed **Iole,** a daughter of
Eurytos, king of Œchalia, but had been ultimately refused her
hand, in spite of his having fulfilled all the conditions laid
down by her father.   Turning elsewhere, he became a suitor
of **Deïaneira,** a daughter of Œneus, king of Kalydon, who
offered his daughter in marriage to the man who should van-
quish the river-god Acheloös in wrestling.   Having proved
himself more than a match for the river-god, Herakles obtained
Deïaneira in marriage, and next proceeded to punish the father
of Iole for his deceit.   Having taken the stronghold of Œchalia,
he put the king and his children to death, with the exception
of Iole, whom he carried off; but instead of returning home
directly, proceeded with her to a promontory in Eubœa, intending to offer a sacrifice to Zeus.   Deïaneira, hearing of
this, and being jealous of a revival of her husband's former
love for Iole, took the white robe in which he had been accustomed to offer sacrifices, steeped it in some preparation given
her by the Centaur Nessos, as a charm to bring back her
husband's love, and sent it by her son Lichas to Herakles.
She was not aware that the preparation contained the deadliest
poison.   Herakles had hardly put on the robe, when he was
seized with violent pain—the poison entering into his frame.
Death appeared to be inevitable.   He caused a pyre of wood
to be erected on Mount Œta, set fire to it, and after handing
over his unerring bow and arrows to his friend Philoktetes,
mounted the pyre, and was consumed in its flames.   His spirit,
it was said, passed away in a cloud, and was conducted by
Iris and Hermes to Olympos, where, after being reconciled

XXXIV.

Theseus.

Laoköon.

to Hera, he was married to the goddess Hebe, and enjoyed immortality and the esteem of all the gods.   Deïaneira, mean-time having heard of the calamity she had caused, put herself to death.

While ancient poets familiarized the people with the exploits of Herakles, artists found in them an endless variety of sub-jects, as the collections of sculptures and painted vases still testify.   In the schools he was held up as an embodiment of heroic virtue, and everywhere honour was done to him.

THESEUS.

(PLATE XXXIV.)

The friend, and in many respects the counterpart of Hera-kles, was **Theseus,** a son of **Ægeus,** king of Attica, and **Æthra,** a daughter of **Pittheus,** king of Trœzene.   While his mother was a descendant of Pelops, his father was of the line of Erechtheus.   Theseus, brought up under the care of his grandfather, Pittheus, whose wisdom and virtue were well known, soon gave promise of great strength and skill in athletic exercises, such as were then prescribed for youths, and more-over became a proficient in playing the lyre.   His father, Ægeus, on taking leave of his mother, Æthra, at Trœzene, had secreted his sword and sandals under a great rock, and told her that when the boy was able to move the rock, he might come to him at Athens, bringing the sword and sandals as a token.   When only in his sixteenth year, Theseus accom-plished this task, and at once set out for Athens, where **Medea,** who was then living with Ægeus, tried to compass his death, but her plan having failed, fled.

On his way to Athens Theseus was the hero of several exploits resembling more or less the feats which Herakles performed in his youth. He slew **Periphates,** whose practice had been to crush with a blow of his iron club all travellers across the pathless district between Trœzene and Epidauros. On the Isthmus of Corinth Theseus met and overcame **Sinis,** the robber, who was the terror of the neighbourhood. It was to commemorate this feat, it was said, that Theseus established the Isthmian games. At Krommyon he slew the wild boar that was laying waste the country round. He threw **Skiron** from a high cliff into the sea—a death to which that robber had doomed many unlucky travellers. At Eleusis he slew the powerful **Kerkyon,** and afterwards **Damastes** (usually called **Prokrustes**), whose manner of killing his victims was to place them on a bed which was always either too long or too short: if too short, he would cut off part of the victim to suit the bed; if too long, he would stretch his victim to the required length.

Arriving at Athens, Theseus was purified from all this bloodshed by the grateful inhabitants. It happened that, because of the long Ionian dress which he wore, and his long hair, which gave him the appearance of a girl, some scoffed at him for going about alone in public. To show that he was far from so effeminate as he seemed, he unyoked a laden wagon that was standing by, and threw it up in the air, to the astonishment of all.

His next exploit was against the family of giants, fifty in number, called Pallantides, sons of his uncle Pallas, who were endeavouring to get rid of Theseus, in the hope of succeeding to the government of Athens at the death of their uncle Ægeus. His extraordinary strength enabled him to overpower them. He then proceeded to Marathon, where, as we have already said, in connection with the labours of Herakles, a furious bull was destroying the plains. He captured and led it off to Athens, where he sacrificed it to the goddess Athene, who had lent him her aid in the enterprise. (See Plate XXXIV.)

But the adventure in which he gained the greatest glory was his slaying the Minotaur, a monster of which we have given a description above in connection with the legends of Crete, where we have also explained why Athens was compelled to send a tribute of young men and maidens as victims to the Minotaur. Theseus offered himself as a victim, and in time arrived with the others in Crete. Before the sacrifice took place, however, he had won the favour of **Ariadne,** the daughter of Minos, and had obtained from her a clue of thread, by holding on to which he might find his way back out of the labyrinth in which the Minotaur lived. The intricacies of its passages would have otherwise been a source of danger against which his great strength would not have served him. On a very ancient vase in the British Museum there is a picture in which Ariadne is represented as holding the one end of the clue, while Theseus in the interior of the labyrinth is slaying the monster. Having by this act freed Athens forever from the cruel tribute, Theseus and his companions set out on the homeward voyage, accompanied also by Ariadne. But at the island of Naxos he abandoned her, fearing to take a stranger home as his wife. Her grief on awaking and seeing the ship far away that conveyed her lover was intense, and has been commemorated frequently both by poets and artists. She was found sorrowing by the young wine-god Dionysos, by whose influence her joy returned.

Meanwhile the arrival of the ship was being anxiously looked for at Athens. That the good news might be known more quickly, Theseus had promised, when he set out, to hoist a white flag when he sighted Attica, if successful. In his joy, however, he had forgotten the promise, and sailed towards the port with the black colours with which he had started. On seeing this, his father, Ægeus, gave way to grief at the supposed loss of his son, and put an end to his life.

Among the other adventures in which Theseus took part were the expedition of the Argonauts and that of Herakles against the Amazons. In the latter expedition he had, it was said, carried off Hippolyte, whose girdle Herakles had been commanded by Eurystheus to obtain. For the carrying off of their queen, a great body of the Amazons invaded Attica, but were repulsed by Theseus.

His warm friendship for the Thessalian prince Peirithöos gave **Theseus** two opportunities of displaying his heroic qualities. The first was at the marriage of his friend—at which, as has been previously related, the Centaurs present at the banquet, becoming fired with wine, raised a tumult, and would have carried off the bride, but for the resistance of Theseus. The second occasion was when Peirithöos, having conceived a passion for Persephone, audaciously resolved to carry her away from the lower world, and was aided by Theseus. The attempt failed, however, and both were kept in chains in the lower world till Herakles released them.

After the death of his father, Theseus succeeded to the government of Athens, lived in splendour, ruled with prudence, and introduced institutions of a most liberal kind among his people. He united the various independent and previously hostile villages of Attica into one state, with Athens at its

XXXIII

Combat between Greek and Amazon.

Meleagros.   The Dioskuri.

head. He enriched and gave a new impulse to the great festival of the **Panathenæa**, that had been established by Erechtheus. In the island of Delos he founded an annual festival accompanied by games, at which the prize was a wreath of the sacred palm-tree. In Athens the festival of **Pyanepsia**, in honour of Apollo, and **Oschophoria**, in honour of Dionysos, were both said to have been established by him. He met his death, it was said, at the hands of **Lykomedes**, to whose court he had retired on the occasion of a tumult in Athens. His wife was **Phædra**, a daughter of Minos, of Crete; according to another report, **Antiope**.

The memory of his deeds was preserved by a beautiful temple in Athens, erected for that purpose, and called the **Theseion**.

THE HUNT OF THE KALYDONIAN BOAR.

At the head of this expedition was **Meleagros**, a son of **Œneus**, the king of Kalydon, and his wife **Althæa**; Deïaneira, the wife of Herakles, being a daughter of the same pair. At the birth of Meleagros the Parcæ appeared to Althæa, it would seem, Atropos telling her that her infant would live as long as a brand which she pointed to on the fire remained unconsumed. Althæa snatched it that moment from the flames, hid it away carefully, and thus secured the invulnerability of her son. On growing to manhood he took part in the Argonautic expedition, and is said to have signalized himself by many acts of bravery; but the enterprise with which his fame was most associated was the successful hunt of the ferocious boar, that was laying waste the country round Kalydon, defying the spears and hounds of ordinary huntsmen.

Meleagros sent messengers round Greece to invite all its bravest heroes to Kalydon to join him in the hunt. There came **Idas** and **Lynkeus** from Messene, **Kastor** and **Poly-deukes** (Pollux) from Lakedæmon, **Theseus** from Athens, **Admetos** from Pheræ, **Ankæos** and the beautiful **Atalante** from Arcadia, **Jason** from Iolkos, **Peleus** from Thessaly, and many other well-proved heroes. After enjoying for nine days, as was usual, the hospitality of Meleagros, they prepared on the tenth for the chase, which, with a few accidents, resulted in the death of the boar by the spear of Meleagros, to whom accordingly fell the trophy of the monster's head and skin.

In Plate XXXIII. he is represented standing beside an altar shaded by a laurel-tree, holding two spears in his hand. His dog looks up to him. The head of the boar lies on the altar.

As, however, Atalante had been the first to wound the boar, Meleagros made that a pretext for presenting her with its skin. But on her way homewards to Arcadia she was met and forcibly robbed of it by the brothers of Althæa, the mother of Meleagros, who considered that they had a superior claim to that part of the booty. A quarrel arose on that account between Meleagros and his uncles; they fought, and the end of it was that the uncles were slain. To avenge their death, Althæa cast the brand, which up till then she had carefully preserved, into the fire, and thereupon her brave son was seized with dreadful pain, and died. Grief at the rashness of her act caused the mother to kill herself.

THE EXPEDITION OF THE ARGONAUTS.

To understand the object of this expedition, it will be necessary to go back a little into the genealogy of the person at whose instance it was conducted. That person was **Jason,** a son of **Æson,** the rightful king of Iolkos in Thessaly, and his wife Alkimede. The father of Æson was Æolos (a son of Hellen and a grandson of Deukalion), at whose death he succeeded to the throne, but was driven from it by **Pelias,** his step-brother, at whose hands he and all his relatives suffered cruel persecution. The boy Jason was saved from harm by some of his father's friends, and placed under the care and instruction of the Centaur Cheiron. At the age of twenty he was told by an oracle to present himself to Pelias, and claim his father's kingdom. Pelias also had learned from the oracle that a descendant of Æolos would dethrone him, and, moreover, that the descendant in question would appear to him for the first time with only one sandal to his feet. Pelias, the usurper, was therefore anxiously looking out for the approach of a person in this plight. It happened that the river Enipeus was swollen when Jason reached it, on his way to put forth his claim against Pelias. But Hera, the patron goddess of Iolkos, taking the form of an old woman, conveyed him across, with no loss except that of one sandal. On his arrival at Iolkos, Pelias recognized him as the rightful heir referred to by the oracle, but, at the same time, was unwilling to abdicate in his favour. He would prefer that Jason should first do something in the way of heroic enterprise, and, as a suitable adventure of that kind, proposed that he should fetch the golden fleece from Kolchis. Jason agreed to this, and set about building the **Argo,** the largest ship that had as yet sailed from Greece. The goddess Athene aided him with her skill and advice in the work, as did also Hera. When the ship was ready, Jason sent messengers to invite the foremost heroes of Greece to join him in his enterprise. Among the many who accepted his invitation were Herakles, Kastor and Pollux, Meleagros, Orpheus, Peleus, Neleus, Admetos, Theseus, his friend Peirithöos, and the two sons of Boreas, Kalaïs and Zetes.

Turning now to the story of the golden fleece, the finding of which was the object of so powerful an expedition, we must go back to Æolos, whom we have mentioned above as grandfather of Jason and son of Hellen. This Æolos had, besides Æson, another son, **Athamas**, who married **Nephele**, and had two children, **Phrixos** and **Helle**. On the death of his wife, Athamas married a second time **Ino,** a daughter of Kadmos, by whom he had two sons, **Learchos** and **Melikertes.** The second wife disliking her two step-children, made several attempts on their lives. To save them from further danger, the shade of their mother, it was said, appeared to Phrixos, bringing at the same time a large ram with a golden fleece, on which she proposed Phrixos and Helle should escape over the sea. They started according to her advice, and Phrixos reached safely the opposite shore, but Helle fell from the ram's back into the sea and was drowned. The name of Hellespont was in consequence given to the strait which they had to cross. Phrixos, having reached the other side, proceeded to Kolchis, on the farthest shore of the Black Sea, and there sacrificed the ram to Zeus, in honour of his safety. He hung the golden fleece up in the temple of Ares.

Previous to starting from Iolkos, Jason offered a sacrifice to Zeus, calling upon the god for a sign of his favour, or displeasure if it should be so. Zeus answered with thunder and lightning, which was taken as a favourable omen. The expedition proceeded first to Lemnos, where the heroes were kindly received, remained a long time, and became the fathers of a new race of heroes. The women of the island had, it would seem, at the instigation of Aphrodite, slain their husbands. One of the Lemnian women, **Hypsipyle,** bore a son to Jason, and called him **Euneos.** Leaving Lemnos and its festive life, the Argonauts continued their journey as far as Kyzikos, where they landed for a short time, and were in the act of leaving, when Herakles, having broken his oar, left the ship, accompanied by Hylas, to cut a new oar in the wood. But some nymphs, admiring the beauty of young Hylas, carried him off; and as Herakles would not leave the country without him, the expedition was compelled to proceed without the assistance and companionship of the great hero. Their next landing was in the neighbourhood of the modern Scutari, where the reigning king, **Amykos,** was famed as a boxer, and for his cruelty to all strangers who entered his territories. Seeing the Argonauts land for the purpose of obtaining fresh water, he sent them, as was his custom, a challenge to match him with a boxer, which Pollux accepted, and proved the skill by which he earned his fame upon the boastful Amykos. Proceeding on their journey, they passed through the perilous entrance to the Black Sea in safety, owing their escape from its dangers to the advice of **Phineus,** the blind and aged king of the district, whom they had found suffering great distress on account of his food being always carried off or polluted by the **Harpys,** just as he sat down to eat it. This punishment, as well as his blindness, had been sent upon him by the gods in consequence of his cruelty to his wife (a daughter of Boreas) and children. The Harpys were driven away effectually by the two sons of Boreas, who accompanied the Argonauts; and it was in return for this kindness that Phineus communicated his plan for a safe passage through the **Symplegades,** two

18

great cliffs that moved upon their bases, and crushed everything that ventured to pass between.   His plan was first to
fly a pigeon through between them, and then the moment that
the cliffs, having closed upon the pigeon, began to retire to
each side, to row the Argo swiftly through the passage.   It
was done, and before the cliffs could close upon her, the ship,
all but her rudder, had got clear of danger.   From that time
the Symplegades were united into one rock.

After many other adventures the expedition at last reached
Kolchis, where they found **Æetes,** a reputed son of Helios
and Perseïs, reigning as king.   He refused to give up the
golden fleece, except to the man who should acquit himself to
his satisfaction in certain enterprises which he proposed.   The
first was to yoke to a plough his unmanageable bulls, that
snorted fire and had hoofs of brass, and to plough the field of
Ares with them.   That done, the field was to be sown with a
dragon's teeth, from which armed men were to spring in the
furrows.   The hero who succeeded so far was then to be permitted to fetch, if he could, the golden fleece, which hung on
an oak in a grove sacred to Ares, and was watched continually
by a monstrous dragon.   **Medea,** the daughter of Æetes,
having conceived a passion for Jason, prepared him for these
dangerous tasks by means of a witch's mixture which made
him proof against fire and sword.   The goddess Athene also
helped him, and his success was complete.

The Argonauts now commenced their homeward voyage,
Jason taking with him Medea.   On missing his daughter,
Æetes gave pursuit.   Seeing that he was overtaking them,
Medea, to divert his course, dismembered her young brother,
Absyrtos, whom she had taken with her, and cast the limbs
about in the sea.   The delay caused to Æetes in collecting

the pieces of his child, enabled Medea and Jason to escape. According to another report, Absyrtos had by that time grown to manhood, and met his death in an encounter with Jason, in pursuit of whom he had been sent by his father.

After passing through many other dangers, Jason at last reached Iolkos, and, presenting the golden fleece to Pelias, claimed the throne, as agreed upon. But Pelias still refused to abdicate. Jason therefore slew him, and assumed the government of Iolkos, together with that of Corinth, where Æetes, the father of Medea, had, it is said, ruled before he went to Kolchis.

Ten years of peace followed the accession of Jason to the throne. The origin of the troubles that fell upon the royal house thereafter was an attachment formed by Jason for the beautiful **Kreusa** (or Glauke, as others called her), whom he made his wife in Corinth. Medea, stung with jealousy, turned to the arts of witchcraft she had learned in Kolchis, and having steeped a dress and a costly wreath in poison, sent them to her rival, and by that means caused her death. Not content with that, she set fire to the palace of Kreon, the father of Kreusa; and further, finding Jason enraged at what she had done, she put to death the children she herself had borne to him, and fled to Athens, where, as we have seen, she lived for a time with Ægeus. Thence also she had to escape, in consequence of an attempt on the life of Theseus. She went back to Kolchis, some believed, in a chariot drawn by winged dragons.

Jason, it is said, depressed by his troubles, repaired to the sanctuary on the Isthmus of Corinth, where the Argo had been consecrated in the grove of Poseidon. On approaching the ship, part of the stern gave way, fell upon him, and caused

his death.   Another version of the story says that he took his
own life.

THE YOUNGER RACE OF HEROES, AND THE WARS AGAINST THEBES AND TROY.

THE heroes of the succeeding age were regarded as sons
or grandsons of those whom we have just described,
the great events of the period in which they lived being the
two wars against Thebes and Troy.   It has already been
observed that the accounts of these wars, though apparently
having some foundation in historical facts, are altogether
mythical in their form, and interwoven with incidents of a
wholly mythical character.

These two events, more than any of the other adventures
of heroes, formed the favourite subjects of the national poetry
of Greece, the incidents of each having been, as a whole, or
in part, worked up into a long series of epic poems and tragedies, of which, with two exceptions, only fragments remain to
our times.   These exceptions are the " Iliad " and " Odyssey "
—the oldest, it is believed, and at the same time the most
celebrated, of the epic poems upon the subject of the war
against Troy, the reputed author of them being Homer.   The
principal epic on the expedition of the seven heroes against
Thebes was entitled the **Thebaïs**, its author being unknown.
We shall relate both these great events in the connection in
which they have come down to us.

THE SEVEN HEROES WHO WENT AGAINST THEBES: THEIR DESCENDANTS, THE EPIGONI.

We have already alluded to the series of grim events by which **Œdipos**, after killing his father, **Laios**, came to the throne of Thebes, and married his own mother, **Jokaste**. It will be remembered that from this union sprang four children, two of them being sons, **Eteokles** and **Polyneikes**, and two daughters, **Antigone**, and **Ismene**; and that, when the criminality of the marriage came to light, Jokaste killed herself, while Œdipos, after putting out his eyes, went into voluntary exile, accompanied only by his high-souled daughter Antigone, who resolved to share all his adversity.

The sons, remaining in Thebes, soon fell into a warm dispute concerning the succession to the throne, but at last agreed to reign year about, **Eteokles**, the elder of the two, having the first period of office. His year, however, having expired, he not only declined to retire in behalf of his brother, but went so far as to expel him from the city.

Polyneikes, brooding revenge, betook himself to **Adrastos**, king of Sikyon, and was there hospitably received, meeting also under the same roof another pretender to a throne, **Tydeus** of Argos. The two youths became friends, and bound themselves to stand by each other in the recovery of their sovereignty. **Adrastos** gave them his two daughters in marriage, and having thus allied himself to their cause, prepared a powerful army to reinstate, first, **Polyneikes** in Thebes, and next, **Tydeus** in Argos.

Mean time both the young men visited many parts of Greece, with the view of obtaining companions in arms, and many a stout hero answered to their summons—such, for example, as Kapăneus, a son of Hipponöos, of Argos, Eteoklos, son of Iphis, and Parthenopæos, a son of Atalanta and Melanion (or of Ares), from Arcadia. These three, together with Polyneikes, Tydeus, and Adrastos, and lastly the princely seer Amphiaraos, the son of Oïkles (or of Apollo), constituted the so-called seven heroes against Thebes. It was, however, with extreme reluctance that Amphiaraos took part in the expedition; for he was a man of profound piety, and a prophet, who knew that the other leaders of the affair had all more or less been guilty of criminal acts. He foresaw that the undertaking, altogether godless as it was—since Polyneikes, though he had suffered injustice, had no right to invade his native town with a foreign army—would have a disastrous issue for all of them. His warnings, however, were unheeded, and he himself, since much was thought to depend on his presence, was forced to take part in the adventure through the following plot :—

Amphiaraos and Adrastos, finding themselves greatly at variance in opinion concerning the projected expedition, at last agreed to intrust the decision of the matter to Eriphyle (the wife of Amphiaraos, who was prevailed on by the costly presents given her secretly by Polyneikes to decide against her husband, though she had been informed by him that Adrastos alone, of all the seven, would ever return from the expedition. On stepping into his chariot to depart for battle, Amphiaraos turned round, and called down upon his wife a curse, which his son, Alkmæon, afterwards fulfilled by slaying his mother to avenge his father's death.

The army was now ready to march under its seven leaders.

We must, however, before tracing its further adventures, return for a moment to Œdipos. After wandering about sad and miserable here and there in Greece, he at last, under the guidance of ·his faithful daughter, **Antigone**, arrived in Attica, where, it had been predicted, he was to find a peaceful end to all his woes. Neither of the sons had troubled himself about the ill-fated old man, until an oracle announced that victory in the approaching battle would be on the side of him who brought back Œdipos to Thebes, and had him in his camp. Thereupon both sought him out, Polyneikes going in person to beg for his blessing on the assault upon their native town. Œdipos cursed the unholy enterprise. Eteokles, as the reigning king, despatched his uncle, **Kreon**, a brother of his mother's, to Attica, with commands to bring back Œdipos by force if necessary. But when Kreon attempted to do so, Theseus interfered, and expelled him and his followers from the land. Œdipos, after calling down upon his undutiful sons a curse, that they might perish each by the hand of the other, died in the sacred grove of the Eumenides at Kolonos, near Athens, and was buried by Theseus with pomp and ceremony. Antigone returned in great grief to Thebes.

About the same time the expedition of the seven set out. On reaching Nemea they found all the springs dry—a judgment sent upon them by Dionysos, it was said, the guardian deity of Thebes. Suffering severely from thirst, and looking about for water, the heroes encountered **Hypsipyle** (see Argonauts), who, because of Jason's love for her, had been sent by the other women of Lemnos to Nemea, and there sold into slavery to the king, **Lykurgos**, her duty being to tend his young child, **Opheltes**. They begged her to take them to a well, which she did ; but before going off with them, had, con-

trary to the warning of an oracle, laid down the child on the
ground in the wood. Returning from the well, they found
the child dead within the coils of a snake. Tydeus and
Kapaneus would have slain the reptile at once, had not Amphiaraos announced it to be a miraculous creature sent by
Zeus as an evil omen. On this account he re-named the child
Archemoros; which means the "dawn of mystery." The
heroes appeased the angry parents by performing splendid
obsequies to the child, the athletic contests and ceremonies
of that occasion being afterwards looked on as the first celebration of the Nemean games (see above). Hypsipyle was
taken back to her home by her son, **Euneos,** who had gone
in search of her.

In spite of this evil omen, the army of the seven advanced
upon Thebes, and after several less important adventures arrived before its walls. There they pitched a camp, and as a
preliminary attempt to settle the matter amicably, sent Tydeus
into Thebes with orders to require that the government be
ceded to Polyneikes, according to the original terms of agreement between the brothers.

Tydeus was, however, received with hostility, and would
have perished in the ambush laid for him by Eteokles, contrary to the universal usages of war, had it not been for his
extraordinary strength. Of the fifty men who surrounded
him, he spared only one to take back to Eteokles the tidings
of the affair.

The dispute must now be decided by force of arms. Thebes
was closely surrounded, each of the seven heroes taking up
his position before one of its seven gates. In a similar manner
Eteokles distributed his forces under seven generals within
each of the gates, reserving for himself the defence of the gate

which his brother was to attack. When the battle commenced, deeds of extraordinary valour were done on both sides; but the gods were against the assailants, the Thebans having gained the divine good-will in a special degree by the sacrifice which Kreon's son, **Menœkeus,** voluntarily made of himself with a view to save his native town, as the oracle announced by the seer **Teiresias** recommended. When the last and fatal day of the siege arrived, Amphiaraos warned his companions in arms of what awaited them, and the death of all their leaders except Adrastos. Intrusting to him tokens of remembrance for their friends, they rushed into battle with all the courage of despair.

Matters soon began to look grave outside the walls of Thebes. The fierce Kapaneus, who had boasted that he would take the town in spite of Zeus and all the divine portents, had reached the parapet of the walls on his storming ladder, when a lightning bolt from Zeus struck and hurled him to the ground. A general onset of the Thebans followed this event, the Argive army falling before them everywhere, and their leaders being slain. Eteokles and Polyneikes pierced each other through the body in a hand-to-hand encounter. The earth, struck by a lightning bolt on the spot where Amphiaraos stood, yawned and swallowed him, from which time forward he continued to exist as a spirit endowed with the gift of prophecy. Adrastos alone escaped, and that by means of the winged horse Arion.

Kreon, the uncle of the fallen sons of Œdipos, succeeded to the throne of Thebes, and, as his first duty, buried Eteokles with great ceremony—a rite which he at the same time denied to the body of Polyneikes, on pain of death to any one who should perform it. The kindly heart of Antigone could not bear this sentence, which caused her brother's soul to wander forever without rest in the lower world; and accordingiy she defied Kreon's strict order, and buried the corpse secretly, as she thought; but his watchman having observed the act she was condemned to be buried alive—the fact of her being betrothed to his son, **Hæmon**, and the tears and entreaties of the latter, being of no avail to mitigate her doom. Antigone was pent in a subterranean chamber, in which, to avoid the pangs of starvation, she hanged herself. Hæmon, unwilling to outlive her, put an end to his existence, and Kreon's inhuman cruelty was punished by the desolation of his house, by which the family of **Œdipos** became extinct.

Thirty years having elapsed since the expedition of the seven, their sons undertook to avenge the death of their fathers by a second attack on Thebes. This was the so called war of the **Epigoni** (that is, "offspring" or sons), which was entered upon with the consent of the gods, and ended in the destruction of Thebes, which for a long time remained a mere open space called "Lower Thebes."

THE TROJAN WAR.

THE CAUSE OF THE WAR.

Contemporary with the conquest of Thebes by the Epigoni, which has been related above, we find on the throne of Troy, or Ilion, a king named **Priamos,** whose chief distinction consisted in his being the father of a noble race of sons. His wife was **Hekabe** (or Hecuba). When the time approached for another son to be born to them, their daughter **Kassandra,** on whom Apollo had bestowed the gift of prophecy, announced that the child would grow up to be the ruin of his country. To prevent such a calamity, the infant was at its birth exposed on Mount Ida, where it was found and brought up by shepherds, in whose society and occupation **Paris, or Alexandros,** spent the early part of his life.

On a beautiful day, as he tended his flocks, three goddesses came to him—Hera, Athene, and Aphrodite—commanding him to decide which of them was the most beautiful. Here we must explain. When Zeus withdrew, as we have already seen, from his proposed marriage with Thetis, on account of a prophecy communicated by Themis, that the issue of such a union would be a son who would surpass his father in might, it was agreed to give the sea-goddess in marriage to Peleus, a young prince of Phthia, in Thessaly, whose piety had endeared him to the gods. "The gods came to their marriage feast," as they did to that of Kadmos and Harmonia, all but **Eris,** the goddess of strife. Angry at not being invited,

she determined to mar the pleasantness of the company, and
to this end threw among them a golden apple, on which was
written, "To the most beautiful." Hereupon the three goddesses mentioned above claimed each the prize, and Zeus referred them to Paris, the shepherd on Mount Ida, for a decision. Unwilling at first to take upon himself so much re-
sponsibility, Paris was at length persuaded to decide, on being
promised the throne of Asia by Hera, immortal fame as a
hero by Athene, and the loveliest wife on earth by Aphrodite.
He assigned the prize to the last-mentioned goddess, and by
so doing drew upon himself and his native country the most
bitter enmity of the other two.

In the meantime it happened that a sacrifice was to be offered in Troy, for which oxen were wanted. Two of the
king's sons, Hektor and Helenos, were sent to the herd on
Mount Ida, to select fitting animals. Their choice included
one that was a favourite of Paris, who boldly refused to give
it up, and followed it to the town, intending to demand its
restoration from the king. But a quarrel ensued on the way,
and Paris would have fallen at his brothers' hands, but for
the timely appearance of Kassandra, who revealed the story
of his birth. Then there was joy in the king's palace at the
return of the lost son, grown up as he was, to be beautiful,
handsome, and brave. The untoward prophecy was forgotten.

The sudden change from the life of a herdsman to that of a
prince surrounded by the pleasures of court and town, made
Paris oblivious of the visit of the goddesses and the promise
that had been made him of the most beautiful wife on earth.
But Aphrodite meant to fulfil the promise, and to this end
commanded him to have ships built to sail to Hellas, and proceed to Sparta, where, in the person of **Helena**, he would

find the wife in question. Paris obeyed, and was accompanied on the journey by Æneas, a son of **Anchises** and the goddess Aphrodite.

Arriving at Amyklæ, he was met and kindly welcomed by the Dioscuri, **Kastor** and **Polydeukes** (Pollux), the brothers of Helena. To the same family (of which Zeus and Leda were the parents) belonged **Klytæmnestra,** the wife of **Agamemnon,** who, like her brother Kastor, was mortal, while the other two, Helena and Pollux, were immortal. Of the close attachment of the two brothers to each other there is a fine instance which we shall here relate, though in point of time it did not take place till a little later. Being present, according to invitation, at the nuptials of **Lynkeus** and **Idas** with **Phœbe** and **Hilæeirə,** the daughters of Leukippos, they became enamoured of the brides, and attempted to carry them off. A fight ensued, in which Kastor, after slaying Lynkeus, fell into the hands of Idas, whom Pollux next slew to avenge his brother's death. Pollux then prayed to Zeus that he might restore his brother to life, proposing as a compensation that both should live only on alternate days. Zeus granted the prayer with its condition. In after times the twin-brothers were regarded as divine beings, and supposed to ride on white horses in the sky, with dazzling spears, and each with a star above his brow. In storms, when a mariner saw a ball of fire in the air, he was assured that the Dioscuri were near to help him.

After spending some time with the Dioscuri, Paris, accompanied by Æneas, set out for Sparta, where he was received by the king, **Menelaos,** and his wife, Helena, in the same spirit of kindly hospitality as the brothers of the latter had displayed at Amyklæ. Of Menelaos we have already mentioned his descent from **Atreus.** The story of his marriage and its consequences is as follows:—

Such, it would seem, had been the astonishing beauty and grace of Helena, that even as a young girl she had captivated the hearts of men, and, among others, of Theseus, who carried her off. The Dioscuri, however, soon found and brought her back, taking with them as a prisoner, Æthra, the mother of Theseus, and presenting her as a servant to Helena. As Helena grew to womanhood, so numerous and so pressing were the noble suitors for her hand, that **Tyndareus,** her foster-father, became alarmed at the prospect of provoking the hostility of so many, by choosing one of them for her. He determined, therefore, to allow her to choose for herself. But first he called upon them all to take an oath, not only that they would be satisfied with her choice, but would assist her husband then and after in whatever danger or difficulty he might be placed. She chose Menelaos, the brother of Agamemnon, her sister's husband, and the marriage was celebrated with great pomp. Tyndareus, however, had omitted to offer a sacrifice to Aphrodite, who, to punish him, made the heart of his foster-daughter readily accessible to unbridled love.

Paris, as has been said, was kindly received by Menelaos, and freely admitted to his hospitality and the society of his wife, Helena, with whom he soon formed an attachment which deepened with time, and under the influence of the costly presents of Asiatic wares which he gave her. Menelaos, meanwhile suspecting nothing, prepared to pay a visit to **Idomeneus** of Crete, leaving his wife under the care of his guest. With her husband safely at a distance, Helena was readily persuaded to elope with Paris to Troy, to become his wife, and there live in oriental luxury and splendour. Reaching the coast under the cover of night, they embarked, and after weathering a storm sent by Hera, the goddess of marriage troth, reached Troy in safety, and were married with great pomp and magnificence.

To Menelaos, at the court of Idomeneus in Crete, Iris, the divine messenger, carried the intelligence of the disgrace that had fallen on his house. Returning at once, and having consulted his powerful brother, Agamemnon, he proceeded to Pylos, to seek the advice of the aged Nestor, whose reputation for prudence and wisdom throughout Greece had been acquired by his services in many wars in the course of the two preceding generations, such was his great age. His counsel on this occasion was that nothing short of a combination of all the armies of Greece would be sufficient to punish the crime that had been committed, and recover the possession of Helena.

Acting on this advice, Menelaos and Agamemnon visited all the princes and heroes of the land, to obtain pledges of their assistance. Those who had been suitors of Helena had been bound by an oath to assist Menelaos whenever called upon by him to do so, and were now ready to carry out their engagement. Others promptly offered their services, from feelings of resentment at the vileness of the act of Paris. Only in two cases was any difficulty experienced, but they were very important cases, as it proved. The first was that of Odysseus (Ulysses), son of Laertes, the king of the island of Ithaka. His beautiful and faithful wife, **Penelope,** had borne him a son, **Telemachos,** and being in the enjoyment of perfect domestic felicity, he was unwilling to exchange it for a part in a war, the issue of which appeared very dubious. But instead of returning a blunt answer, he pretended insanity, put on a fisherman's hat, yoked a horse and an ox together, and commenced to plough. But Palamedes, detecting the sham, set the infant Telemachos on the ground in front of the plough. In saving the child Odysseus revealed the sobriety of his senses, and was compelled to join the expedition. The other case was that of **Achilles,** the son of Peleus and Thetis, a nymph of the sea.

Thetis having been offered by the gods the choice in behalf of her son, of either a long life spent in obscurity and retirement, or a few years of dazzling martial fame, chose the life of obscurity, and with that view conveyed him, dressed as a girl, to the court of **Lykomedes,** in the island of Skyros. There he was brought up among the king's daughters, and gained the love of one of them, Deidamia, who bore him a son, Neoptolemos, who afterwards took part in the war against Troy. Meantime it was known to be of the highest importance for the Trojan expedition to discover the concealment of the young son of Thetis, and to enlist his services. For that purpose Odysseus was sent in the dress and character of a trader to Skyros. On the pretext of offering his trinkets and wares for sale to the king's daughters, he obtained admittance to the palace, and discovered Achilles, disguised as he was. Odysseus ordered a magnificent suit of armour to be displayed before the youth, and a call to arms to be sounded on a military horn. The scheme was successful—an impulse to achieve military glory seized upon Achilles, who forthwith offered his services to the projected expedition. Peleus sent **Patroklos,** the son of Menœtios, to be a companion for his son.

The harbour of Aulis was where the various contingents of ships and soldiery were appointed to assemble; and when they had all arrived—more than 1,000 ships, each with at least 150 men—it was a sight such as had never been seen in Greece before. Agamemnon, the most powerful prince in Greece, was elected to the position of commander of the expedition.

While the fleet lay in Aulis, a serpent was observed coiling itself round a plane-tree, on which was a sparrow's nest with nine young birds. The serpent devoured the young ones, but on turning to the mother-bird was instantly changed into stone. Kalchas, the high-priest, was summoned to divine what the strange occurrence might betoken. He replied: "Nine years we must fight round Ilion, and on the tenth take the town." Thereafter the fleet sailed, crossed the Ægean, and landed by mistake in Mysia, which the Greeks prepared to lay waste. They were, however, stoutly opposed by the king of the country, Telephos, a son of Herakles. In the contest Patroklos proved his bravery, fighting side by side with Achilles. He received a wound, which Achilles—thanks to his early training under the Centaur Cheiron, and the knowledge of medicine then obtained—was able to cure. Telephos also had received a wound from a spear of Achilles in the engagement, and, finding that it would not heal, consulted an oracle regarding it. The reply of the oracle was that it could be healed only by him who had caused it. Meantime another oracle was communicated to the Greeks, to the intent that Telephos should lead them to Troy. How this came about we shall see presently.

The Greek fleet had returned again to the harbour of Aulis. While lying there, Agamemnon had chanced to see a beautiful stag, sacred to Artemis. His passion for the chase led him to draw upon the stag, and kill it, while in the pride of his success he dared to boast that he could excel the goddess of the chase herself. This was the cause of a series of misfortunes that then befel him. The injured goddess first sent a calm

19

which detained the fleet week after week. In spite of Palame-des' invention of the game of draughts and other means of amusement, the prolonged inactivity began to tell upon the force, and to create serious discontent. At last Kalchas, being ordered to discover what the gods desired, explained that Artemis required, on the part of Agamemnon, the sacrifice of his daughter **Iphigeneia.** His fatherly feelings had to yield to his sense of duty as commander of the expedition. He sent a message to his wife Klytæmnestra, to come to Aulis, bringing Iphigeneia with her,—to be married, he said to Achilles. They came ; but it was as a victim, not as a bride, that Agamemnon led his daughter to the altar of Artemis. The goddess, satisfied with his intentions, suddenly appeared on the scene, provided a goat for the sacrifice, carried off Iphigeneia in a cloud to Taurus, and appointed her to the care of her temple there. Klytæmnestra could not forgive her husband for the deception he had practiced. How she avenged herself shall be afterwards related.

In consequence of the oracle concerning the wound which he had received from the spear of Achilles, Telephos proceeded to Aulis, where the Greek fleet lay, and presented himself in disguise to Agamemnon, seized his infant son, **Orestes**, whom Klytæmnestra had brought with her, and threatened to slay the child, if healing were refused him. Odysseus interposed, and scraping some of the rust from the spear of Achilles, applied it to the wound, and healed it. Thereupon Telephos offered his services in leading the expedition to Troy, and, the oracle being thus fulfilled, the Greeks set sail a second time for Troy landing on their way at Lemnos, to sacrifice at an altar raised there by Herakles, Philoktetes, who had inherited the bow and arrows of Herakles, was bitten in the

foot by a snake, and suffered agony that made him scream
continually.   Unable to heal the wound, and unwilling to
endure his screams, the Greeks left him behind, and proceeded
on their journey, reaching at last the Trojan shore.

THE FIRST YEARS OF THE WAR.

The Trojans having received intelligence of the hostile preparations of the Greeks, prepared on their part also to meet
the enemy, assembling in and around the city of Troy all the
forces they could obtain from neighbours and allies.   Their
foremost hero, whom they chose to lead them in assaults, was
Hektor, the eldest son of the king.   The first engagement
of the two forces occurred while the Greeks were in the act of
landing from their ships, the result of it being that the Trojans
were driven back within their walls, but not without inflicting
considerable loss on their enemy.   The first attempt of the
Greeks to take the town by storm entirely failed, and, finding
that the Trojans would not surrender Helena to her husband,
the Greek commander could see no other means of compelling
them to do so than by a siege.   Accordingly a well-fortified
camp was constructed round the ships, which had been hauled
up on the shore, and with that camp to fall back upon, the
Greek army proceeded to lay waste the territory and towns in
the neighbourhood.   The Trojan forces, acknowledging the
superiority of the besiegers, did not seek a battle, and excepting such incidents as when Achilles and Hektor fought in
single combat, or when **Troïlos**, the youngest son of Priam,
was captured and put to death by Achilles, nothing of moment transpired.

In the course of the raids made by the Greeks in the neighbourhood, it happened that having taken the town of Pedasos, and come to divide the spoils, Agamemnon obtained as his captive **Chryseïs,** a daughter of **Chryses,** the priest of Apollo in the island of Chryse, while to the lot of Achilles fell **Briseïs,** a maiden as beautiful as the priest's daughter. Chryses entreated Agamemnon to restore him his daughter, offering a heavy ransom for her, but was met with refusal and contumely.   Having one other resource—an appeal to the god in whose service he was—Chryses implored the aid of Apollo, who, being for other reasons also hostile to the Greeks, visited them with a plague which carried them off in great numbers.   Agamemnon called a muster of the army, and inquired of the high-priest, Kalchas, by what the angry god could be appeased.   Kalchas, being assured of the protection of Achilles, boldly declared that the wrath of Apollo had been caused by the unjust detention of Chryseïs, a daughter of one of the priests.   Upon this, Agamemnon, who had borne a grudge against Kalchas ever since the sacrifice of Iphigeneia, rated the priest in reproachful terms, charging him also in the present instance with being in league with Achilles—a charge which the latter would have resented with force, had not the goddess Athene interposed.   Agamemnon felt his dignity as king and commander of the army insulted by the threat of Achilles, and demanded as satisfaction for this the person of the beautiful Briseïs, apparently to take the place of Chryseïs, whom he had been compelled to give up. Achilles having been warned by Athene to be calm, confessed his inability to resist the demand, and from that time withdrew with all his men from the camp.

Thetis having beseeched Zeus to take measures to compel Agamemnon to atone for this insult to her son, obtained a divine decree setting forth that so long as Achilles held aloof the Greeks would be defeated in every engagement with the Trojans. Emboldened by the intelligence of the step taken by Achilles, the Trojans sallied from their walls, and after numerous battles, skirmishes, and personal encounters, always attended with serious loss to the enemy, drove the Greeks back to the shelter of their fortified camp beside the ships. At last, abased and humiliated by disasters, Agamemnon sent an embassy to Achilles, offering to restore Briseïs, and in addition to bestow on him his daughter's hand, with seven towns for a dowry. But the wrath of Achilles would not relent, and still the need of his countrymen grew worse.

The end seemed to be near when Hektor, at the head of the Trojans, had stormed the wall of the camp, and set several of the ships on fire. Seeing this, Patroklos begged Achilles to lend him his armour, and allow him to lead the **Myrmidons** to the fight. The request being granted, Patroklos and his men were soon in the heat of the battle, their sudden reappearance striking the Trojan army with terror, and causing it to fall back. Not content with thus deciding the battle, Patroklos, disregarding the advice of Achilles, pursued the enemy till Hektor, turning round, engaged him in a hand-to-hand fight, the issue of which was the death of the Greek hero. Hektor stripped him of the armour of Achilles, which he wore, but left the body for the Greeks to take possession of. The grief of Achilles at the loss of his friend was as violent as had been his anger against Agamemnon. He called for vengeance on Hektor, and with the object in view of obtaining it, yielded to a reconciliation which all the sufferings of his countrymen could not previously induce him to submit to. With armour more dazzling and

superb than had ever been seen before, forged by the god He·
phæstos, and brought by Thetis in the hour of her son's need,
he went forth to battle, seeking Hektor in the Trojan ranks,
which everywhere hurried back like sheep before a wolf. The
Trojan hero stepped forth to meet his adversary, but not without sad misgivings. He had said farewell to his faithful wife,
Andromache, and to his boy, **Astyanax.** But even the
strong sense of duty to his country, which had supported him
in this domestic scene, deserted him utterly when the young
Greek hero approached with the dauntless bearing of the god
of war himself. Hektor fled; but Achilles, having a faster step,
cut off his retreat, and thus imbued him with the courage of
despair. The combat did not last long, the victory of Achilles
being easily won.

Unappeased by the death of Hektor, Achilles proceeded to
outrage his lifeless body by binding it to his war-chariot.
After dragging it thus three times round the walls of Troy in
the face of the people, he returned with it to the Greek camp,
and there cast it among dust and dirt. Displeased by such
excess of passion, the gods took care of Hektor's body, and
saved it from corruption, while Zeus in the meantime softened
the heart of Achilles, and prepared him for the performance
of an act of generosity which was to blot out the memory of
his previous cruelty. On the one hand, Thetis was employed
to persuade her son to give up the body without a ransom.
On the other hand, Hermes was sent to bid Priam go stealth-
ily in the night to Achilles' tent, and beg the body of his
son. The aged king of Troy obeyed, and coming to the
young hero's tent, besought him, as he valued his own father,
to give him leave to take away the lifeless body, and pay to it
the customary rites of burial. Achilles was touched by the

gentleness of his beseeching, raised the old man from his knees, shared with him the hospitality of his tent, and, in the morning, having given up the body, sent him back under a safe escort. In the pause of hostilities that took place then, the Greeks buried the body of Patroklos with great ceremony.

THE DEATH OF ACHILLES.

The loss of Hektor had so dispirited the Trojans, that without fresh succours they could not face the enemy again. Such succours, however, consisting of an army of Amazons, under the command of the beautiful **Penthesilea,** arrived in the interval of mourning for Hektor in the one camp and for Patroklos in the other. When hostilities commenced again, the valiant Penthesilea, being eager to measure her strength with that of Achilles, and to avenge the death of Hektor, led the Trojan army into battle. The leaders of the Greeks were Achilles and **Ajax,** the son of Telamon. While the latter hero was engaged in driving back the Trojan ranks, Achilles and Penthesilea met in single combat. He would have spared her willingly, and did not, till compelled in self-defence, strike with all his might. Then she fell mortally wounded, and as she fell, remembering the fate of Hektor's body, implored Achilles to spare hers that disgrace. There was no need of this; for he, to save her still if possible, and if not, to soothe her last moments, lifted her in his arms, and there held her till she died. The Trojans and Amazons made a combined rush to rescue the body of their leader; but Achilles made a sign to them to halt, and praising her valour, youth, and beauty, gave it to them freely—a kindly act which touched friends and foes alike. Among the Greeks, however, there was one **Thersites,** mean and deformed in mind as well as body, who not only dared to impute a scandalous motive to Achilles, but, approaching the fallen Amazon, struck his spear into her lightless eye.   A sudden blow from Achilles laid him lifeless on the ground.

All who saw this punishment inflicted approved of it, except **Diomedes,** the son of Tydeus, a relation by blood of Thersites, who stepped forward and demanded of Achilles the usual reparation, consisting of a sum of money.   Feeling himself deeply wronged because his countrymen, and especially Agamemnon, did not unconditionally take his part in the matter, Achilles abandoned for a second time the cause of the Greeks, and took ship to Lesbos.   Odysseus was sent after him, and by dint of smooth words, cleverly directed, succeeded in bringing him back to the camp.

What made the return of Achilles more urgent at that time was the arrival of a new ally to the Trojans, in the person of **Memnon,** a son of Eos (Aurora) and Tithonos, who besides being the son of a goddess, as well as Achilles, appeared further to be a proper match for him, inasmuch as he also carried armour fashioned by Hephæstos.   When the two heroes met, and were fighting fiercely, Zeus received in Olympos a simultaneous visit from their respective mothers, Thetis and Eos, both imploring him to spare their sons.   He answered that the issue must abide the will of Fate, Mœra, to discover which he took the golden balance for weighing out life and death, and placing in one scale the fate of Achilles and in the other that of Memnon, saw the latter sink to denote his death.   Eos made haste to the battle-field, but found her son dead.   She carried away his body, and buried it in his native land, in the distant east.

Achilles did not long enjoy his triumph; for, animated by success, he led on the Greeks, and would have captured Troy, however clearly the Fates might have decreed the contrary, had not Apollo given unerring flight to an arrow drawn by Paris. By that shaft from an unworthy source, as far as could be judged, Achilles fell. Ajax, the stout hero, and Odysseus, clever as well as brave, seized his body, and fighting all the way carried it back to camp, where its burial was attended with extraordinary pomp and ceremonial, the Muses chanting dolorous lays, and the heroes who had known him personally taking part, as was the custom on such occasions, in athletic competitions. The armour which he had worn in the fight was offered by Thetis to the most deserving. Only two claims were preferred, and those were on behalf of the two heroes who had rescued his body. The award being given in favour of Odysseus, Ajax, from grief at what he deemed neglect, sank into a state of insanity, in the course of which he intentionally fell upon his sword, and died.

A cessation of hostilities was obtained on the death of Achilles and Ajax, the two foremost of the Greek heroes. This period of peace having expired, and the former conditions of war having been resumed, the first event of importance that occurred was the capture of **Helenos,** a son of Priam, who, like his sister, Kassandra, was endowed with the gift of prophecy. Odysseus, who had made the capture, compelled Helenos to disclose the measures by which it was decreed that the siege should be brought to a determination. The answer was, that to take the city of Troy, and thus close the siege, three things were necessary: 1, the assistance of the son of Achilles, **Neoptolemos;** 2, the bow and arrows of Herakles; 3, the possession of the Palladium (an image of the goddess

Pallas-Athene), which was carefully preserved in the citadel of Troy. In satisfying the first condition no difficulty was ex‧ perienced. Odysseus, always ready to be of service for the common good, proceeded to Skyros, where he found Neop‧ tolemos grown to manhood, and thirsting for martial renown. A present of the splendid armour which his father, Achilles, had worn and which Odysseus now magnanimously parted with, fired the youth's ambition, and led him easily to Troy, where he distinguished himself in a combat with **Eurypylos** (a son of Telephos), who had joined the Trojan ranks.

A more serious matter was the fulfilment of the second con‧ dition, seeing that the bow and arrows of Herakles were then in the possession of **Philoktetes**, whom, as we have already said, the Greeks abandoned at Lemnos, not caring to endure the screams caused by the wound in his foot. His feelings were known to be rancorous towards the Greeks. Notwith‧ standing that, Odysseus, accompanied by Diomedes (or, as others say, by Neoptolemos), went to Lemnos, and successfully tricked Philoktetes into following him to Troy, where his wound was healed by Machæon, a son of Asklepios, and a reconciliation was effected between him and Agamemnon. The first on whom his fatal arrows were tried was Paris, after whose death Helena married his brother, **Deiphobos**. The Trojans were now completely shut up within the town, no one daring to face the arrows of Philoktetes.

There remained, however, a third condition—the seizure of the Palladium. Odysseus, successful in the other two, and undaunted by the greater difficulty of the new adventure, pro‧ posed to steal alone within the walls of Troy in the disguise of a beggar, and as a first measure to find out where the Pal‧ ladium was preserved. He did so, and remained unrecognized except by Helena, who, having felt ever since the death of Paris a yearning for Menelaos, proved to be a valuable ally. Odysseus, in the meantime, returned to the Greek camp to obtain the assistance of Diomedes. The two having made their way back to Troy, laid hold of the Palladium, and, carrying it off in safety, fulfilled the third and last condition.

The next difficulty was the plan of assault to be adopted. It was proposed by Odysseus, on the suggestion of the goddess Athene, that Epeios, a famous sculptor, should make a great wooden horse, sufficiently large to hold inside a number of the bravest Greeks, and that the horse being ready, and the heroes concealed within it beyond detection, the whole Greek army should embark and set sail, as if making homeward. The plan of Odysseus was agreed to, and great was the joy of the Trojans when they saw the fleet set sail. The people, scarcely trusting their eyes, flocked to the abandoned camp, to make sure. There they found nothing remaining but a great wooden horse, about the use of which various opinions arose—some thinking it an engine of war, and demanding its instant destruction. But the opinion that prevailed most was that it must have been an object of religious veneration, and if so, ought to be taken into the city. Among those who thought otherwise was **Laoköon,** a priest of Apollo, who had arrived on the scene, accompanied by his two young sons, to offer a sacrifice to the god in whose service he was. Laoköon warned his countrymen in no case to accept this gift of the Greeks, and went so far as to thrust his spear into the belly of the horse, upon which the weapons of the heroes within were heard to clash, and the bystanders were all but convinced of the justice of the priest's opinion. But the gods had willed it otherwise, and to turn the opinion of the people

against Laoköon, sent a judgment upon him in the shape of
two enormous serpents, which, while he and his two sons were
engaged in sacrificing at an altar by the shore, issued from
the sea, and casting their coils round the two boys first, then
round the father, who came to their assistance, caused him to
die in great agony.   The scene is represented in a marble
group now in the Vatican, from which the figure in Plate
XXXIV. is taken.   The mysterious fate of Laoköon was
readily believed to be a punishment for the violence he had
done to the sacred horse.

   But to carry out effectually the stratagem of the horse,
Odysseus had left behind on the shore his friend **Sinon**, with
his hands bound, and presenting all the appearance of a victim
who had escaped sacrifice, which he professed to be.   The
good king Priam was touched by the piteous story which Sinon
told, ordered his bonds to be struck off, and inquired the
purpose of the horse.   Sinon replied that it was a sacred
object, and would, if taken into the city, be a guarantee of
the protection of the gods, as the Palladium had been before.
The city gates being too small, part of the wall was broken
through, and the horse conducted in triumph towards the
citadel.   This done, the Trojans, believing that the Greeks
had abandoned the siege in despair, gave way to festivity and
general rejoicing, which lasted well into the night.

   When the town had become perfectly quiet, the inhabitants,
exhausted by the unusual excitement, being fast asleep, Sinon
approached the horse, and opened a secret door in its side.
The heroes then stepped out, and made a fire signal to the
fleet, which lay concealed behind the neighbouring island of
Tenedos, and now advanced quietly to the shore. The troops
having disembarked and made their way silently to the city,

there ensued a fearful slaughter, the surprised inhabitants falling thickly before the well-armed Greeks. Finally the town was set on fire in every corner, and utterly destroyed. Priam fell by the hand of Neoptolemos. The same fate befel the son of Hektor—not for anything that he had done, but that he might not grow up to avenge his father's death. Of the few Trojans who escaped were Æneas, his father Anchises, and his infant son Askanios. Carrying his aged father on his shoulders, Æneas fled towards Mount Ida, and thence to Italy, where he became the founder of a new race.

Menelaos became reconciled to his now penitent wife, Helena, and took her back with him. The Trojan women of rank and beauty were distributed among the Greek heroes as captives in war, Neoptolemos obtaining Andromache, the widow of Hektor, and Agamemnon carrying off Priam's daughter, Kassandra. The extensive booty from the king's palaces having been divided, preparations were made for returning home. While some—as, for example, Nestor, Idomeneus, Diomedes, Philoktetes, and Neoptolemos—had favourable voyages, and reached their respective homes in safety, others, like Menelaos, were driven hither and thither by storms, which delayed their passage for years. But the heroes to whose return the greatest interest attaches, were Agamemnon and Odysseus.

Agamemnon, returning after an absence of ten years, found that his wife, Klytæmnestra, had in the meantime accepted as her husband Ægisthos, a son of Thyestes, and therefore of an accursed line. These two proposed to compass the death of Agamemnon; and he, though warned of their designs by Kassandra, whose prophetic power enabled her to foresee the issue, lent himself easily to their purpose, innocently accepting

as genuine his wife's expression of joy. He entered the warm
bath that had been prepared for him, but on coming out of it,
found himself entangled in a piece of cloth which his wife
threw over his head. In this helpless condition he was slain
by her and Ægisthos, Kassandra and many of his followers
perishing with him. His young son **Orestes** contriving to
escape with the help of his sister **Elektra,** fled to Phokis,
where he was received hospitably, and remained several years,
during which Ægisthos ruled over Argos on the throne of
Agamemnon.

A few years after the murder of Agamemnon an oracle of
Apollo was communicated to Orestes, commanding him to
revenge that foul deed, and promising the assistance of the
god. Without being recognized he arrived at Mykenæ, accompanied by his faithful friend **Pylades,** and there revealed
himself to his sister Elektra, while to his mother he professed
to be a messenger come with intelligence of the death of her
son Orestes. Seeing her and Ægisthos rejoice at the news,
he was enraged, and slew her, while her husband fell at the
hands of Pylades.

The shedding of a mother's blood was regarded as the
blackest crime on earth; and though the fact that Orestes had
perpetrated the deed to avenge the murder of his father, and
at the instigation of Apollo, went far to exculpate him, it did
not satisfy the malignant Erinys (Furies), who pursued him
from land to land, permitting no peace to his throbbing heart.
Arriving, in the course of his wanderings, at Delphi, Orestes
complained to Apollo of his sufferings, and was told by the
god that he might expect relief if he could fetch the ancient
statue of the goddess Artemis from Taurus. The difficulty of
the task consisted in this, that it was the practice of the Tauric

Artemis to secure the immolation of all strangers that approached her temple. Fortunately for Orestes, as it happened, his sister Iphigeneia held the office of priestess there, having been carried away, as we have already seen, by the goddess at the moment when she was to be sacrificed by her father Agamemnon. On arriving at the temple, Orestes, who was accompanied by Pylades, was seized, and would have been sacrificed by the hand of his own sister, had not an accident revealed the relationship. He told her all that had happened, and how Apollo had commanded him to carry away the statue of the goddess. With the assistance of Iphigeneia he obtained possession of the image, and in her company returned with it to Greece.

The task imposed by Apollo was accomplished, but still the relentless Furies continued to persecute the unhappy youth. Apollo then advised him to proceed to Athens, and there to call for a trial in the Areopagus, a court appointed to hear causes of murder, especially the murder of a relative. (See "Ares"). The goddess Athene appealed for justice in his behalf. Apollo defended him at the trial. The Erinys appeared as plaintiffs. When the pleadings had been heard, and the votes of the judges came to be taken, they were found to be equally divided for and against. The right of giving the casting vote was reserved on this occasion for Athene, who, stepping forward, took up a white voting-stone, and placing it among the votes favourable to Orestes, declared his lawful acquittal. The Erinys professed themselves appeased, desisted from persecution, and from that time enjoyed the title of **Eumenides.** (See "Erinys"). Thus acquitted, and purified from the stains of crime, Orestes ascended the throne of his father Agamemnon, in Mykenæ, married **Hermione,**

the daughter of Helena and Menelaos, and at their death succeeded to the dominion of Sparta also.

Turning now to Odysseus, we find him, long after the other
heroes of the Trojan expedition had reached their homes, still
being tossed about by storms, passing through great perils,
encountering strange beings, and ultimately succeeding in
many unhopeful adventures. He had left Troy with a well-
manned fleet richly laden with spoil, and after several adventures of less moment, in which, however, he lost a number
of men, reached the country of the Kyklopes—enormous
giants with only one eye. In a cave which was the habitation
of one of them, **Polyphemos** by name, a son of the sea-
god Poseidon, Odysseus and his fellow-travellers took shelter,
while their ships lay anchored beside a neighbouring island.
Polyphemos, who was absent at the time of their arrival,
returned with his sheep to the cave. The first thing he did
on entering was to close up the entrance with a great stone,
which a hundred men could not have moved. The next thing
was, having discovered the strangers, to eat two of them for
his supper, after which he slept soundly. The following
morning, after driving out his sheep, he replaced the stone at
the mouth of the cave, to prevent the escape of his victims,
and the consequent loss of several suppers. The history of
the first day having repeated itself on the two following days,
a plan of escape occurred to Odysseus. The giant having
had his usual supper, Odysseus offered him some wine, which
had the effect of creating a desire for more. His goblet
being constantly replenished, Polyphemos at last sank helpless, through sleep and intoxication. Seeing this, Odysseus,
with the help of his companions, laid hold of a great pole,
and having made the end of it red hot, let it down on the

giant's eye, and burned it out. Polyphemos sprang up in great fury, and after groping in vain for his supple enemies, made for the doorway of the cave, removed the stone, and sat down in its place, determined to permit no one to escape. But Odysseus and his companions fastened themselves each under the belly of one of the great sheep within the cave, knowing that the giant would let them pass out unmolested. And so it was; for, feeling the fleece as they passed, he was quite satisfied. Odysseus once outside the cave, and with what remained of his crew safe in the ship, shouted jeeringly back to the Kyklops, telling him also his name. Polyphemos then implored his father, the god Poseidon, to punish Odysseus for what he had just done. It was in answer to this prayer that Odysseus was driven hither and thither, detained here and there, and at last, after ten years' wandering, and the loss of all his men, reached home in a miserable plight.

Of the adventures that befel him after leaving the country of the Kyklopes, the most important were the following:— After leaving Æolos, the king of the winds, and suffering the misfortune already related (see "Æolos"), he reached the habitation of the sorceress **Circe** (a sister of Medea, it was said), whose first act was to transform his companions into swine. For Odysseus himself her charms had no potency. He compelled her to restore his men to their proper human form. Changing her manner, Circe now exhibited a cordial feeling towards Odysseus, entertaining him and his companions very hospitably for the period of a year, on the expiry of which she advised him to make a journey to the lower world, to question the shade of the seer Teiresias as to the fate in store for him. Acting on her advice, Odysseus penetrated to the region of Hades, saw and conversed with the shades of some of his

20

former companions in the siege of Troy, and then returned to Circe, who gave him good counsel in regard to his future journey. On his voyage homeward he passed the **Sirens** safely (see "Sirens"), passed Scylla the sea-monster, with loss of six men, and afterwards, in spite of the warnings both of Teiresias and Circe, landed on the island of Trinakia, where his companions plundered the sacred flocks of the sun-god. As a punishment for this they were afterwards overtaken by a fearful storm at sea, and all perished except Odysseus, who, clinging to a piece of his ship for nine days, was at length driven on shore on the island belonging to the nymph **Kalypso**, who received him kindly, and out of love detained him as her prisoner for seven years.

Despising her love and her offer of immortality, Odysseus sat disconsolate by the sea-shore, thinking of his home in Ithaka, and yearning to see it again before he died. The gods, taking compassion on him, prevailed on Kalypso to let him go. He made a raft, and put to sea; but Poseidon, not yet appeased for the wrong done to his son Polyphemos, raised a storm which shattered the small craft, and would have caused Odysseus to perish but for the timely aid of the sea-nymph **Leukothea.** Swimming to land, he found himself in the island of the Phæakians, was discovered on the shore by the king's daughter, Nausikäa, and entertained hospitably by the king, Alkinöos, to whom he related his adventures. After receiving many costly presents, he was conveyed home to Ithaka in a well-manned ship. There he found his wife, Penelope, still faithful to him, in spite of the incessant wooing of all the princes of the neighbouring islands in the course of her husband's long absence.

His son, Telemachos, whom he left an infant, had now

grown to manhood, and having just arrived from a journey in search of intelligence concerning his missing father, was staying in the house of a shepherd when Odysseus arrived, and heard the story of how the suitors of Penelope were vexing her and consuming her husband's possessions. Odysseus and his son appeared among them in disguise, raised a quarrel, and with the help of Athene, slew them all. Then took place the touching meeting with his wife. After crushing an insurrection raised by the friends of the slain suitors, Odysseus spent the rest of his life in reigning peacefully over his island kingdom of Ithaka.

ROMULUS AND REMUS.

The Romans had no heroes in the sense in which we have come to regard that word from a study of the Greek legends. **Romulus** and **Remus**, it is true, have a legendary character, which may be compared in some respects with that of several Greek heroes. They were the offspring of a god (Mars) and a vestal virgin. They were exposed to death at their birth, were suckled by a she-wolf, were preserved and brought up among herdsmen. On arriving at manhood, they returned to claim their inheritance, and founded the city of Rome, Romulus naming it after himself. They instituted festivals—the **Palilia** and **Lupercalia**—the latter to commemorate their having been nourished by a wolf. They established the priesthood of Arval Brothers. Remus, less fortunate in his adventures, was slain. His brother Romulus was at last carried up bodily to heaven in the presence of the people, and in the course of a storm of thunder and lightning. A simple hut on the Palatine hill was preserved with veneration as the sanctuary of Romulus. But the demand for historical truth, or the appearance of it, was too strong in Rome to permit a poetic embellishment of the story, such as it would have experienced in Greece.

HORATIUS COCLES.

The ancient Roman ballads sang of the brave Horatius, who had fought so well in the old wars raised by the exiled Royal family and their partisans. A golden statue of him stood in the market-place, and beside it sacrifice was offered in his memory. Such honours were the same as were appointed for Greek heroes. But the story of the deeds of Horatius wanted, nevertheless the true legendary character, and was probably accepted by the people with more of pride than pious feeling.

NORSE AND OLD GERMAN MYTHOLOGY.

___

U NLIKE their Aryan kinsfolk—the Greeks—the Teutons
were not a literary people. Their mythical tales were
preserved not in books, but in memory. And Christianity,
as represented alike by the missionaries and by Charlemagne
himself, did its best to destroy Teutonic paganism root and
branch. Hence it happens that of the myths of the gods and
heroes of those great nations who, in pre-Christian times, inhabited the territories now included under the general name
Germany, no complete and systematic account has been trans-
mitted to modern times.

But the old Germans were of the same race with the people
of Norway, Sweden, and Denmark. Their speech was essen-
tially the same. They had the same social and domestic
customs, and the same religion. Further, during the time
when Christianity was spreading over Germany and Scandina-
via, that exodus of the Norsemen was likewise taking place
which ended in the colonization of Iceland—or Snowland, as
it was also named by its discoverers in the middle of the ninth
century. There, "on the verge," as Dr. Dasent says, "of
the polar circle," the Vikings established their little independent principalities or republics; unmeddled with by Christian

priests, and disdaining the continental kings who were aping the customs of the new times, the Icelandic Norsemen preserved, for five centuries more, the pure faith of their forefathers.

Lastly there appears to have been less antagonism, less friction, between the two rival religions—Odinism and Christianity—in Iceland than in other countries. Its Christian priests would seem to have felt the loyalty of children towards their old faith, then dying away. Hence, in a measure, the complete and systematic form in which the Icelanders were able to leave a permanent record of their mythology. It was a Christian priest—Sigmund Sigfusson—who, in the middle of the eleventh century, composed the compilation of mythical poems known as the elder Edda. To the succeeding century belongs the younger Edda, which is merely a prose rendering of those portions of the first work which narrate the creation of the world and man, and the generation, adventures, functions, and ultimate fate of the gods. As a cosmogony and theogony this Edda, or, as the word might be paraphrased, "Tales of a Grandmother," is as complete even as its Greek prototype, the Theogony of Hesiod. And as a record and expression of the spiritual life of those Teutons, who also were the progenitors of our English race, it is, or surely ought to be, incomparably more interesting.

THE CREATION.

In the prose Edda, Ginki, the wise king, travels in search of knowledge to the home of the Asa folk—the Norse gods—each of whom supplies the visitor with some piece of special information. The cosmogonic history thus patched up between

them closely corresponds in main points with that contained in
the Hesiodic poem; while its special details, tone, and colour-
ing are the expression of special climatic conditions. Where
the earth now is there was in the beginning, says the Edda, no
sand, sea, or grass, but only an empty space (Ginnunga-gap),
on whose north side lay the region of mist, ice, and snow,
(Niflheim) and on its south side the region of warmth and
sunlight, (Muspelheim). The warm breaths from the sun-land
caused the ice to melt, and topple over into Ginnunga-gap;
and from the matter so accumulated sprang the huge Ymir, ancestor of the Reimthursen, Rime, or Frost,—giants. Ymir
fed on the milk of the cow Audhumbla, whose name, it may
be observed, in the Zendavesta, stands indifferently for
"cow" or mother-earth. The cow herself lived by licking
the ice-blocks; from which, in consequence of the licking,
was produced Bori, who is alike the fashioner of the world,
and the father of Bor, who was the father of Odin. Odin's
brothers were Wili and We: and just as in Hesiod the deities
Zeus, Poseidon, and Hades supplant Kronos, so the sons of
Bori overthrow and succeed the primitive dynasty of Ymir
and the Frost Giants. Also, the dead Ymir is turned to account similarly with the dead Kronos. His flesh becomes
earth; his blood, the sea; his bones, the mountains; his
teeth, cliffs and crags; his skull, the heavens, wherein his
brains float in the form of clouds. The heavens, are supported by four Dwarves—Austri (east), Westri (west) Nordri
(north), and Sudri (south); and the stars in it are the sparks
from the fire-land of Muspelheim. The new world thus
fashioned was called Midgard, as being placed midway between the lands of frost and fire. To preserve it and its inhabitants from the giants, who dwelt in Jötunheim, Odin and

his brother surrounded it with a fence made from the eye-brows of Ymir. The inhabitants themselves were said to have been produced from two pieces of wood which the brothers found floating on the sea, and changed into a man, whom they named Ash, and a woman, whom they named Embla.

From this middle world, or Midgard, arose the Norse Olympos, or Asgard, whereon dwelt the Asa folk—Odin and the twelve Aesir. It contained two mansions—Gladsheim for the gods, and Vingolf for the goddesses. There also was Walhalla, wherein Odin placed one-half of the heroes slain in battle, the other half being received by Freija, the wife of Odin. Besides those already named there were, as the Edda says, other homesteads, such as Elfheim, where the elves dwelt; Breidablick, where dwelt the bright and beautiful, far-seeing Baldur; Himinbiorg, or the Heaven-tower of the thunder-god Thor; and Valaskialf, whence Odin could watch all gods and men. The gods also met in daily council beneath the branches of the tree Yggdrasil, one of whose roots grew in Asgard, the second in Niflheim, and the third in the realm of Hela, or Death: and their way thither lay over the bright Asa-bridge, or Bifraust, or Rainbow, which was said to burn all a-fire, so as to keep away the Frost giants of Jötunheim. Lastly, the

LOWER WORLD

was ruled by the goddess Hel; and to it were consigned those who had not died in battle. It was so far away that Odin's swift horse Sleipnir took nine nights to reach it. The river Gioll—the Norse Styx—surrounded this lower world on every side. Nastrand was the name of the worst spot in the Norse hell. Its roofs and doors were wattled with hissing snakes,

XXXV

Odin.

ejecting poison, through which perjurers and murderers were forced to wade by way of punishment.

THE AESIR,

Whose thrones were in Gladsheim, were twelve in number. Their names were—Thor, Baldr, Freyr, Tyr, Bragi, Hödr, Heimdall, Vithar, Vali, Ullr, Ve, Forseti. Thus, with Odin, the "All-father," whose throne rose above the other twelve, the great gods of the Norse Pantheon were thirteen in number.

ODIN.

(PLATE XXXV.)

The physical origin of the idea of Odin is evident, fir**.** from the meaning of his name, and, secondly, from the various attributes assigned to him. The word Odin is simply another form of Woden, or Wuotan, which Grimm connects with the Latin *vadere*. He is thus the moving, life-giving breath or air of heaven; and as such corresponds to the Hindoo Brahmin =Atman (German, Athem), or ever-present life and energy. His Greek correlative is, of course, Zeus, who is likewise spoken of as All-father. The name Zeus is derived from a root signifying "to shine," and thus the King of the Greek Asgard was originally "the glistening ether." It was but natural that Odin, as the personification of the blue sky, should rule the rain-clouds and the sunlight; hence as Odin the rain-giver he corresponds with Zeus Ombrios (the showery Zeus), while as the light-god he is merely a Norse Phœbos or Apollo, whose spear—the sun rays—disperses the darkness. As sky-god, and god of the moving air, he was, no less natu·

rally or inevitably, invoked as the protector of sailors. In this respect he corresponds or is interchangeable with Thor. But this interchange, or overlapping, of functions is as distinc-tive of Norse as of Greek mythology. Finally, Zeus and Odin resemble each other in their development from purely physical into spiritual beings. Odin, the ever-present ether, becomes the ever-present and ever-knowing spirit, the Father of all. And as Zeus is the father of the Muses, so Odin is the father of Saga, the goddess of poetry. The two ravens that sat on the shoulders of Odin, and every morning brought him news of what was passing in the world, were called Hunin and Munin—Thought and Memory. Memory, or Mnemosyne, was the mother of the Greek Muses. A trace of the worship of Odin survives even to the present day. In one of the Orkney islands is an Odin stone, in a hollow of which super-stitious people thrust their hands, by way of testifying on their most solemn oath. The island of Heligoland is said to have derived its name from Odin, who was also named Helgi (*der Heilige*), or the Holy. "Charles's Wain," as we now call it, was named Odin's Wain; and the "Milky Way" was also known as Odin's Way. Unlike Zeus—the Greek All-father—Odin was also a god of war. Hence it was that, as already ob-served, he received into Walhalla one-half of the heroes slain in battle.

The two goddesses *Frigg* and *Freija*, who were at different times believed to be each the wife of Odin, appear to be the one simply a development of the other. Of all the goddesses, Frigg was the best and dearest to Odin. She sat enthroned beside him, and surveyed the world. She knew all, and exercised control over the whole face of nature. In Plate XXXVI. she is represented seated with the golden spindle by

Frigg.

Freija.

Thor.

her side, with which she used to spin. She is attended by her handmaiden *Full* or *Fulla*. Freija was also a goddess who presided over smiling nature, sending sunshine, rain, and harvest. She was further a goddess into whose charge the dead passed. As has been said, half the number of heroes who fell in battle belonged to her. She is represented in Plate XXXVII. driving in a cart drawn by two cats.

In Plate XXXV. Odin is figured seated on his throne, and attended by the ravens, Hunin and Munin, and the two dogs.

THOR,

(PLATE XXXVIII.,)

Or Donar, simply meant the Thunderer—*der Donnerer;* and he dwelt in the vault of heaven. As he was likewise said to be the son of Odin, or of Heaven, it is evident that, as in the case of the All-father, he had a purely physical origin. As the god of thunder and lightning Thor resembles Zeus; and as the thunderbolts of Zeus were forged by the smith-god Hephæstos, who dwelt below ground, so the hammer of Odin was smithied by the Dwarves (*zwerge*), or black elves, who dwelt within the earth. Thor is represented driving through the clouds in a car drawn by two goats. Among the pagan Norsemen, Thor's hammer was held in as much reverence as Christ's cross among Christians. It was carved on their grave-stones; and, wrought of wood, or of iron, it was suspended in their temples. Thor, under the symbol of the hammer, was invoked as the deity who made marriages fruitful. He was also the god of the hearth and of fire.

As a sky-god Thor is identical with Odin much in the

same way as Vishnu is with Indra.   While the other Asa folk
ride to their trysting-place, Thor goes on foot: he is the
striding god, as Vishnu is, who traverses heaven in three
steps. Thor is perhaps identical with the Gallic god Taranis,
whose name resembles in sound the Scottish Celtic word for
thunder. Thor has also been identified with the Slavonic
god Perkunes, or Perune, whose name, according to a well-
known law of phonetic change, is thought to be connected
with the Greek word for thunder—Keraunos.

In Plate XXXVIII. Thor is represented driving in his car
drawn by two goats, with his hammer raised to strike.

BALDR

Means the shining god.   His son Brono means daylight, in
the Anglo-Saxon theogony.   His home is called Breidablick
—the far or wide-shining; and the name evidently conveys
an idea similar to that suggested by such Greek words as
Euryphassa, Eurynome, and Eurydike.   The story of Baldr
—the most lovely and pathetic not only in Norse but in any
mythology—leaves no doubt whatever as to its physical origin
and significance.   The joy of the world in the presence of
Baldr means only the gladness inspired by sunlight.   The
solemn oath sworn by all living things not to hurt the bright
god, and their speechless dismay at his death, only mean the
gloom of the northern climes during the winter months,
when, in the purely concrete language of the primitive race,
Baldr, or the sun, was dead.

The myth says that only the mistletoe had not sworn not
to hurt Baldr; that Loki discovered the fact, and then
directed Hödr—the blind god of the winter months—to
shoot him with a twig of it.   This mistletoe-bough is another

Freyr.

form of the thorn with which Odin puts to sleep the spring maiden Brynhild; of the thorn of the Persian Isfeudyar; or of the boar's tusk which kills the bright, spring-like Adonis. Loki, it was said, fled from the wrath of the gods, changed himself into a salmon, was then caught by them in a net, and bound fast until the twilight of the gods—or, in Christian terminology, until the judgment-day. The unlucky Hödr was killed by Odin's son, Bali, whose home was among the willows and in the dry grass.

FREYR,

(PLATE XXXIX.,)

Is likewise named Fro. The functions ascribed to him are another instance of that interchange or overlapping to which we have referred above, and which seems to be accounted for by the hypothesis that whole groups of mythical beings are in reality but personified epithets of one and the same thing. Thus Freyr, as the cause of fruitfulness, is merely the sun-lit and air-breathing heaven as represented by Odin. Like Odin he is the patron of seafarers. Not only is Freyr repeated, so to speak, in Odin, but also—or if not the god himself, then his servant, Skirnir—in the Volsung and Niblung heroes, Sigurd, Sigmund, and Gunnar. And as Sigurd can win the maiden Brynhild only by riding through the flaming fire which surrounded and guarded her dwelling, so by the same exploit must Skirnir win Gerda for the master. In later times, when the old religion had given way before Christianity, and its myths were being explained on the Euhemerist method, it was alleged that Freyr had only been a Swedish king, whose sorrowing subjects buried his body in a magnificent tomb, to which, for three whole years, they continued to bring their presents, as if Freyr were alive.

This Euhemerism is, however, inconsistent with the most authoritative source of all—the Eddas.   In Dasent's "Prose Edda" Freyr is described as the god of rain, sunshine, and fruits—as Odin, in fact, in another shape. His wife was Gredr, whose beauty—as he saw her leaving her father's house, and shedding a lustre over air and sea—captivated the god, and allowed him no rest till he won her.

In Plate XXXIX. Freyr is represented riding on a wild boar through the air, at a speed greater than that of the swiftest horse.   Sometimes he was drawn by it in a car.   In crossing the sea he also used a boat.

TYR

Is likewise named Ziu, and Saxnot.   Our word Tuesday is a memorial of his name.   Once more, this god seems to be an instance of personifying an epithet.   Ziu is identical with the root—meaning "shine"—of the Sanscrit *Dynaus*, the Greek *Zeus*, and the Latin *Deus*.   Tyr, therefore, is another glistening god.   He is pre-eminently the god of war and of athletic sports.   "On him it is good for wrestlers to call."   Tyr had only one hand, the other having been bitten off by the wolf Fenris, into whose mouth the god had placed it as a pledge of security, when the wolf allowed himself to be bound in the net that shall hold him fast till the judgment-day.

BRAGI

Is the god of poetry and eloquence.   "He is famous for wisdom, and best in tongue-wit and cunning speech.'' A sort of counterpart of this god was his wife Iduna, who dwelt in the under world. She is spoken of in terms that recall the Hindoo description of Ushas—Eos—or the Daure goddess. For as Ushas—the Dawn—makes the world young every new morning, so Iduna is said to preserve in a box the golden apples which the gods ate, and so made themselves young again.

HEIMDALL

Was the watchman of the bridge Bifröst, leading to the underworld. The sound of Heimdall's horn is heard over the world, and shall be the signal for the great battle between the gods on the day of their ending, or twilight. The name of his horse, Gulltopr (Goldropf, or golden mare), connects him with the sun-gods and sun-horses of classical mythology. Heimdall was so sharp a watchman that he could even hear the grass grow on the earth, and the wool on the backs of sheep!

Vithar was next in strength to Thor. As the "twilight,'' or *Götterdämmerung*, Vithar shall destroy the wolf Fenris, the devourer of the gods, by placing one foot on the monster's lower jaw, and pushing up the upper one—thus wrenching them asunder. **Ulle** is the god of the chase; a skilful bowman, and a fast runner on stilts. Like Bragi and Iduna, **Mimir** is the deity of wisdom and knowledge. He dwelt by the ash-tree, Yggdrasil, beneath whose roots bubbled forth the well of wisdom, Mimir's well, from whose waters Mimir drank his daily draught.

Loki dwelt in the land of the dead. He was the son of the giant Farbanti, whose duty it was to ferry the dead over the waters of the lower world. Loki had three children as cruel and hateful as he himself was full of mischief. One was the huge wolf **Fenris** (Plate XL.), who, at the last day, shall hurry gaping to the scene of battle, with his lower jaw scraping the earth and his nose scraping the sky! The second was the serpent of Midgard—the serpent which Odin threw into the sea, where the monster grew to such length that it embraced the whole world in its folds. The third was the goddess **Hel**, who was half black and half blue, and lived daintily on the brains and marrow of men.

Hel is, in fact, that dreadful Hindoo goddess Kali, who, in these modern days, has degenerated into a Doorga of quite a pathetic and interesting character. Loki was at the bottom of all the mischief that ever happened in the society of the gods. The character of this god, and his close relationship with a personage who figures conspicuously in modern theology, are pretty well indicated in the following adage, with its equivalents in German and English: Loki er or böndum —der Teufel ist frei gelassen—the devil is loose.

Of the almost countless beings who figure in Norse mythology we must say but very little. Like the great gods, they appear to be representative of the good and evil powers of nature. Among them are the Elves (Alfen, Elfen,) who live in Alfheimr (Elf-home). Their king is the Erlkönig (Elfen Konig). In the night hours they come in troops to dance in the grass, leaving, according to popular belief, their traces in the form of fairy-rings. The dwarves (Zwerge), whose father is named Ivaldr, dwell in the heart of the hills. To them belong precious stones and metals, on which they prove their skill in workmanship. As guardians of hidden treasures they were propitiated by the seekers of the same with a black goat or a black cock. An echo is called by the

The Wolf Fenris.

Icelanders Dwergmaal-Zwergsprache—or dwarf-voice. The evil beings who stole the light every evening, and the summer every year, were called giants. Such were the Reifriesen (Hrimthursen) who brought the winter. The giant Hrungnir had a head of stone, and a heart of stone; and a giantess, mother of Gmir, as many as nine hundred heads. Another giant was Thiassi, who slew Thor and cast his eyes up to heaven, where they shone thereafter as stars. In the extreme north dwelt the giant Hresvelgr, the motion of whose wings caused wind and tempest, in which respect he resembles the gigantic bird of the Buddhist play, *Nagananda*, who raises the waves on the sea by the flapping of his wings. On the extreme south was Surtr, whose flaming sword guarded the bounds of Muspelheim. Besides these there were the Tröll-weiber (troll arvis), phantoms from the land of the dead, who in the dark nights rode to the earth on a wolf bridled with snakes. The three Nornen were the Norse Fates. The Valkyrien were fair maidens who hovered over the field of battle, woke up the dead heroes with a kiss, and led away their souls to fight and drink ale as of old in the happy Valhalla.

THE TALE OF THE VOLSUNGS AND NIBLUNGS.

THE Volsunga Saga and Nibelungenlied hardly differ in anything but the name. The one is merely the Norse, the other the German, form of one and the same nature myth, or epic. According to the "Solar myth" theorists, this epic serves the common purpose of all Aryan nations; in India being known under the names of Ramayana and Mahabharata; in Greece as the Iliad and the Odyssey; in our more northern lands as the Tale of the Volsungs, and the Nibelungen Lay;

and in England as the tale of King Arthur and his Knights of the Round Table.   Whatever objections may be urged against the "Solar myths" explanation of these stories, it is quite indisputable that the main incidents in all of them completely coincide.   Indeed it is not too much to affirm that fully to appreciate the spirit of any one of these great epics of the world, the student must possess some acquaintance with its co-ordinate ones.   But not only do the main incidents in the Northern Epics coincide with those in the Iliad and Odyssey, but they even contain episodes which correspond in everything except the name with plots in Greek tragedy. Gudrun, for example, is only a Norse Medea.   We now proceed to give a slight sketch of the Volsunga Saga.

Volsung was the son of Rerir, the son of the Sigi, the son of Odin.   Volsung lay for seven years in his mother's womb; and they said the youngling kissed his mother or ever she died.   Volsung had a daughter called Signy, who was married to Siggeir, King of Gothland.   During the marriage festivities in Volsung's house, and as the good folk sat round the evening fire, there entered an old man wrapped in a cloak, who drove a sword into a log of wood right up to the hilt, predicted great things of the hero who should be able to draw it out again, and immediately disappeared.   The old man was Odin; and the sword was the sword of Gram, which has its counterpart in the sword of Chrysaor, in Roland's Durandal, and in King Arthur's Excalibur.   And as only Theseus could lift the huge stone, and none but Ulysses could draw his own bow, so among the assembled heroes only Sigmund the son of Volsung could pull out Gram.

Volsung was afterwards murdered in the land of Siggeir; wherefore Sigmund avenged the death of his father by killing the children of his brother-in-law, Siggeir. After that he returned to his own land, and married Borghild, by whom he had two children, Helgi and Hamund. But Sigmund was no more constant in his loves than other heroes of whom we read in classical literature. He fell in love with Hjordis, who was beloved by the son of King Hunding. Between the two heroes there ensued a fight, during which the one-eyed man in a blue cloak, and a bill in his hand, appeared: whereupon Sigmund was slain. The dying Sigmund comforted his wife Hjordis, and entrusted to her charge his sword Gram, wishing her to preserve it for their unborn boy. "And now," said he, "I grow weary with my wounds, and I will go to see our kin that have gone before me." So Hjordis sat over him till he died at the day dawning.

Hjordis after that married Hialprek, King of Denmark, a character who corresponds to the Grecian Laios and Akrisios. At Hialprek's court was born Sigurd, the son of Hjordis and Sigmund—the favourite hero of Norse mythology. Sigurd was taught in all the arts and sciences by Regin, the cunning blacksmith, who was also the brother of the otter killed by Odin, and the serpent—or worm—Fafnir, who guarded those golden treasures which, according to the Solar theory, mean the gladdening and revivifying sunlight, Fafnir himself being the evil power, the cloud, or the darkness which steals the light. Regin wished to secure the treasure for himself, and forged a sword for Sigurd to slay the worm with. But it shivered into pieces on its very first trial; and Sigurd, in contempt at Regin's smithing, procures the fragments of his paternal sword Gram, and Regin welds them together. Gram stood every test. Sigurd drove it, right to the hilt, into Regin's anvil: and after that, a lock of wool, borne on the surface of the stream, divided into two against the motionless edge. Sigurd slew Fafnir, and procured the treasure; and next he slew Regin, who wished to possess the whole of the prize on the plea that his forging of the weapon had really won the victory. After that Sigurd went to free the Valkyrie Brynhild, according to the Solar myth the Maiden of Spring, for whom the cold earth is longing. Brynhild lay in the sleep into which she had been thrown by the thorn of Odin—that is, by the thorn, or cold, or frost of winter.

Sigurd, like his mythical relatives in Norse and Greek stories, was unfaithful in his loves. He fell in love with Gudrun, the sister of Gunnar, and that, too, in spite of those love scenes and speeches of his with Brynhild, for the beauty of which the Volsung Saga is perhaps unequalled by any other epic story whatever. Brynhild had sworn to marry only the man who could ride through the fire which surrounded her dwelling. This Gunnar could not do; but Sigurd did it in Gunnar's shape, whereafter Brynhild agreed to marry Gunnar. But Gudrun, in her triumph, revealed the secret; and just as Œnone procured the death of the unfaithful Paris, and Deianeira that of the fickle Herakles, so Brynhild compassed the death of Sigurd. Brynhild also, like another Deianeira, dies, in grief, on the funeral pile of her husband. Next, Gudrun, also grieving for Sigurd, leaves her home; but she marries Atli, King of Hunland. It would seem that this Atli must be another name for the powers of darkness, for he invited his wife's brothers to his court, in order that he might seize the golden treasure, "the sunlight," which they had received from the dead Sigurd. These treasures the brothers buried in the Rhine river, and went on their way to Hunland, though they well knew they were destined never to return. The scene in which the brothers are slain by the treacherous Atli is unsurpassed for power and terror by any fighting story, except, perhaps, by that one in the Mahabharata which describes the final struggle on the battle-field of Hastinapur. Next follows Gudrun's revenge for the death of her brothers; like, as we have already said, a Norse Medea, she slew her own and Atli's children.

But we cannot further pursue those final tragedies in which all the various kinsfolk die by each other's hands, and in obedience to that stern, inevitable fate which in these tales seems to be personified in Odin, and looms so terribly in the background of the dramas of Sophocles and Æschylus.

We would in conclusion recommend the student to read the translation of the Volsung Saga, recently published by Messrs. Morris and Magnusson, as also Dr. Dasent's translation of the prose Edda. Those who know German may also consult Wilhelm Mannhardt's *Die Götter der deutschen und nordischen Völker*, published in Berlin, 1860. For an exhaustive exposition of the "Solar myth" theory, alike of the subjects embraced in the foregoing sketch, and of Aryan myths in general, we recommend the student to the work of the Rev. George W. Cox on "The Mythology of the Aryan Nations."

THE MYTHOLOGY AND RELIGION OF THE HINDOOS.

IN the Veda, the earliest record of the Sanscrit language, many of the myths common to the Aryan nations are presented in their simplest form.   Hence the special value of Hindoo myths in a study of Comparative Mythology.   But it would be an error to suppose that the myths of the Greeks, Latins, Slavonians, Norsemen, old Germans, and Celts were *derived* from those of the Hindoos.   For the myths, like the languages, of all these various races, the Hindoos included, are derived from one common source.   Greek, Latin, Sanscrit, etc., are but modifications of a primitive Aryan language that was spoken by the early "Aryans" before they branched away from their original home, wherever that may have been, to form new nationalities in India, Greece, Northern Europe, Central Europe, etc.   The Sanscrit language is thus not the mother, but the elder sister of Greek and the kindred tongues: and the Vedic mythology is, in like manner, only the elder sister of the other Aryan mythologies.   It is by reason of the discovery of the common origin of these languages that scholars have been enabled to treat mythology scientifically. For example, many names unintelligible in Greek are at once explained by the meaning of their Sanscrit equivalents. Thus, the name of the chief Greek god, Zeus, conveys no meaning in itself.   But the Greek sky-god **Zeus** evidently corresponds to the Hindoo sky-god **Dyaus,** and this word is derived from a root **div** or **dyu,** meaning "to shine." Zeus, then, meant originally "the glistening ether;" and the Sanscrit **devas,** Greek **theos,** and Latin **deus,** meaning "god," are from the same root, and signify "shining" or "heavenly." Similarly other Greeek names are explained by their counterparts, or cognate works in Sanscrit. Thus the name of Zeus's wife, Hera, belongs to a Sanscrit root **svar,** and originally meant the bright sky, the goddess herself being primarily the bright air; and Erins is explained by the Sanscrit **Saranyu.** In India there have been two dynasties, as it were, of gods— the Vedic and Brahmanic. The Vedic gods belong to the very earliest times, appear obviously as elemental powers, and are such as would have been worshipped by a simple, uninstructed, agricultural people. The Brahmanic religion was, in great part at least, a refined development of the former; and was gradually displacing the simpler worship of Vedism many centuries before the birth of Christ. Five or six centuries before the last event, Dissent, under the name and form of Buddhism, became the chief religion of India; but in about ten centuries Brahmanism recovered its old position. Buddhism now retains but comparatively few followers in India. Its chief holds are in Burmah, Siam, Japan, Thibet, Nepaul, China, and Mongolia: and its nominal followers at the present day, perhaps outnumber those of all other religions put together.

THE VEDIC GODS.

DYAUS

Was, as we have already indicated, the god of the bright sky, his name being connected with that of Zeus through the root *div* or *dyu*. That the god-name and the sky-name were interchangeable is evident from such classical expressions as that "Zeus rains" (*i. e.*, the sky rains). In such expressions there is hardly any mythological suggestion: and the meaning of the name Dyaus,—like those of the names Ouranos and Kronos in Greek,—always remained too transparent for it to become the nucleus of a myth. Dyaus, however, was occasionally spoken of as an overruling spirit. The epithet, Dyaus pitar, is simply Zeus pater—Zeus the father; or, as it is spelled in Latin, Jupiter. Another of his names, *Janitar*, is the Sanscrit for genetor, a title of Zeus as the father or producer. *Dyaus pitar*, "father sky," and *prithus matar*, "mother earth," are generally spoken of together.

VARUNA

Is also a sky-god: but in later times he becomes god of the waters. The name is derived from the root *var*, to cover, or envelop: and so far Varuna (accent Váruna) means the vault of heaven. Here, then, we seem to find a clue to the meaning of the Greek Ouranos, whom we already know to have been a sky-god ; Ouranos means the coverer; but, as observed above, the name would have remained unintelligible apart from its reference to the Sanscrit name. The myth of Varuna is a wonderful instance of the readiness and completeness with which the Hindoo genius spiritualized its sense-impressions. From the conception of the thousand-eyed (or starred) Varuna, who overlooked all men and things, the Indian Aryans passed to the loftier conception of Varuna as an all-seeing god or providence, whose spies, or angels, saw all that took place. Some of the finest passages in the Vedic hymns are those in which the all-seeing Varuna is addressed : as in the following verses, translated by Muller from the Rigveda :—

"Let me not yet, O Varuna, enter into the house of clay; have mercy, Almighty, have mercy!

"If I go along trembling like a cloud driven by the wind; have mercy, Almighty, have mercy!

"Through want of strength, though strong and bright god, have I gone to the wrong shore; have mercy, Almighty, have mercy!

"Thirst came upon the worshipper, tho' he stood in the midst of the waters; have mercy, Almighty, have mercy!

"Whenever we men, O Varuna, committed offence before the heavenly host, whenever we break thy law through thoughtfulness; have mercy, Almighty, have mercy!"

INDRA.

(PLATE XLI.)

The connection, or identity, between Zeus and Dyaus seems to be chiefly limited to the names. There is greater resemblance between Indra and Zeus than between Zeus and Dyaus. Indra, as the hurler of the thunderbolts, and as a "cloud compeller," coincides with Zeus and Thor.

The myth of Indra—the favourite Vedic god—is a further instance of that transition from the physical to spiritual meaning to which we have referred; though Indra is by no means so spiritual a being as Varuna. It is also a good instance of the fact that, as the comparative mythologists express it, the further back the myths are traced the more " atmospheric " do the gods become. First, of the merely physical Indra. Indra shatters the cloud with his bolt, and releases the imprisoned waters. His purely physical origin is further indicated by the mythical expression that the clouds moved in Indra as the winds in Dyaus—an expression implying that Indra was a name for the sky. Also, the stories told of him correspond closely with some in classical mythology. Like Hermes and Herakles, he is endowed with precocious strength ; like Hermes he goes in search of the cattle, the clouds which the evil powers have driven away; and like Hermes he is assisted by the breezes—though in the Hindoo myth by the storm-winds, rather—the *Maruts*. His beard of lightning is the red beard of Thor. In a land with the climatic conditions of India, and among an agricultural people, it was but natural that the god whose fertilizing showers brought the corn and wine to maturity should be regarded as the greatest of all.

" He who as soon as born is the first of the deities, who has done honour to the gods by his exploits; he at whose might heaven and earth are alarmed, and who is known by the greatness of his strength ; he, men, is Indra.

" He who fixed firm the moving earth; who tranquillized the incensed mountains; who spread the spacious firmament; who consolidated the heavens; he, men, is Indra.

" He who, having destroyed Ahi, set free the seven rivers : who recovered the cows detained by Bal ; who generated fire in the clouds ; who is invincible in battle : he, men, is Indra.

" He under whose control are horses and cattle, and villages, and all chariots; who gave birth to the sun and to the dawn ; and who is the leader of the waters : he, men, is Indra.

" He to whom heaven and earth bow down ; he at whose might the mountains are appalled ; he who is the drinker of the Soma juice, the firm of frame, the adamant-armed, the wielder of the thunderbolt: he men, is Indra.

" May we envelop thee with acceptable praises as husbands are embraced by their wives !"

The first verse in the preceding hymn from the Rigveda perhaps refers to Indra as a sun-god, and to the rapidity with which, in tropical climates, the newly-born sun grows in heat-giving powers. The Ahi, or throttling snake, of the third verse, is the same as the Greek Echidna, or the Hindoo Vritra; and is multiplied in the Rakshasas—or powers of darkness—against which the sky-god Indra wages deadly war. He is likewise spoken of in the same hymn in much the same kind of language that would naturally be applied to the creator and sustainer of the world. But so is almost every Hindoo deity. Absolute supremacy was attributed to each and every god, whenever it came to his turn to be praised or propitiated.

SURYA

Corresponds to the Greek Helios. That is, he was not so much the god of light as the special god who dwelt in the body of the sun. The same distinction exists between Poseidon and Nereus; the one being the god of all waters, and even a visitor at Olympos, the other a dweller in the sea. Sûrya is described as the husband of the dawn, and also as her son.

SAVITAR

Is another personification of the sun. His name means the " Inciter or enlivener," and is derived from the root su, to drive or stimulate. As the sun-god he is spoken of as the golden-eyed, golden-tongued, and golden-handed; and the Hindoo commentators, in their absurd attempts to give a literal prosaic explanation of a highly appropriate poetic epithet, say that Savitar cut off his hand at a sacrifice, and that the priests gave him a golden one instead. Savitar thus corresponds to the Teutonic god Tyr, whose hand was cut off by the wolf Fenris. Like other gods in the Hindoo and Norse mythologies, Savitar is regarded as all-powerful. That Savitar is a sun-god appears from the following passages, among many others, from the Rigveda:—

" Shining forth he rises from the lap of the dawn, praised by singers; he, he, my god Savitar, stepped forth, who never misses the same place.

" He steps forth, the splendour of the sky, the wide-seeing, the far-shining, the shining wanderer; surely enlivened by the sun do men go to their tasks, and do their work.

" May the golden-eyed Savitar arise hither !

" May the golden-handed, life-bestowing, well guarding, exhilarating, and affluent Savitar be present at the sacrifice !"

The second passage seems to identify Savitar with Odin, who was also " the wanderer "—*Wegtom,* and who was one-eyed, as Savitar was one-handed.

SOMA.

In some respects the myth of Soma is the most curious of all. Soma, as the intoxicating juice of the Soma plant, corresponds to that mixture of honey and blood of the Quoasir, which, in the Norse mythology, imparts prolonged life to the gods. In the Rigveda the Soma is similarly described; as also the process by which it is converted into intoxicating liquid. But in the same hymns Soma is also described as an all-powerful god. It is he who gives strength to Indra, and enables him to conquer his enemy Vritra, the snake of darkness. He is further, like Vishnu, Indra, and Varuna, the supporter of heaven and earth, and of gods and men; thus it would seem as if the myth of the god Soma is but an instance of that fetishistic stage in the history of the human kind during which men attributed conscious life and energy to whatever hurt or benefited them. The following passages from the Rigveda are adduced to show in what terms Soma was spoken of as a god, and as a mere plant:—

"Where there is eternal light, in the world where the sun is placed, in that immortal, imperishable world, place me, O Soma . . .

"Where life is free, in the third heaven of heavens, where the worlds are radiant, there make me immortal."

And again,—

"In the filter, which is the support of the world, thou, pure Soma, art purified for the gods. The Usijas first gathered thee. In thee all these worlds are contained.

"The Soma flowed into the vessel for Indra, for Vishnu; may it be honeyed for Vâyu!"

AGNI

Is the god of fire, his name evidently being connected with the Latin *ignis*. He corresponds to the Greek Hephæstos. Of this god Mr. Wheeler, in his introduction to his History of India, thus writes: "To man in a primitive state of existence the presence of fire excites feelings of reverence. Its powers raise it to the rank of a deity whose operations are felt and seen. It burns and it consumes. It dispels the darkness, and with it drives away, not only the imaginary horrors which the mind associates with darkness, but also the real horrors—such as beasts of prey. . . . It becomes identified with the light of the sun and moon; with the lightning which shoots from the sky and shatters the loftiest trees and strikes down the strong man; with the deity who covers the field with grain and ripens the harvest; with the divine messenger who licks up the sacrifice and carries it to the gods."

As another curious instance of the sort of fetishism to which we have referred, the Veda describes Agni as being generated from the rubbing of sticks, after which he bursts forth from the wood like a fleet courser. Again, when excited by the wind he rushes amongst the trees like a bull, and consumes the forest as a raja destroys his enemies. Such expressions of course prove the purely physical origin of the god Agni; and it is hardly necessary to observe that, like Indra, Varuna, Soma, Vishnu, etc., he is an all-powerful god, and supporter of the universe.

VAYU

Is the god of the winds, or of the air. Allied to him are the Maruts,—the storm-gods, or "crushers," whose name has been derived from a root meaning to grind, and regarded as connected with such names as Mars and Ares. The same root appears in Miolnir, an epithet of Thor, conceived as the crashing or crushing god. The Maruts are the Hindoo counterparts of the Norse Ogres—the fierce storm-beings who toss the sea into foam, and who, in the Norse Tales, are represented as being armed with iron clubs, at every stroke of which they send the earth flying so many yards into the air. The primary meaning of the name is clear from the Vedic passages which describe the Maruts as roaring among the forest trees, and tearing up the clouds for rain.

Among all the personifications of Hindoo mythology, one of the purest and most touching and beautiful is

USHAS,

Whose name is the same as the Greek Eos—or the Dawn. The name Ushas is derived from a root *us*, to burn. The language in which the physical Ushas was spoken of was especially capable of easy transformation into a purely spiritual meaning. The dawn-light is beautiful to all men, barbarous or civilized; and it did not require any great stretch of poetic fancy to represent Ushas as a young wife awakening her children, and giving them new strength for the toils of the new day. It happens that the word which in Sanscrit means "to awake," also means "to know;" and thus, like the Greek Athene, Ushas became a goddess of wisdom. The following passages show how Ushas was regarded by the Vedic worshippers :—

"Ushas, daughter of heaven, dawn upon us with riches; diffuser of light, dawn upon us with abundant food; beautiful goddess, dawn upon us with wealth of cattle.

"This auspicious Ushas has harnessed her vehicles from afar, above the rising of the sun, and she comes gloriously upon men with a hundred chariots.

"First of all the world is she awake, trampling over transitory darkness; the mighty, the giver of light, from on high she beholds all things; ever youthful, ever reviving, she comes first to the invocation."

Had we space for discussion of so interesting a subject, it would be easy to show how naturally monotheistic conception would grow out of the polytheism of the Vedic religion. Meantime we content ourselves with the following monotheistic hymn, translated by Dr. Max Muller :—

"In the beginning there rose the source of golden light. He was the only lord of all that is; he established this earth and this sky: who is the god to whom we shall offer our sacrifice?

"He who gives life, he who gives strength; whose blessings all the bright gods desire; whose shadow is immortality; whose shadow is death: who is the god to whom we shall offer our sacrifice?

"He who through his power is the only king of all the breathing and awakening world. He who governs all, men and beasts: who is the god to whom we shall offer our sacrifice?

"He whose power these snowy mountains, whose power the sea proclaims, with the distant river. He whose these regions are as it were his two arms: who is the god to whom we shall offer our sacrifice?

" He through whom the sky is bright and the earth firm. He through whom the heaven was established—nay, the highest heaven; he who measured out the light in the air: who is the god to whom we shall offer our sacrifice?

He to whom heaven and earth, standing firm by his will, look up, trembling inwardly; he over whom the rising sun shines forth; who is the god to whom we shall offer our sacrifice?

      *   *   *   *   *   *   *   *   *

" May he not destroy us, he the creator of the earth; or he the righteous, who created heaven; he who also created the bright and mighty waters: who is the god to whom we shall offer our sacrifice? "

THE BRAHMANIC GODS.

Of the later Hindoo religion the chief deities are Brahma, Vishnu, and Siva—forming the Hindoo Trinity, or Trimûrti. These are not regarded as separate, independent gods, but merely as three manifestations or revelations or phases of the spirit or energy of the supreme incomprehensible being **Brahm**. This trinity is a comparatively late formation. The trinity of the later Vedic writings is composed rather, of the representative gods of earth, air, and sky. Agni, Vayu, and Surya. Again, no such trinity as the Brahmanic, appears to be known in the Mahabharata, which represents Brahma, Vishnu, and Indra as being the sons of Mahadeva, or Siva. Perhaps, however, the reason of this is to be found in the mutual jealousy of the two great sects, Vaishnavas and Saivas, into which the Hindoo religion came to be divided. To Brahm as the self-existent—of whom there is no image— there existed neither temples nor altars. As signifying, among other things, the principle of divinity, the name Brahm is of the neuter gender, and the divine essence is described as that which illumines all, delights all, whence all

XLI

Trimûrti, or Hindoo Trinity.

Indra.

proceeds, that of which all live when born, and that to which all must return.

BRAHMA

(PLATE XLII.)

Is that member of the triad whose name is best known to Englishmen, and most familiar to the Hindoos themselves. Images of him are found in the temples of other gods, but he has neither temples nor altars of his own. The reason of this is that Brahma, as the creative energy, is quiescent, and will remain so until the end of the present age of the world —of the *Kali Yuga*, that is—only a small portion of whose 432,000 years has already passed.

It appears, however, that an attempt was made to represent even the divine spirit of Brahm; for the god Narayana means the spirit moving on the waters. Narayana is figured as a graceful youth lying on a snake couch which floats on the water, and holding his toe in his mouth.

Brahma is figured as a four-headed god, bearing in one hand a copy of the Vedas, in another a spoon for pouring out the lustral water contained in a vessel which he holds in a third hand, while the fourth hand holds a rosary. The rosary was used by the Hindoos to aid them in contemplation, a bead being dropped on the silent pronunciation of each name of the god, while the devotee mused on the attribute signified by the name.

Brahma, like each god, had his *sacti*, or wife, or female counterpart, and his *vâhana* or vehicle, whereon he rode. Brahma's *sacti*, is **Saraswati**, the goddess of poetry, wisdom, eloquence, and fine art. His *vahana* was the goose— *hansa*, in Latin, *anser*, in German, *gans*.

22

VISHNU

(PLATE XLII.)

Is the personification of the *preserving* power of the divine
spirit. The Vaishnavas allege that Vishnu is the paramount
god, because there is nothing distinctive in the act of an-
nihilation, but only a cessation of preservation. But of
course the argument would cut all three ways, for it might as
well be said that creation, preservation, and destruction are
at bottom only one and the same thing—a fact thus pointing
to the unity of God. Of the two Hindoo sects the Vaish-
naivas are perhaps the more numerous. Vishnu is represented as being of a blue colour ; his *vâhana* is Garuda, the
winged half-man, half-bird, king of birds, and his *sacti*, or
wife, is the goddess Lakshmi. He is said to have four hands
—one holding a *shankha*, or shell, the second a *chakra* or
quoit, the third a club, and the fourth a lotus Plate XLII.
represents Vishnu lying asleep on Ananta, the serpent of
eternity. At the end of the *Kali Yuga*, Vishnu will rest in
that position ; from his navel will spring a lotus stalk, on the
top of which—above the surface of the waters, which at that
time will cover the world—Brahma will appear to create the
earth anew.

SIVA

(PLATE XLIII.)

Is the destroyer—the third phase of Brahm's energy. He is
represented as of a white colour. His *sacti* is Bhavani or
Pracriti, the terrible Doorga or Kali, and his *vâhana* a white

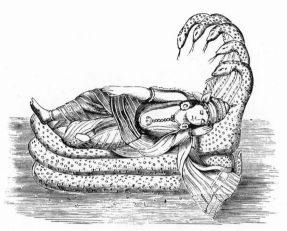

XLII

Vishnu.

Brahma with Saraswati.

XLIII.

Kamadeva.

Siva.

bull. Sometimes Siva is figured with a trident in one hand, and in another a rope or *pasha*, with which he, or his wife Kali, strangles evil-doers. His necklace is made of human skulls; serpents are his ear-rings; his loins are wrapped in tiger's skin; and from his head the sacred river Ganga is represented as springing.

Among the minor deities may be mentioned **Kuvera,** the god of riches; Lakshmi, being the goddess of wealth; **Kamadeva,** the god of love, who is represented (see Plate XLIII.) as riding on a dove, and armed with an arrow of flowers, and a bow whose string is formed of bees; and thirdly, **Ganesha,** the son of Siva and Prithivi, who is regarded as the wisest of all the gods, is especially the god of prudence and policy, and is invoked at the opening of Hindoo literary works.

AVATARS OF VISHNU.

The word *avatar* means, in its plain sense, Descent—that is, from the world of the gods to the world of men. In these descents, or incarnations, the purpose of Vishnu has always been a beneficent one. His first avatar is named **Matsya,** wherein, during the reign of King Satyavrata, Vishnu appeared in the form of a fish. For the world had been deluged by water for its wickedness, and its inhabitants had perished, except the king and seven sages, with their families, who together with pairs of all species of animals, entered into an ark prepared for them, and of which the fish took care, by having its cable tied to its horn. In the second, or **Kurma** avatar, Vishnu appeared in the form of a tortoise, supporting Mount Mandara on his back, while the gods churned the sea for the divine ambrosia. In the **Varâha,** or third avatar, Vishnu appeared as a boar to save the earth when it had been drowned a second time. The boar went into the sea and fished the earth out on his tusks. In the fourth he appeared as **Narasingha,** the man-lion, to free the world from a monarch who, for his austerities, had been endowed by the gods with universal dominion. In this shape Vishnu tore the king to pieces. Subsequently he appeared as a dwarf; then as Rama, the hero of the Ramayana, who likewise was a beneficent being. His chief incarnation appears in Krishna, the god who is most loved by the Hindoos. Buddha, the founder of the Buddhist religion, was also said to be an incarnation of Vishnu. Nine of these avatars have already passed. In the tenth, or **Kalki Avatâra,** he will appear armed with a scimitar, and riding on a white horse, when he will end the present age; after which he will sleep on the waters, produce Prama, and so inaugurate a new world.

THE MYTHOLOGY AND RELIGION OF EGYPT.

EGYPTIAN myths undoubtedly originated and were developed similarly to the myths of all other nations with which we are acquainted. Yet an indication of the various stages of that development, and an understanding of the system as a whole, and as it is now known to us, are far more difficult in the case of Egyptian than of Greek, Norse, Germanic, or Hindoo mythology. The reason of this is very evident. The Egyptian religion seems to have reached its abstract or metaphysical stage long before any of the religions to which we have referred ; and as its records belong wholly to that stage, there are no means of enabling the student to bridge over the gap between its earliest and its latest formations.

Indeed, it would appear as if precisely the same kind of difference existed between the Egyptian and the Greek genius as between the Greek genius and that of the Hindoos. The temperament of the Greek was open, joyous, sensuous ; that of the other two races was self-repressive, brooding, and mystical. The bias or mental bent of these was not so much towards what was artistically or logically preventible, as towards the elusive, mysterious spirit of which they imagined all things visible and tangible to be merely the veil. The

341

Greek was artistically sensuous; the Hindoo was mystically religious. Or, the difference between them may be said to resemble that between form and colour. The contrast in intellectual bias between the Egyptians and their adversaries, the Greeks, is sufficiently indicated in what Herodotus says of the Egyptian contempt for the claims made by the Greeks of descent from the gods. The priests of Egypt could only laugh at the absurdity of the belief according to which a god was said to be the sixteenth ancestor of Hecatæos. *Our* gods, said they, never lived on earth.

However, it appears as if a comparison of it with other systems shows that the mythology of Egypt is, in great measure at least, explicable by the general doctrines implied in the title "Solar Myth." Even that very readiness with which the Greeks identified the Egyptian gods with their own affords, if not proof, at all events some countenance, to the supposition that both Pantheons were, so to speak, peopled after the same manner. Again, the functions and characters of the Egyptian gods interchange like those of the Greek and Norse gods. Their names have in both cases similar physical meanings. In both cases also the birth and genealogy of the gods appear to be but an expression of physical, visible sequences. We find in both cases the same confusion, or identity, between a god's mother and his sister; and what appears to be the same conflict between the light-giving and the light-stealing powers of nature. The old German religion is, perhaps, of a more spiritual character than that of Egypt. Yet there is no doubt that the idea of the contest between the purely spiritual powers Ormuzd and Ahriman was originally only the idea of the contest between the sunlight, Indra, and the clouds or darkness, Vritra. This seems a strong indirect proof that Osiris and Typho are the same as Indra and Vritra. The idea of dynastic overthrow and succession common to the Aryan religions, and presented with such weird and pathetic grandeur in Norse mythology, is, if at all, but faintly defined in the religion of Egypt. Yet it seems to be implied in such phrases as "Osirian divinities," and "three orders of the gods." Lastly, it appears that many of the Egyptian deities are only personified attributes of one and the same thing or person.

The eight great gods of Egypt were, **Neph, Amun, Pthah, Khem, Sati, Maut,** and **Bubastis.**

NEPH

Is also named Num, Nu, Nef, Cnouphis, and Cenubis. Now Nef means spirit or breath, in which sense it is still retained in Arabic. He is "the spirit of God moving on the face of the waters." Therefore in this special, physical sense Neph corresponds to the Teutonic Woden, or Wuotan (see p. 313); as also Brahma and Zeus. Neph was worshipped in Ethiopia and the Thebais. He is represented as having a ram's head with curved horns. His wife, or in Hindoo phraseology *sacti*, was named Auka.

PTHAH

Is only Neph under a new name; or, to express it otherwise, he represents a special energy of that god. He is the creator, or the universal life in *action*. Jamblichus calls him the *demiourgos*, or artisan of the world; and the Greeks regarded him as the counterpart of their own artisan god, Hephæstos or Vulcan. As the creator he was thought of as the father and sovereign of the gods. He was worshipped chiefly in

Memphis.   He appears as a mummy-shaped male figure; also as the pigmy-god.

KHEM,

Like the former god, is only a special energy or activity of the universal life.   He is a personified attribute, or epithet. He is the god of generation and reproduction, and was identified as Pan by the Greeks, who called his chief city—Chemmis, in the Thebais—by the name of Panopolis.   But Khem not only merges into the god Num or Neph, he also usurps the functions of, or is the same as, the garden-god **Ranno.** It was but natural that the god of reproduction should also be a garden-god.   This garden-god, Ranno, was represented under the form of an asp, whose figure is found on wine-presses and garden and agricultural implements. It should here be observed that Priapus, the classical counterpart of the procreative Khem, was the tutelary deity of gardens.

AMUN

Was the chief god of Upper Egypt.   From the signification of the name—"hidden"—it would appear that Amun was a deity of a highly spiritual character.   As in the preceding instances, he is identified or connected with various other gods, *e. g.*, he is named as Amun-ra (**Ra** being the sun-god), and Amun-num (**Num**, the living breath or spirit).   His companion goddess was Mut or Maut; and the two deities, with their son Khuns, formed the Trinity of Upper Egypt.

SATI

The Greeks imagined to be the same as Hera.   As such she

would be the queen of heaven; but a distinction was made between her and

NEITH,

Who was said to be the goddess of the upper heaven (or ether), whereas Sati was the goddess of the lower heaven (or air). If Neith be a sky-deity, and if she be also the mother of the sun-god, the facts are another instance from Egyptian mythology of that same process through which the Greeks peopled their Olympos and the Norsemen their Asgard. But further, the functions attributed to Neith seem to show that the idea of this goddess was developed much in the same way as that of the Greek Athene. As Athene in Greek, and Ahana in Sanscrit, meant originally the light of the dawn, and finally, moral and intellectual light, so we find that Neith also came to be a deity of wisdom. This goddess was worshipped especially at Saïs in the Nile delta.

MAUT,

To whom we have already referred as the second person of the Theban Trinity, meant the Mother,—Mother Nature,— and thus corresponded to the Greek Demeter.

BUBASTIS

Was chiefly worshipped in the town of Bubastus in Lower Egypt. She was said to be the daughter of the great goddess Isis. She was represented with the head of a cat, the animal specially sacred to her.

RA

Comes first in the second class of deities. The Greeks

identified him with their own sun-god, Helios, and called the city in which he was principally worshipped Heliopolis. He is represented with a hawk's head, over which is a solar disc. His purely physical origin seems to be proved by the myths that Neith, or the upper air, was his mother; and that he married Mut (Demeter): this merely signifying the interaction of earth and sunlight in producing vegetation. But again, Ra was said to have for children Athor, Mu, and Mat. Athor was identified with Aphrodite, who was originally the goddess of light; while Mu means physical light, and Mat moral light. Precisely the same transition in meaning happens in the story of Neith, and in that of Athene, Ahana, Ushas, and Eos. The wide prevalence of this god's worship shows in what importance he was held, an importance naturally attaching to the sun-god among all nations given to elemental worship. From Ra, with the prefixed syllable Pi, was derived the name Phrah, or, in Old Testament spelling, Pharaoh. Every Pharaoh was thus entitled son of the sun. All this suggests that Sabæism, or fire-worship, was originally practised in Egypt. Ra is also identical with Baal, a name implying "lord," and applied to the sun. Baalbek means "city of the sun," and was so named by the Greeks—Heliopolis.

SEB

Is said to be the son of Ra. He is a sort of Egyptian Kronos, being represented in the hieroglyphics to be the father of the gods. Here again we have an interchange of functions; for it has been seen that Neph, Pthah, etc., have been similarly described. Also, like other gods in and out of Greek mythology, Seb marries his own sister, Nutpe. These

XLIV

Osiris.

Nile God.

two were at the head of the " Osirian divinities "—Osiris, Isis, Seth, Nephthys. Nutpe or Nepte has been identified with Rhea. She is supposed to coincide with Lucina, and to preside over births and nursing. As being the mother of Isis and Osiris, she was called the mother of the gods.

OSIRIS,

(PLATE XLIV.,)

The great deity of the Egyptians, has been by some identified with the sun, or sunlight, or the vivifying powers in nature. According to this view the sleep or death of Osiris means the sleep of the spring-maiden Brynhild (see p. 324), or the imprisonment of Persephone in the dark realm of Hades. His contest with Seb (by the Greeks called Typho) would certainly seem to be another instance of the plausibility, at least, of this view. At any rate, Osiris, being restored to life, became the judge of the under-world. There he listens to Thoth's tale of the character of the disembodied souls, who are introduced to the judge by Horus (the son of Osiris), after their good and bad deeds have been weighed by Anubis in the scale of truth.

These trials in the under-world were attended by forty officers, called Assessors of the Dead, who are thus described by Sir Gardner Wilkinson: "These assessors were similar to the bench of judges who attended at the ordinary tribunals of the Egyptians, and whose president, or arch-judge, corresponded to Osiris. The assessors were represented in a human form with different heads. The first had the head of a hawk, the second of a man, the third of a hare, the fourth of a hippopotamus, the fifth of a man, the sixth of a hawk, the seventh of a fox, the eighth of a man, the ninth of a ram, the tenth of a snake, and the others according to their peculiar character . . . They are supposed to represent the forty-two crimes from which a virtuous man was expected to be free when judged in a future state; or rather the accusing spirits, each of whom examined if the deceased was guilty of the peculiar evil which it was his province to avenge."

The worship of Osiris was universal throughout Egypt, where he was gratefully regarded as the great example of self-sacrifice, as the manifester of good, as the opener of truth, and as being full of goodness and truth. As Osiris was the personification of physical and moral good, so his brother Seb (Typho) was the personification of all evil. Of the analogy between these two on the one hand, and the old Persian deities of good and evil, we have already spoken.

Another explanation of the Osirian myth has thus been given: Osiris was the Nile god. (Plate XLIV.) The river, in its periodical inundations, was said to have married the earth (Isis, Rhea), and in its retreat to have been killed by the giant of Sterility (Seb, or Typhon), who was jealous, perhaps, of the wondrous fruitfulness of the marriage between the soil and the great river.

APIS

Was the great beast-god of Egypt. This sacred bull was known as Apis at Memphis, and as Mnevis, or Onuphis, at Heliopolis. His worship was so prevalent and popular, because he was regarded as an avatar, or incarnation, of the favourite deity Osiris, whose soul had transmigrated into the body of a bull. The sacred bull was allowed to live for no more than twenty-five years, at the end of which it was taken to the Nile, and drowned in one of the sacred wells. His death was followed by national mournings, which, however, gave place to national thanksgivings, as soon as a new Avatar, or sacred bull discovered himself by the following marks: a black coat, a white triangular spot on the forehead, a spot like a half-moon on its right side, and under its tongue a knot like a beetle. The following quotations from Ælian, as given in Wilkinson, narrate the ceremonies consequent on the re-discovery of Osiris:—

"As soon as a report is circulated that the Egyptian god has manifested himself, certain of the sacred scribes, well versed in the mythical marks, known to them by tradition, approach the spot where the divine cow has deposited her calf, and there, following the ancient ordinance of Hermes, feed it with milk during four months, in a house facing the rising sun. When this period has passed the sacred scribes and prophets resort to the dwelling of Apis, at the time of the new moon, and placing him in a boat prepared for the purpose, convey him to Memphis, where he has a convenient and agreeable abode, with pleasure grounds and ample space for wholesome exercise. Female companions of his own species are provided for him, the most beautiful that can be found, kept in apartments to which he has access when he wishes. He drinks out of a well, or fountain of clear water : for it is not thought right to give him the water of the Nile, which is considered too fattening . . The man from whose herd the divine beast has sprung is the happiest of mortals, and is looked upon with admiration by all people." Cambyses, it is said, found a set of villagers rejoicing over a new sacred bull, and fancying they were making merry over his recent defeat in Ethiopia, the king of kings at once ran the bull through the body, and had the priests flogged. It was considered a good omen if the bull ate food offered to it. Men also listened at the ears of Apis, then put their hands to their own ears to prevent the escape of the secret, which they interpreted according to the nature of the first words they chanced to hear uttered.

SERAPIS

(PLATE XLV.)

Was another name of Osiris, although the Greeks said that his worship was not known in Egypt until the time of Ptolemy Philadelphus, when it was introduced from Sinope, under the name of Serapis. Serapis was known as the judge of the under-world.

ISIS

(PLATE XLV.)

Was the wife of Osiris, also a counterpart of him; for, as he was judge of the dead, so she is described as the giver of death. She is identified with Ceres and Persephone, and, in this view, the grief of Isis for her husband may be regarded as an Egyptian version of the myth representing Demeter as mourning for the loss of her daughter. Apuleius makes her declare: "I am nature, the parent of all the gods, mistress of all the elements, the beginning of all the ages, sovereign of the gods, queen of the manes, and the first of the heavenly beings." But as the mother of all she is convertible with Mat and Nutpe (see pp. 346, 347). And then Apuleius proceeds: "My divinity, uniform in itself, is honoured under numerous forms,

XLV.

Isis.

Serapis.

various rites, and different names. . . . but the sun-illumed Ethiopians, and the Egyptians renowned for ancient lore, worship me with due ceremonies, and call me by my real name, ' Queen Isis.' " Plutarch considers Isis to be the earth, the feminine part of nature, while Diodorus says that the Egyptians, considering the earth to be the parent of all things born, called her Mother, just as the Greeks called earth Demeter.

ANUBIS,

With **Hor**, or **Horus**, and **Har-pi-chruti**, or Harpocrates, were the children of Osiris and Isis. The first was a jackal-headed god ; and, according to another myth, was the son of Osiris and Nephthys, a sister of Isis, who, fearing the jealousy of Isis, concealed the child by the sea-shore. The office of Anubis was to superintend the passage of souls to their abode in the unseen world. As such he corresponded to the Greek Hermes Psychopompos. Anubis presided over tombs ; and he is frequently introduced in sculpture as standing over a bier on which a corpse is deposited. Horus was a hawk-headed god. As the avenger of his father Osiris, who was slain by Typhon, he was identified by the Greeks as Apollo. He also corresponded in some degree to the sun-god Ra, and was worshipped by the Egyptians as representing the vivifying power of the sun. Harpocrates seems to be merely another version of Horus—he is a personification of the sun. He is represented as a child sitting on a lotus flower, with his finger on his lips. Under this figure he was thought of as the god of silence. Perhaps in placing a representation of him in front of each of their temples, the wise Egyptians meant to symbolize the fact that worship ought to be conducted with silence.

THOTH

Was the god of letters, the clerk of the under-world, and the keeper of the records for the great judge Osiris. He is represented with the head of an ibis, and bearing a tablet, pen, and palm-branch. So great was the respect in which the sacred ibis was held—on account, no doubt, of its usefulness in destroying venomous reptiles—that any one guilty of killing it was himself punished with death.

ANOUKE

Was the third member of the trinity of Northern Ethiopia, the other two members being Sati and Neph.

THE SPHINX,

Unlike her Greek representative—who was a cruel monster born of the evil powers Typhon and Echidna—was a beneficent being who personified the fruit-bearing earth, and, like the sun and sky powers we have named above, was a deity of wisdom and knowledge. Her figure—lion-bodied, with the head and breast of a woman—was placed before every temple. The Egyptian Cerberus, or hell watch-dog, must have been a more forbidding and strange-looking animal than his Greek brother. He had the trunk and legs of a hippopotamus, with the head of a crocodile.

INDEX.